Paul, the Law, and the Jewish People

Paul, the Law, and the Jewish People

E. P. SANDERS

FORTRESS PRESS   MINNEAPOLIS

For P. D. K.

COPYRIGHT © 1983 BY FORTRESS PRESS

First paperback printing 1985

Library of Congress Cataloging in Publication Data

Sanders, E. P.
  Paul, the law, and the Jewish people.

  Bibliography: p.
  Includes indexes.
  1. Law (Theology) – Biblical teaching. 2. Bible. N.T.
Epistles of Paul – Criticism, interpretation, etc.
3. Paul the Apostle, Saint – Attitude towards Judaism.
4. Judaism – History – Post-exilic period, 586 B.C.–210 A.D.
I. Title
BS2655.L35S26 1983   241'.2   82–17487
ISBN 0–8006–1878–5

Printed in the USA   AF 1-1878

00 99 98 97 96 4 5 6 7 8 9 10 11 12 13

Contents

CONTENTS

Abbreviations

ARNA	Aboth de Rabbi Nathan, version A
ATANT	Abhandlungen zur Theologie des Alten und Neuen Testaments
BBB	Bonner biblische Beiträge
BEvTh	Beitrage zur evangelischen Theologie
BJRL	*Bulletin of the John Rylands Library*
BNTC	Black's New Testament Commentaries (-HNTC)
BZ	*Biblische Zeitschrift*
CNT	Commentaire du Nouveau Testament
ConBNT	Coniectanea biblica, New Testament
DSS	Dead Sea Scrolls
ET	English Translation/English Translator
EvTh	*Evangelische Theologie*
FRLANT	Forschungen zur Religion und Literatur des Alten und Neuen Testaments
Hermeneia	Hermeneia—A Critical and Historical Commentary on the Bible
HNT	Handbuch zum Neuen Testament
HNTC	Harper's New Testament Commentaries (-BNTC)
HTKNT	Herders theologischer Kommentar zum Neuen Testament
HTR	*Harvard Theological Review*
ICC	The International Critical Commentary
JBL	*Journal of Biblical Literature*
JSJ	*Journal for the Study of Judaism*
JSNT	*Journal for the Study of the New Testament*
JTS	*Journal of Theological Studies*
KEK	Kritisch-exegetischer Kommentar über das Neue Testament
KuD	*Kerygma und Dogma*
Migr.	Philo, *De Migratione Abrahami*
NEB	*New English Bible*
NTS	*New Testament Studies*
PPJ	E. P. Sanders, *Paul and Palestinian Judaism*
lQM	*Milhāmāh (War Scroll)*

ABBREVIATIONS

1QS	*Serek hayyaḥad (Rule of the Community, Manual of Discipline)*
1QSa	Appendix A *(Rule of the Congregation, The Messianic Rule)* to 1QS
4QpPs	*Psalms Commentary*
Quest. Ex.	Philo, *Quaestiones et Solutiones in Exodum*
RB	*Revue biblique*
RSR	*Recherches de sciences religieuse*
RSV	Revised Standard Version
SBLDS	Society of Biblical Literature Dissertation Series
SBT	Studies in Biblical Theology
SNTS	Society of New Testament Studies
SNTSMS	Society of New Testament Studies Monograph Series
ST	*Studia theologica*
TDNT	G. W. Bromiley (ET and ed.), *Theological Dictionary of the New Testament*
TZ	*Theologische Zeitschrift*
UNT	Untersuchungen zum Neuen Testament
USQR	*Union Seminary Quarterly Review*
WUNT	Wissenschaftliche Untersuchungen zum Neuen Testament
ZNW	*Zeitschrift für die neutestamentliche Wissenschaft*
ZTK	*Zeitschrift für Theologie und Kirche*

Preface

The present work consists of two essays, each of which treats a question of importance for understanding Paul's relationship to Judaism. The first essay (Part One), on the law, deals with the central problem for understanding Paul's thought about his native faith. The first and third chapters expand and clarify, and sometimes correct, the account of Paul's view of the law which was sketched in *Paul and Palestinian Judaism*. The essay also takes up aspects of Paul's treatment of the law which were not previously touched on, and I attempt to consider the problem of Paul and the law as a whole. In the endnotes, some of which are quite discursive, I have taken into account some of the most important critical assessments of my earlier work. The second essay deals with a question which I did not consider in that volume, Paul's thought about and relationship to his fellow Jews. This question requires also us to consider Paul's self-understanding and activity as apostle of Jesus Christ.

One point should be made here. In *Paul and Palestinian Judaism* I did not intend to explore Paul's Jewishness, his overall relationship to Jewish tradition and thought. Despite the length of that book, the subject was limited to how "getting in and staying in" were understood by Paul and his near contemporaries in Judaism. The present work, however, does focus more closely on Paul's general relationship to contemporary Judaism, and consequently it includes sections on such topics as Paul's use of Scripture, the degree to which he was a practicing Jew during his career as apostle to the Gentiles, and his thought about the fate of his "kin by race" who did not accept Jesus as Messiah. Thus the present work, though in some aspects a fuller exposition of positions which I have already published, is intended to be an independent monograph which deals with Paul's thought about the law and his own people, and with the consequences of his views and his practice for the relationship of his churches to Judaism.

More precisely, the work addresses an important chapter in the history of the emergence of the Christian movement as a separate religion. It may be that the survival of Galatians and Romans leads us to put too much emphasis on Paul's role in that development, but it is nevertheless important to understand his role, and in particular his thought about the law, the Gentiles, and the Jews. This emphasis of the work, and in fact its appearance at this time, are due to a five-year research program at McMaster University on the movement toward normative self-definition in Judaism and Christianity during the first centuries of the common era. Our research was generously funded by a grant from the Social Sciences and Humanities Research Council of Canada, and the basic work on the present chapters was done under the auspices of that grant. I share the indebtedness of many to the Council for their encouragement and interest, as well as for financial assistance. I, again along with my colleagues, am also indebted to the officers of McMaster University for their enthusiastic support of the research project.

An earlier form of the essay on the law was presented at the meeting of Studiorum Novi Testamenti Societas in Toronto in August 1980. I am grateful to the members of the Committee for the opportunity of presenting the major thesis of the present work, and some of its details, to the members of the Society. The original paper would ordinarily have appeared in the Society's journal, *New Testament Studies;* but it was of awkward length, and the Secretary of the Society, Professor Graham Stanton, and the editor of the journal, Professor R. McL. Wilson, encouraged me to expand it for publication in another format rather than to shorten it for inclusion in the journal. I am indebted to them for their advice and permission.

The presentation before the members of SNTS led to several very helpful exchanges with other scholars. I am especially grateful to Professors Heikki Räisänen, Paul Meyer, J. Louis Martyn, Robert Gundry, and Walter Wink. I am also indebted to Professor Räisänen for making available to me his own manuscript on Paul and the law, from which, as the reader of the endnotes will see, I learned a great deal.

An appointment as Walter G. Mason Visiting Professor at the College of William and Mary in Virginia during the autumn of 1981 provided the opportunity to complete the drafting of the work. The members of the Department of Religion provided an excellent atmosphere for work, as well as stimulation and encouragement. My deep thanks to them all.

I owe thanks to Mrs. Sue Hodge for her assistance in the preparation of the subject index, and to the editorial staff of Fortress Press for their careful work.

By no means the least benefit of the grant from the Social Sciences and Humanities Research Council was that it allowed the employment of Phyllis DeRosa Koetting as editorial assistant, secretary, and bibliographer.

McMaster University generously continued her employment for a year after the conclusion of external funding in June, 1981. I have thanked numerous people for encouragement, advice, and support. No one deserves more thanks for enabling this work to appear at the present time, complete with accurate footnotes, bibliography, and indexes, than Ms. Koetting.

PART ONE

PAUL AND
THE LAW

Introduction

Different Questions, Different Answers

It is with more than a little hesitation that one picks up again the question of Paul and the law. It is a topic that has been discussed by numerous scholars in great detail, with the result that one pauses before thinking that fresh light can be shed on it. This consideration points to others: the subject is difficult,[1] and all the scholarly labor that has been spent on it has resulted in no consensus. The difficulty of the topic, however, is matched by its importance, and it merits the effort that has been expended. It is a subject which must be penetrated if one is to understand Paul's thought, and it is no less crucial for understanding an important moment in the divorce of Christianity from Judaism. If despite the difficulty and the scope of the problem I venture to address it in relatively short compass, it is in the hope that a few clarifying proposals can be made, even if every exegetical problem cannot be solved.

There is a tantalizing quality to the study of Paul's view of the law. He says a lot about it, and one should be able, by using the normal tools of exegesis, to determine precisely what he thought. The subject is not like the study of the historical Jesus, where one has to distinguish redaction from tradition, probe to find the earliest traditions, and try to establish criteria for determining authentic material. Nor is it like the study of "wisdom" in 1 Corinthians, where there is too little material at hand to allow us to be sure just which "wisdom" Paul was replying to. In the study of "Paul and the law" we have before us a lot of unquestionably authentic statements by Paul on the subject; and, further, we know what law Paul was talking about. With a few exceptions, he meant the *Tanak*, the Jewish Torah.[2] Yet the search for what he "really meant" goes on. One may ask, of course, whether or not he did have a single and well-thought-out position on the law, and that question will be posed here. But a priori one would expect him to have had a clear position on the law. The law, it would appear from his own testimony, had been his life before God revealed his son to him (Phil. 3:4–6; Gal. 1:13–15). His break with it was self-conscious.[3] His re-

3

action to the possibility that his Galatian converts might accept the law was so forceful that one expects him to have had a clear and decisive reason for responding as he did. And yet, to repeat, there is no agreement among scholars as to what that reason was, and still less is there agreement as to how to understand the relationship of his numerous other statements about the law to the position which he took in the Galatian controversy.

One of the factors which makes Paul's statements about the law hard to unravel is the general difficulty of distinguishing between the reason for which he held a view and the arguments which he adduces in favor of it. To take an example: It is clear in 1 Corinthians 11 that Paul thinks that men should pray with heads uncovered and that women should pray with heads covered. In favor of this view he says that for a woman to pray with head uncovered is the same as if her head were shaved (1 Cor: 11:5). He also says that she should pray with her head covered "because of the angels" (11:10).[4] He then asserts that nature itself teaches that men should have short hair and women long hair (11:14f.; although how this supports his main point is not quite clear).[5] Finally he says to those still unconvinced that "we recognize no other practice," nor do the other churches (11:16). In this particular case he may never state the real reason for his position: he was Jewish.[6] Nevertheless, we see how he can mingle all sorts of arguments. This fact, as we shall see, helps to explain why scholars disagree about why he said what he said about the law: reason and argument are not always easy to distinguish.

The proposal of the present monograph is that the different things which Paul said about the law depend on the question asked or the problem posed. Each answer has its own logic and springs from one of his central concerns; but the diverse answers, when set alongside one another, do not form a logical whole, as might have been expected had he set out to discuss the problem of law as such. The primary aim is to show that this is the case and to sketch the principal questions and answers. Each category is not treated in equal exegetical detail, and the first category — why Paul said that no one is justified by works of law — receives more attention than the others. Before launching into the first category, however, it will be helpful to describe the general understanding of Paul's thought which governs much of the following discussion.

Central Convictions and
Soteriological Scheme

I have previously argued, and I wish here simply to repeat, that much of what Paul says in the very divergent circumstances of his surviving let-

4

ters is controlled by certain central and identifiable convictions: that God had sent Jesus Christ to provide for the salvation of all; that salvation is thus available for all, whether Jew or Greek, on the same basis ("faith in Christ," "dying with Christ"); that the Lord would soon return; that he, Paul, was called by God to be the apostle to the Gentiles; and that Christians should live in accordance with the will of God.[7] There are doubtless other views which Paul consistently held, and some of these are brought forward to justify his arguments at various points. Thus, since he was Jewish, he undoubtedly always thought that "God is one," and he used this conviction to undergird the argument about the equality of Jew and Gentile in Rom. 3:29f. I do not, however, regard this conviction as "central" in the way the ones first listed are, because, as a Pharisee, he was a monotheist, but he probably did not then draw from that conviction the conclusion that Jews and Gentiles can be saved on the same condition.[8]

There seems to be fairly wide agreement that Paul's thought was christologically determined,[9] but not all who hold that basic position agree about its precise meaning and ramifications. W. D. Davies, for example, urges the centrality of Christ for Paul, but puts the stress on Christ as Jewish messiah rather than Christ as universal lord.[10] J. Christiaan Beker mentions as central to Paul's thought "the Christ-event in its apocalyptic meaning" (a phrase which he can reverse: the christological interpretation of apocalyptic),[11] but he proceeds to argue that the real center for Paul is "the triumph of God."[12] I fully agree that the nearness of the end is crucial for Paul and conditions his view of his own work and, indeed, all his thought.[13] I should want to emphasize — and here I think that Beker would agree — that there is no dichotomy in Paul's thought between the lordship of Christ and the triumph of God. For precision, however, I should urge that it is the *christological* interpretation of the triumph of God that is the central characteristic of his thought.[14]

Although I do not wish to prolong the discussion of the central and determining features of Paul's thought, one more distinction must be made. There is a difference between the center of his thought and the central *terminology* by which he discusses the transfer from the unsaved to the saved state. Both Beker and Hans Hübner have attributed to me the view that "participation in Christ" is the center of Paul's thought, despite my effort to make it clear, in discussing "dying with Christ" and "righteousness by faith," that I was discussing only the terminology which is most revealing for understanding Paul's conception of how one *enters* the body of Christ.[15] Entering the body of Christ, important as it is for Paul, is not the whole of his thought, and one must distinguish between "the center of his thought" (or, in my terms,

5

his "primary convictions") and "the most telling terminology by which he expresses the transfer from the old life to the new."

I do wish now, however, to focus on the latter topic, for it is especially important for understanding what he says about the law. Much of what Paul wrote falls within a framework which I call "getting in and staying in." The framework, besides those two topics, includes what happens to those who do not "get in" and what happens to those who get in but who do not behave in the way which Paul considers appropriate to life in the Spirit. In discussing getting in and the behavior appropriate to staying in, Paul employs appreciable diversity of terminology. The terminology for entering the body of those who will be saved has been illuminatingly discussed by Gerd Theissen. He divides the terms into two principal types, sociomorphic and physiomorphic. He makes the important observation that all the terms are metaphorical depictions of a change from an unsaved to a saved state.[16]

Equally diverse, and sometimes equally metaphorical, is Paul's terminology for behavior appropriate to those whose state has changed. The terminology which one would expect from one of Paul's background, that of being righteous or unrighteous, upright or wicked, does not often appear in his discussions of proper behavior.[17] The righteousness terminology, especially the passive verb "be righteoused,"[18] is employed in his discussions of transferring from one status to another and does not often appear in discussions of maintaining the new status.[19] Paul often draws on the purity language of the Bible in describing behavior appropriate to being Christian,[20] and he can also discuss that behavior as the "fruit" of living in the Spirit.[21] Most striking for our present purpose is the fact that he can use the language of living by the law in this context.

It may be helpful to illustrate the framework of getting in, staying in, and the consequences of behavior by a diagram and some lists. The intention is to show at the same time the basic framework and the diversity of terminology. While it may be helpful to present the framework in diagram form, I realize that it is also risky. One can readily be understood to be reducing complexities of thought to a simple chart. For the sake of clarity, however, I shall run the risk. Let me emphasize that I do not regard all the terms in the diagram and the lists as simply synonymous, nor do I think that everything that Paul thought can be reduced to or encompassed within the framework, much less the diagram which illustrates it. I do think, however, that the diagram and the lists illustrate some of Paul's basic convictions about becoming and remaining Christian and help to reveal a coherence which underlies diversity of expression.[22]

6

The diagram has two basic elements: the transfer from one status to another (the horizontal arrow) and behavior within each state and its consequences (the vertical arrows). It should be further explained that the diagram should be studied together with the lists which follow it. The first list gives the passages in which the transfer terminology occurs; the second those in which behavior terminology is used. Neither list is intended to be completely exhaustive.

The framework illustrated by the diagram is this: Humans start in a condemned state: they are "in sin" and "sinners." Thanks to God's action in Christ they may transfer to the body of those who will be saved. Those who do not transfer will be destroyed. Those who do transfer are to live in a certain way. There are divergent possibilities in the case of those who sin after the transfer: they may be punished and saved; they may correct their way and be saved; they may refuse to correct their way and be excluded from the body of those who will be saved.[23]

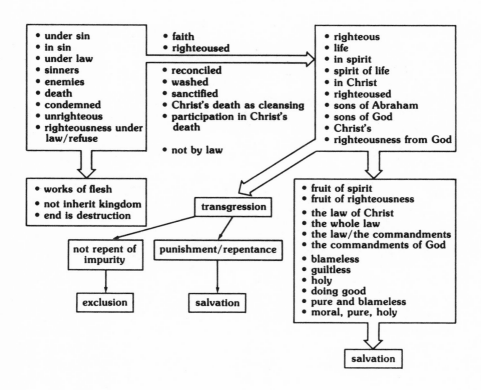

TRANSFER TERMINOLOGY

sinners enemies	righteoused } by death reconciled } of Christ		Rom. 5:8-10
condemnation	death of Christ	acquittal (dikaiōsis)/life	Rom. 5:18
sinners	death of Christ	righteous (dikaioi)	Rom. 5:19
in sin	death with Christ	life	Rom. 6:4
in sin	righteoused by sharing Christ's death	life	Rom. 6:7
enslaved to law/flesh	death with Christ	new life of spirit	Rom. 7:4-6
condemnation/ sin/death	death of Christ	in Christ no condemnation	Rom. 8:1f.
unrighteous	washed, righteoused, sanctified [in baptism]	[righteous]	1 Cor. 6:9-11
Jews or Gentiles (sinners)	righteoused by faith		Gal. 2:16
	by faith	spirit	Gal. 3:2, 14
	by faith	sons of Abraham	Gal. 3:7, 14
	by law X	righteousness/life	Gal. 3:21
	through faith	sons of God	Gal. 3:26
righteous under law/refuse	faith/sharing sufferings	in him/righteousness from God	Phil. 3:6-11

TERMINOLOGY FOR BEHAVIOR AND CONSEQUENCES

works of flesh	Gal. 5:19; cf. 1 Cor. 5:9f.; 1 Cor. 6:9f.
not inherit kingdom	Gal. 5:21; 1 Cor. 6:9
end is destruction	Phil. 3:19; cf. 2 Cor. 4:3; 2 Cor. 11:15
fruit of spirit	Gal. 5:22
fruit of righteousness	Phil. 1:11
just requirement of law	Rom. 8:4
law of Christ	Gal. 6:2; cf. 1 Cor. 9:21
whole law	Gal. 5:14
law/commandments	Rom. 13:8–10
commandments of God	1 Cor. 7:19
blameless	1 Thess. 3:13; cf. 5:23; Phil. 2:15f.
guiltless	1 Cor. 1:8
holy	1 Cor. 7:34; cf. 2 Cor. 7:1
doing good	Gal. 6:9
pure and blameless	Phil. 1:9–11
moral, pure, holy	1 Thess. 4:3–7

(Christian)
transgression
↓
punishment   } 1 Cor. 3:12–15 (cf. 4:4–5); 1 Cor. 5:1–5;
↓   1 Cor. 11:30–32; cf. 2 Cor. 5:10
salvation

transgression
↓
repentance   } 2 Cor. 7:9–10
↓
salvation

not repent
↓   } 1 Cor. 5:11–13; 2 Cor. 12:21
exclusion

Special attention should be paid to the use of the *dik-* (right-) root. The passive verb is used to denote the act of the transfer, and thus it appears along with "faith" and "dying with Christ" in the second column from the left on the Transfer Terminology chart. Even in this sense there are two distinguishable uses: one is righteoused from concrete sins (1 Cor. 6:9–11) or from (the power of) Sin (Rom. 6:7). Perhaps needless to say, for Paul the two went together: one in Sin also sinned, and in Christ God provided for the cleansing of sin and for freedom from Sin.[24] Three forms of the *dik-* root appear along with "life" and "in the Spirit" to denote the state of those who transfer from sin: *dikaiōsis*, (Rom. 5:18), *dikaios*, (Rom. 5:19), and *dikaiosynē* (Gal. 3:21; Phil. 3:9). Again, these three terms do not have precisely the same nuance. A person who is *dikaios* is apparently one who is upright, who does not sin. Having been cleansed, he no longer bears the burden of his former transgressions. Thus he also has *dikaiōsis*, acquittal, having been forgiven. The person who participates in Christ's sufferings may also be said to have the *dikaiosynē ek theou*, which appears to be equivalent to being "in Christ" (Phil. 3:9). I make these observations in order to emphasize not only the importance of the *dik-* root, but also the importance of observing flexible usages and variations of precise meaning within a coherent framework.

The diagram will, I hope, make it clear that Paul used the term *nomos* in at least two quite distinct contexts, one in discussing how one gets "in" (not by works of law), the other in discussing how one who is "in" behaves (he keeps the law). Thus we come already to one of our principal conclusions: the question being addressed determines what Paul says about the law. The fact that there are "negative" and "positive" statements by Paul about the law has always been observed, and there have been various explanations. We shall return to the principal ones at the end of chapter 2. Here I shall only comment that the explanation which proceeds from determining what *question* is being addressed differs from the explanation which is based on *distinctions of meaning* which Paul consciously had in mind (e.g. the law as an external code legalistically performed and the law as the ethical principle of love.).[25]

When one starts from the principal contexts thus far noted and looks for others, it turns out that there are some. There are four principal questions in reply to which Paul used the word *nomos*, and we shall now take up each of them. In discussing principal contexts it is necessary to leave aside some of the appearances of *nomos* in Paul, particularly those in which it appears to mean "principle."[26]

NOTES

1. H. J. Schoeps (*Paul: The Theology of the Apostle in the Light of Jewish Religious History* [Philadelphia: Westminster Press, 1961], p. 168) commented that the law is the most difficult aspect of Paul's thought. Cf. Peter Stuhlmacher, "Das Ende des Gesetzes," *ZTK* 67 (1970): 35; "Das Gesetz als Thema biblischer Theologie," *ZTK* 75 (1978): 272.

2. See below, n. 26.

3. Already the problems begin: is it correct to say he broke with it; and, if so, in what way and to what extent did he do so? For the self-consciousness of some sort of break, however, one may point to Phil. 3:7.

4. It is not necessary for the present purpose to discuss the reason for which he uses *exousia* in 11:10. The general point is clear enough.

5. Perhaps the reasoning is this: a woman should have long hair; uncovered hair is the same as a shaved head; therefore she must pray with her head covered.

6. Cf. *Sifre Num.* 11 (on 5:18).

7. Cf. E. P. Sanders, *Paul and Palestinian Judaism* (Philadelphia: Fortress Press, 1977), pp. 44lf. (hereafter cited as *PPJ*). Correct behavior is an addition to the earlier list. C. J. A. Hickling, in a thoughtful and helpful article, offers as the center of Paul's thought something more fundamental than these "closely linked statements": "God has already brought about in Christ a decisive and final *transformation of time*." The center of Paul's thought and religion is "not simply, or even principally in the content of his assertions about God and Jesus and his own calling, but in the sense of fundamental and paradoxical contrast, as of one standing at a cosmic frontier, with which this content was perceived." This puts the center in "an aspect of Paul's experience of being Christian." (See C. J. A. Hickling, "Centre and Periphery in the Thought of Paul," *Studia Biblica 1978, Vol. 3, Papers on Paul and Other New Testament Authors* [Sheffield: JSOT Press, 1980], pp. 199–214, quotations from pp. 208f., 200.) I believe that Hickling puts his finger on a vital point, and at the end of this chapter we shall return to an aspect of Paul's experience as the source of Paul's thought about the law. Most attention, however, will be given to Paul's arguments and consequently to convictions that are subject to propositional formulation.

8. On this see Nils A. Dahl, "The One God of Jews and Gentiles (Romans 3:29–30)," in *Studies in Paul* (Minneapolis: Augsburg Publishing House, 1977), pp. 178–91, esp. 189f.

9. Thus, for example, Georg Eichholz, *Die Theologie des Paulus im Umriss* (Neukirchen-Vluyn: Neukirchener Verlag, 1972), pp. 224f.; Peter Stuhlmacher, "Interpretation von Römer 11:25–32," in *Probleme biblischer Theologie* (Munich: Chr. Kaiser, 1971), p. 556 (The center of all Pauline preaching, which gives meaning to the rest, is the crucified and resurrected Christ; summarizing and agreeing with Ulrich Luz, whose work will be cited below); Stuhlmacher, "Das Ende des Gesetzes," pp. 14–39. For the christological determination of Paul's view of the law, see also Andrea van Dülmen, *Die Theologie des Gesetzes bei Paulus* (Stuttgart: Verlag Katholisches Bibelwerk, 1968), e.g., p. 7; Karl Hoheisel, *Das antike Judentum in christlicher Sicht* (Wiesbaden: O. Harrassowitz, 1978), esp. p. 182; Heikki Räisänen,

"Legalism and Salvation by the Law," in *Die paulinische Literatur und Theologie* (Aarhus: Forlaget Aros, 1980), p. 71.

10. See *PPJ*, p. 514; W. D. Davies, *Paul and Rabbinic Judaism*, 4th ed. (Philadelphia: Fortress Press, 1980), pp. xxxi, 324.

11. J. Christiaan Beker, *Paul the Apostle: The Triumph of God in Life and Thought* (Philadelphia: Fortress Press, 1980), p. 17.

12. Ibid., p. 362: "Paul is an apocalyptic theologian with a theocentric outlook."

13. In *PPJ*, pp. 44lf., I identified as one of Paul's "central convictions" that the Lord would "soon return to bring all things to an end," and the nearness of the end, in Paul's view, was emphasized in my summary of his "pattern of religion" (*PPJ*, p. 549). Further, I gave to his soteriological thought the tag "participationist eschatology" (p. 552). I am thus at a loss to understand the criticism that I rejected apocalyptic as important for understanding Paul (Davies, *Paul and Rabbinic Judaism*, p. xxxi).

14. Note Beker's christocentric definitions of Paul's thought on pp. 17 and 135, the theocentric statement quoted in n. 12, and the apparent harmonization of the two on pp. 365–67. One finishes the book wishing for a final, crisp statement which relates the early christocentric definitions to the theocentric conclusion. Does the emphasis fall on the statement that "Christology . . . serves theology" (p. 365) or "the imminent triumph of God is defined by the death and resurrection of Christ" (p. 367)? At any rate, there is no doubt that the two go together.

15. Beker, p. 12: "The *Mitte* (center) of Paul's thought is located either in justification by faith . . . or sacramental participation . . . or both (Sanders)." On p. 286, in an asterisked footnote, he says that although I say that the two are ultimately the same, my position is ambivalent since I " play down" the importance of justification. This simply overlooks my own statement of Paul's "central convictions" (in *PPJ*, pp. 44lf.; they have just been reiterated), as well as my detailed explanation of how it is that justification and participation are two terms which point toward the same reality, while the latter tells us more about how Paul thought (*PPJ*, pp. 502–8).

Hans Hübner ("Pauli Theologiae Proprium," *NTS* 26 [1980]: 445–73) argues, intending to address my work, that *the doctrine* of righteousness by faith, not "being in Christ," is the "centre of Pauline theology" (the phrase appears on p. 449). Hübner in fact simply fails to deal with my principal positions:

1. There is no recognition of my distinction between Paul's central convictions and the varieties of his transfer terminology (*PPJ*, pp. 44lf.; 463–72; 502–8).

2. There is no acknowledgment of my view that the different opinions about "righteousness" and "participation" are in large part a terminological dispute (*PPJ*, pp. 507f.).

3. Throughout, Hübner discusses "the doctrine of righteousness by faith" (*die Rechtfertigungslehre*) as if it were unquestionably a unified, established doctrine, ignoring my argument that the righteousness terminology is used in diverse ways by Paul (*PPJ*, pp. 491–95).

4. Having noted some agreements between my position and Schweitzer's, Hübner spends a substantial part of his paper criticizing Schweitzer (and occasionally Wrede), as if he were refuting my position, when in fact I agree with many of his criticisms of Schweitzer (see, e.g., Hübner, p. 453, at n. 40; p. 454, at nn. 46, 47).

Hübner has some fresh arguments in favor of considering "righteousness by faith," forensically understood, to be the center of Paul's thought. I do not find them convincing, especially since they are not actually addressed to my previous arguments to the contrary; noteworthy though they are, I cannot pursue the discussion here.

Finally, I am indebted to Professor Hübner for bringing to my attention a regrettable error on my own part. On p. 441 of *PPJ* I agreed with Schweitzer that "righteousness by faith can be derived from and understood on the basis of other aspects of Paul's thought such as possession of the Spirit and living in the Spirit, but not vice versa" (quoted by Hübner, p. 449). Here I went too far in agreeing with Schweitzer, and the phrase "derived from" does not represent my own view. As my later discussion shows, my own view was — and is — that "being justified by faith" and "being in Christ" point to the *same* reality, while the "participatory" categories serve to *define* the "juristic ones" (*PPJ*, pp. 502–8, esp. 507f.). Further, other points of Paul's theology do "derive from" the participatory categories, not from the juristic ones (*PPJ*, pp. 439f. and nn. 47 and 51). I should not, however, have said that the juristic language as such "derives from" the participatory.

16. Gerd Theissen, "Soteriologische Symbolik in den paulinischen Schriften," *KuD* 20 (1974): 282–304.

17. Paul's own usage is outlined on p. 9 below and discussed briefly in chapter 3 of this essay. For the terminology in more or less contemporary Jewish literature, see *PPJ*, pp. 624f., s.v. "The Righteous" and "Righteousness." More recently, see Benno Przybylski, *Righteousness in Matthew and His World of Thought* (New York: Cambridge University Press, 1980).

18. The problem of the translation of the verbal forms of the *dik-* root into English is well known. Recently see A. J. Mattill, Jr., "Translation of Words with the Stem *Dik-* in Romans," *Andrews University Seminary Studies* 9 (1971): 89–98. Kendrik Grobel's proposal (in his ET of Bultmann's *Theology of the New Testament* [New York: Charles Scribner's Sons, 1951–1955]) to revive "rightwisen" seems not to have caught on. I have decided to attempt the standard English expedient of making a verb directly from the noun or the adjective. Note Hardy's famous "to small" (from the adjective).

A scholar whose regard I greatly treasure, since he stands so high in my own, has frankly told me that his opinion of me will be diminished if I persist in this barbarism. Since I am persisting, I wish to explain why. I entirely agree that there is no justification for "to loan," "to author," "to exegete," and the like. The British are entirely correct to regard these as barbarisms coined by my compatriots, most of whom now live to the south of me. But "to righteous" and "to faith" are different matters. The point and mode of Paul's argument in Gal. 3:6–8, for example, is entirely lost on the English reader when *dikaiosynē* in 3:6 is translated "righteousness" and *dikaioun* in 3:8 is translated "justify." The argument depends on the fact that the verb in 3:8 is cognate with the noun in the scriptural quotation in 3:6. Paul uses Scripture to prove his point, and his argument is terminological in character.

There are numerous such passages. Attempts to finesse the problem in the standard English translations have not succeeded. That is part of the justification (no pun intended) for the frontal, though brutal, assault.

There is a second reason for the neologism, one that seems to me finally overwhelming. The verb, especially the passive form of it, varies significantly in meaning, while in the most common phrase the meaning is, for good reason, in dispute. Yet *dikaioun* is too important in Paul's vocabulary to allow it to disappear behind varying translations. The RSV quite reasonably translated the passive of *dikaioun* "freed" in Rom. 6:7; in 1 Cor. 6:11 the meaning is probably either "forgiven" or "purified," in 1 Cor. 4:4 "acquitted," and in Rom. 2:13 "will be found innocent." The question of the precise meaning in the most important phrase for our present topic, "righteoused by faith, not by law," is moot; it is clear that the verb there as elsewhere (with a few exceptions) signifies the transfer to the Christian life, but the precise connotation is difficult to determine. It is a standard debate as to whether "be made righteous" or "be justified" catches the meaning better. There are sound objections to both translations, and it seems to me that we should refuse to be impaled on either horn of the dilemma. Since "justified" is the common English verb, I shall remark about it that it conveys to most English speakers the meaning of "be declared or found innocent," when the question is precisely whether or not Paul has shifted the meaning beyond that of the law court.

19. *PPJ*, pp. 470–72; 518 n. 5; 544f. The plural adjective *dikaioi* in Rom. 5:19 does not constitute an exception. "Many will be made righteous" *(dikaioi katastathēsontai hoi polloi)* means the same as if Paul had written "many will be righteoused" *(dikaiōthēsontai hoi polloi)*.

20. *PPJ*, pp. 450–53. See now the full analysis in Michael Newton, "The Concept of Purity at Qumran and in the Letters of Paul" (Ph.D. diss.; Hamilton, Ontario: McMaster University, 1980).

21. Gal. 5:22; cf. Phil. 1:11.

22. Xavier Léon-Dufour ("Jugement de l'homme et jugement de Dieu. 1 Co 4, 1–5 dans le cadre de 3, 18–4, 5," in *Paola a una Chiesa Divisa [1 Co 1–4]* [Rome: Abbazia di S. Paolo, 1980], pp. 137–75) offers a very interesting diagram to illustrate Paul's thought (p. 152). There are some points of correspondence, but the diagrams serve different purposes, and there is no point in trying to reconcile them. A study of Professor Léon-Dufour's article and his diagram, however, will help drive home the point that any diagram is intended only to illustrate an aspect of thought.

23. There are two complexities with regard to Paul's thought about "transferring" from one state to another that cannot be represented by the chart. (1) The arrow from left to right shows the logical sequence. I have argued elsewhere *(PPJ,* pp. 442–47) that organically Paul's solution preceded the problem. (2) Prof. J. Louis Martyn has pointed out to me that the language of "transferring" makes it appear that Paul regarded the change of status as entirely volitional, whereas in fact he thought of it as something which happens to a person. This is a very complicated matter. I at least partly accept Martyn's point, but I do not intend the chart to clarify this aspect of Paul's view of God and humanity. It shows what happens, which Paul, of course, thought of as being "by grace," but which also involves human commitment.

24. Or perhaps it is necessary to say. Brendan Byrne (*"Sons of God" – "Seed of Abraham"* [Rome: Biblical Institute Press, 1979], p. 231), intending to counter my position, stresses that Paul "held in essential unity" the conceptions "of Christ as both dying *for* us and allowing us to die with him." That, of course, is precisely what I said (*PPJ*, pp. 463–68; 487; 498f.; 502f.; and esp. 507). This fact, however,

does not prove that the repentance/forgiveness scheme is central to Paul, which is Byrne's contention.

25. Ernest deWitt Burton especially explained the different things said about the law on the basis of Paul's having different definitions consciously in mind. See *The Epistle to the Galatians* (Edinburgh: T.&T. Clark, 1921), pp. 447–60, esp. p. 451. See further the next note and pp. 83–86 below.

26. Rom. 3:27; 7:21, 23; 8:2 (the phrase "the law of the Spirit of life"). Some have recently argued that "*nomos* of faith" (Rom. 3:27) and "*nomos* of the Spirit of life" (8:2) mean the biblical law as viewed or encountered by believers. This enables them, among other things, to bridge Paul's negative and positive statements about the law — a point to which we shall return in chapter 3. This line of argument has been convincingly answered by Heikki Räisänen, "Das 'Gesetz de Glaubens' (Röm. 3.27) und das 'Gesetz des Geistes' (Röm. 8.2)," *NTS* 26 (1979): 101–17, discussing the views of G. Friedrich, E. Lohse, P. von der Osten-Sacken and H. Hübner. Hübner has responded to Räisänen in the appendix to the second edition of *Das Gesetz bei Paulus* (Göttingen: Vandenhoeck & Ruprecht, 1980), pp. 136f.; and Räisänen has met this response in *Paul and the Law* (forthcoming). The single most decisive point is this: according to the interpretation of Hübner and others, the Mosaic law (viewed through the eyes of faith) would have to be the *means* through which boasting is excluded (Rom. 3:27) and also the *means* through which Christians are freed from the (perverted) law (8:2). This seems clearly impossible. It would, among other things, make nonsense of Paul's view of the death of Christ. It is much better in both cases to take *nomos* to refer to the saving *principle* of faith or of the Spirit. See further pp. 92f. below.

It should be added that until very recently scholars generally (and correctly) understood *nomos* in Rom. 3:27 and the other passages referred to here to mean "rule" or "norm"; so, e.g. Wolfgang Schrage, *Die konkreten Einzelgebote in der paulinischen Paränese* (Gütersloh: Gerd Mohn, 1961), p. 99.

1

The Law Is Not
an Entrance Requirement

Our first category is the one which has attracted the most extensive
exegetical work and which is usually taken as being the most characteristic
thing which Paul says about the law: one is righteoused by faith, not by
works of law. Three principal problems have arisen in the course of scholarly
debates. (1) Against whom is the statement directed? (2) Why does Paul
hold that righteousness cannot come by law? (3) What is the relationship
between saying that righteousness is not by law and the statement that judgment is on the basis of deeds or that, at the judgment, those who have done
the law will be righteoused (Rom. 2:13)? The third problem is postponed
to a subsequent chapter, and we shall now consider the other two.

There is a narrow range of answers possible to the first question. The
statement "no one is righteoused by works of law" can be understood as
directed against the Jewish understanding of salvation, against Paul's Christian opponents (whether Jewish or Gentile), or both. The second question
produces more debate and a wider range of answers. Paul holds the view
which he so often asserts because it is impossible to do the entire law (the
"quantitative" answer); because doing the law itself estranges — doing it is
worse than not doing it, as Heikki Räisänen has remarked[1] (the "qualitative"
answer); because of his exclusivist soteriology (only by faith in Christ,
therefore not by law); because of the exigencies of the Gentile mission.[2] It
is naturally possible to combine some of these explanations of Paul's view,
and Hans Hübner has recently proposed that the quantitative answer appears in Galatians, the qualitative in Romans.[3]

I do not plan to take up and assess each problem and the various answers
to it one by one, but rather to discuss the principal passages and to draw
conclusions at the end.

Galatians 2—3

We first meet the formulation "not by works of law" in Galatians, which
is in many ways fortunate, for both the setting and the main thrust of Galatians are relatively easy to determine, and they tell us rather a lot about

Paul's treatment of the law in the letter. To understand the statements about the law in Galatians, it is important to be clear about two points: (1) The subject of Galatians is not whether or not humans, abstractly conceived, can by good deeds earn enough merit to be declared righteous at the judgment; it is the condition on which Gentiles enter the people of God. (2) Paul's arguments about the requirement for admission are largely taken from Scripture, and he is in all probability replying to topics introduced by the rival missionaries. While both these points are important for understanding Paul's treatment of the law, the first is absolutely vital. Nevertheless, I do not propose to prove either in advance. The evidence will appear as the argument proceeds. We begin with a sketch of the situation in Galatia; the burden of discussion with other scholars will be borne by the notes.

Missionaries were attempting, apparently with some success, to convince Paul's Gentile[4] converts that to be heirs of the biblical promises they had to accept the biblical law. To put it in the terms used earlier: the Gentile converts could enter the people of God only on condition that they were circumcised and accepted the law. In their own terms, the missionaries held the position that those who wanted to be true sons of Abraham and heirs of the promises must do as Abraham did and be circumcised (Gen. 17:9-14, 26f.).[5] Precisely who these missionaries were remains uncertain, but their position seems to be materially the same as that of the people whom Paul calls "false brethren" in Gal. 2:4. It thus seems likely that they were "right wing" Jewish Christians.[6]

Theirs was an entirely reasonable position, and its great strength was almost certainly the support which reading the Bible would give it. The most forceful passage is Gen. 17:9-14, where God tells Abraham that he and his seed (*to sperma*; cf. Gal. 3:16, 19) must be circumcised and that any male who is not circumcised will be destroyed (cf. Paul's reply, Gal. 5:4). The opposing missionaries could also have read to the Galatians Isa. 56:6-8, where the "foreigners" who join the people of God are expected to hold fast to the covenant (circumcision) and especially to keep the Sabbath. Thus most of Paul's arguments against the opposing position are based on the Bible (Gal. 3:1-5 is a notable exception), as he apparently wished to counter his opponents on their own ground and to show, *by Scripture*, that the biblical commandments were not a necessary or sufficient condition for admission to "the Israel of God."[7]

It is easy to imagine how the disagreement arose. Many Jews, and all the Jewish Christians whose views are known to us, expected Gentiles to be brought into the people of God in the messianic period.[8] There was, however, no accepted *halakah* governing the conditions of their admission.

The prophetic and poetic passages (e.g., *Sib. Or.* III.772–75) which envisage the entry or submission of the Gentiles in the last days generally do not give legal detail.[9] The Jewish Christians, who considered the end to be near, however, had to make practical decisions. The normal requirement for entering the people of God was to make full proselytization,[10] and some Jewish Christians obviously thought that the same condition should be maintained even in the last days.[11] It is this view which the "false brethren" of Gal. 2:4 held and this view which Paul attacks in the body of Galatians. Paul's view was at the other extreme: Gentiles were to be brought into the people of God without being required to accept the law of Moses, but by faith in Christ alone, and it was his mission to bring them in. We shall later have to consider whether or not, or the degree to which Paul applied to native Jews the admission requirement of faith to the *exclusion* of circumcision and the law, but the problem as it meets us in Galatians is that of the admission of the Gentiles.[12] Peter and James appear basically to have agreed with Paul on the question of the Gentiles. It was not their mission to bring them in, but it was correct for Paul to do so without requiring proselytization. It was probably Peter's responsibility to the circumcised, which might be hindered if he himself were not Torah-observant, not disagreement with Paul's mission as such, which led him to withdraw from the Gentiles in Antioch.[13]

If we assume that all the parties named or referred to in Galatians were Christians, we should also assume that the rival missionaries did not argue against "faith in Christ." The latter is a common Christian formulation,[14] though doubtless it meant different things to different people.[15]

If this description of the situation is at all correct, then we can readily grasp the broad outline of Paul's argument. The argument of Galatians 3 is against Christian missionaries, not against Judaism, and it is against the view that Gentiles must accept the law *as a condition* of or as a basic requirement for membership.[16] Paul's argument is not in favor of faith per se, nor is it against works per se. It is much more particular: it is against requiring the Gentiles to keep the law of Moses in order to be true "sons of Abraham."[17]

We have become so sensitive to the theological issue of grace and merit that we often lose sight of the actual subject of the dispute. Many scholars who view the opposing missionaries as Jewish Christians nevertheless see Galatians 3 as Paul's rebuttal of Judaism.[18] But the quality and character of Judaism are not in view; it is only the question of how one becomes a true son of Abraham, that is, enters the people of God. I believe that the reason for which Galatians 3 is seen as Paul's argument against Judaism is this: Paul's argument about righteousness by faith or by works of law in Galatians 2 and 3 is viewed as if he were arguing that an individual cannot merit salvation by achieving enough good deeds to present a favorable balance before God.[19] It is believed to be characteristic of Judaism to hold such a position, so that Paul's argument is perceived to be against Judaism. A study of Jewish material does not reveal such a position. More to the point, that is not Paul's argument in any case. The question is not about how many good deeds an individual must present before God to be declared righteous at the judgment, but, to repeat, whether or not Paul's Gentile converts must accept the Jewish law in order to enter the people of God or to be counted truly members.

In focusing on the controversy as one regarding "entry," I do not mean to imply that the requirement of faith alone for entry (to be a descendant of Abraham; to be righteoused) is a fleeting one which has no significance for continuing life in the people of God. The debate in Galatians is a debate about "entry" in the sense of what is essential in order to be considered a member *at all*.[20] Paul holds that faith is the sole membership requirement; his opponents would require also circumcision and acceptance of the Mosaic law. As we shall see more fully below, it is not doing the law in and of itself which, in Paul's view, is wrong. Circumcision is, from one perspective, a matter of indifference (Gal. 6:15). It is completely wrong, however, when it is made an essential requirement for membership.

The controversy centers on the admission rite, circumcision, but includes other aspects of the law as well, such as food and "days" (Gal. 2:11–14; 4:10). It thus appears that Paul's opponents took the position — which is, to repeat, entirely understandable — that Gentile converts to the people of God had to be circumcised and accept the rest of the law. (The significance of Gal. 5:3 for understanding their position will be considered below.) Paul's view is equally straightforward, although the reason for which he held it is not immediately evident. Gentiles do not need to accept the Mosaic law in order to be members of the people of God. Thus we have a debate which is both understandable and of obvious importance.

These general observations are, I hope, sufficient to clarify what is at stake and the major position taken by Paul's opponents. Now I wish to give a closer analysis of the role of Gal. 3:10–12 in the argument, in order to approach the question of *why* Paul held that Gentiles should not accept the law of Moses. It is primarily on the basis of this passage, especially when it is coupled with 5:3, that the argument is made that Paul objected to the law because it could not be satisfactorily fulfilled.[21]

It is certainly true that the word "all" appears in the quotation of Deut.

27:26 in Gal. 3:10. It may nevertheless be asked whether or not the thrust of Paul's argument is that the law should not be accepted because it is impossible to do all of it.[22] I wish to bring forward three considerations against that view.

In the first place, we should consider how Paul chooses the quotations in Galatians 3. The argument is terminological. It depends on finding proof-texts for the view that *Gentiles* are *righteoused* by *faith*. Those three words are crucial, and Paul is able to link Gentiles to "righteoused by faith" through the Abraham story. Abraham is thus the middle term, being connected with Gentiles in one proof-text and righteousness by faith in another. In the course of this argument Paul cites the only two passages in the Septuagint (LXX) in which the *dik-* root is connected with *pistis* (Gen. 15:6; Hab. 2:4). Hab. 2:4 apparently would have suited his argument better if it had had a passive form of *dikaioun* instead of the adjective *dikaios;* he takes *ho dikaios ek pisteōs zēsetai* ("the one who is righteous by faith will live") to prove that *en nomōi oudeis dikaioutai* ("no one is righteoused by the law").[23] But, nevertheless, the passage will serve his purpose; it connects righteousness with faith. The quotation which brings Gentiles into the picture by connecting them with Abraham is the first passage in the Abraham story which mentions the blessing of the Gentiles, which Paul apparently took to mean their inclusion in the messianic era. The quotation in Gal. 3:8 is based on Gen. 18:18, not 12:3 (as is sometimes said), since Paul's major intention is to include the Gentiles, and the term *ethnē* does not appear in 12:3.[24] Again, from Paul's point of view it might have been preferable for the verb *dikaioun* to appear in Gen. 18:18; but "blessed" serves quite well and he repeats it in 3:9. The verse, however, was not chosen because of "blessed," but because of *ethnē.* Thus by quoting Gen. 18:18 Paul "proves" that *Gentiles* are blessed in Abraham; while Gen. 15:6 is used to "prove" that Abraham was *righteous* by *faith.* Abraham, to repeat, is the link between the key terms in the argument.[25]

After these observations it is not surprising to note that Deut. 27:26 is the only passage in the LXX in which *nomos* is connected with "curse." There are passages which say that one who does not keep the commandments (*entolai;* see e.g. Deut. 28:15) will be cursed, but that does not suit Paul's argument. He wants a passage which says that the *nomos* brings a curse, and he cites the only one which does. Thus I propose that the thrust of Gal. 3:10 is borne by the words *nomos* and "cursed," not by the word "all," which happens to appear.[26]

Our second consideration has to do with how to read the relationship between the argument of 3:10–12 and the proof-texts. It is a fairly common view that one should interpret what the proof-texts say in order to discover what Paul means.[27] I think that what Paul says in his own words is the clue to what he took the proof-texts to mean. Thus in 3:10 Paul means that those who accept the law are cursed.[28] This consideration also points to the conclusion that the emphasis is not on the word "all."

Thirdly, we should take account of the place of Gal. 3:10–13 in the argument of 3:8–14 as a whole. I take the argument of 3:8–14 to run like this: The main proposition is that God *righteouses* the *Gentiles* by *faith* (3:8),[29] which is proved by citing Gen. 18:18, which says that in Abraham the Gentiles will be blessed. The word "blessed" naturally leads to its opposite: cursed. Gal. 3:10, then, announces the negative proof of the positive statement of 3:8. Deut. 27:26 proves that "those who are of works of law are under a curse" (Paul's own statement of the meaning of the quotation). Having named the law, Paul reiterates that "no one can be righteoused" by it, to prove which he cites Hab. 2:4 (3.11). But does faith exclude the law? Yes: "the law is not of faith," a statement which he proves by citing Lev. 18:18, which specifies that one must do the commandments (3:12).[30] Gal. 3:11–12, taken together, argue that righteousness is by faith and that the law is not by faith. This is, in effect, a repetition of the argument that faith, not obeying the law, is the condition for being righteous.[31] The argument continues with the explanation of how God has provided for the removal of the curse of the law (3:13). Verse 14 summarizes the preceding argument in chiastic fashion, the first *hina* clause ("in order that") reiterating the positive point of 3:8 (the blessing of Abraham for the Gentiles), the second, the positive assertion of 3:1–5 (the Spirit is received through faith).[32] These two positive assertions, in turn, serve the larger negative argument against the requirement to keep the law (announced in 2:16 and implied throughout). The summary in 3:14 shows where the emphasis of the argument in 3:1–13 falls.

Thus I regard 3:10–13 to be subsidiary to 3:8[33] and to consist of a chain of assertions which are stated by Paul in his own words and which are proved by the citation of proof-texts which contain one or more of the key words in his argument.

These three considerations—the character of the terminological argument in favor of *Gentiles* being *righteoused* by *faith*, which is based on proof-texts; the fact that Paul states in his own words what he takes the proof-texts to mean; and the subordination of vv. 10–13 to v. 8—seem to me to be decisive against the view that the thrust and point of the argument are directed toward the conclusion that the law should not be accepted because no one can fulfill all of it.[34] The argument seems to be clearly wrong that

Paul, in Galatians 3, holds the view that *since* the law cannot be entirely fulfilled, *therefore* righteousness is by faith.[35]

Even if it be granted that the thrust of the argument is not that the law cannot be fulfilled, we must still ask whether or not Paul held that view. Does it play, for example, a subsidiary role? Some would argue — I was once one of them — that Gal. 3:10-11 contains two arguments against the law: (1) The law cannot be fulfilled (presupposed, not stated, in 3:10); (2) even if it could be, righteousness comes only by faith. In this construct the emphasis is on the second argument (v. 11).[36]

Thus Räisänen, noting that Paul nowhere explicitly says that the law cannot be fulfilled, nevertheless maintains that such a view is presupposed in Gal. 3:10-12. "This is borne out by Rom. 1:18 — 3:20; the same thought is reflected in Gal. 5:3 and probably 6:13."[37] My own understanding of each passage is different. Gal. 6:13 recalls Paul's attack on Peter in 2:14[38] and probably reflects the dilemma of many Jewish Christians.[39] They wanted to maintain full fellowship with Gentile converts and thus sometimes did not observe the law with entire strictness, although they still thought that the Gentiles should be brought into full observance of the law. To meet with the Gentile converts and argue their case, in other words, they would run the risk of undermining it. Paul uses the dilemma of the other missionaries against them in Gal. 6:13. I see here no evidence of the view that they were *unable* to fulfill the law.

Gal. 5:3 and Rom. 1:18 — 3:20 will be discussed more fully below, and I shall here do little more than observe that neither one says that the law could not be fulfilled. Indeed, this is made clear with regard to Rom. 1:18 — 3:20 in Räisänen's own discussion. That passage contains the charge that *everyone* commits *heinous* sins, while holding open the possibility that some, both Jew and Gentile, could be righteous *by the law*. Räisänen points out that the exaggeration of Rom. 1:18 — 3:20 is forced by Paul's prior conclusion that, if the law could save, Christ died in vain.[40] It does not seem to be motivated in the least by the view that the law is so difficult that it cannot be fulfilled.

In Phil. 3:6, one of the passages in which Paul deals with "righteousness by the law," he says of himself that he once had such righteousness, having been blameless. It agrees with this that, in his admonitions to Christians, he calls on them to be "blameless" or "guiltless" (1 Thess. 3:13; 5:23; 1 Cor. 1:8), although not "according to righteousness under the law." We thus see that, at least for rhetorical purposes, Paul could entertain the possibility of human blamelessness. As a counterweight to Phil. 3:6 may be cited Rom. 3:23f.; Romans 5, especially 5:12; and Romans 7, all of which directly state

23

or presuppose universal sinfulness. Of these passages only Rom. 3:23f. directly mentions "righteousness by the law," and as far as I can see it is the only passage in Paul which can reasonably be read the way Hübner wants to read Gal. 3:10–12: "*since* everybody sins, *therefore* righteousness is by grace, through faith." Even here the "since . . . therefore" construct is by no means certain. Further, there is general acknowledgement that at least part of this passage is the quotation of a pre-Pauline tradition, and it would be very precarious to cite it as the source of Paul's view of the law.

But what of the apparent conflict between Phil. 3:6 and Rom. 5:12? Is one exaggeration and the other Paul's real view? We may be permitted, in discussing an obviously speculative question, to propose a somewhat speculative answer. The view that everyone, at some time or other, commits a sin is commonplace in rabbinic and other Jewish literature, although the conclusion which Paul draws from that is unique to him. On the other hand, the admonition and claim to be perfect of way are also known from Jewish literature, especially the Dead Sea Scrolls.[41] Thus we might reasonably suppose that both views were known in the Judaism of Paul's day. Paul, in different contexts, makes use of both sorts of statement. It would be hazardous to suppose that Paul must have held one position as his true view, while using the other only for the sake of argument. He could quite easily have held both, without ever playing them off against each other so that he became aware that they are mutually exclusive. He could have thought, that is, that obeying the law perfectly was difficult but not entirely impossible and thus say of himself that he was blameless; and also that, in a general way, everyone at some time or other transgresses. One may recall the story of R. Eliezer, who taught that "there is none that is righteous," but who was still surprised that he had committed a sin for which he had to suffer.[42]

This attempt to explain Phil. 3:6 and Rom. 5:12 is not necessary to the argument against the view that Paul *grounded* his opposition to the law as the way to righteousness on the fact that it could not be obeyed, but considering Romans 5 does cast indirect light on the reason for Paul's view. Romans 5 shows that Paul was perfectly well acquainted with the view that everyone sins; but nevertheless he does not make use of that argument in the principal debates about righteousness. Romans 5 is written on the assumption that he has already, in Romans 4, proved that "righteousness is by faith, not by law" (see 5:1), and it itself is not an argument against the possibility of righteousness by law. There is, in fact, a certain awkwardness when Paul attempts to connect universal sin with the law (5:13f.), an awkwardness which is revealing, as we shall see.[43] Meanwhile, what is important to note is that Paul does not cite human inability to fulfill the law in his principal arguments against his opponents, Galatians 3 and Romans 4, when he undertakes to prove that righteousness *cannot* be by law.

We cannot, then, say that Paul never thought that everybody sins; simply that that view is not put forward as the ground of his own view that righteousness must be by faith, to the exclusion of doing the law.

Some have read Gal. 3:13 as revealing another issue at the center of Paul's rejection of the law: the messiah was judged by the law as guilty but was vindicated by God; therefore "the law has been judged by God in Christ 'on the tree.'"[44] As A. E. Harvey puts it, "since Jesus, in the eyes of God, was right, then the law was wrong.[45] In support one may point to 1 Cor. 1:23, where the cross is said to be a stumbling block to Jews. The reasoning is that Jews cannot believe in a messiah condemned and cursed by the law, but that those who accept Jesus as messiah must, by that very fact, reject the verdict of the law. One can then add that the Christian movement was persecuted for confessing as messiah one whom the law had condemned.[46]

This is all plausible as a line of reasoning. But, while it is reasonable to surmise that Paul saw a fault in the law for its supposed role in Christ's death,[47] neither he nor other first-century Jewish Christians — or non-Christian Jews — seem to have reasoned in this way.[48] I shall itemize the arguments against putting this point as the central one in explaining Paul's rejection of righteousness by the law.

1. The argument sketched above makes the substitutionary view of Christ's death central.[49] It is, I think, generally conceded that, while Paul repeats that view, it is not the one most characteristic of his thought. Thus Christ's death as taking on the curse of the law is not likely to be the key understanding behind Paul's own view.

2. It is very likely that Gal. 3:13 came to Paul ready-made as a reply to the charge that the crucified one cannot be the messiah. The answer is introduced because of the *Stichworte* which lead the argument from "Gentiles" to "blessing" to its opposite, "curse." Thus Gal. 3:13 is not the keystone of the argument, but has a subsidiary place in explaining how the curse (3:10) is removed.

3. This leads to a further point: the Christians who developed the argument probably did not themselves reject the law. The argument is effective, if anywhere, in a Jewish environment, and it probably came from such an environment. But we do not know of any Christian Jews who drew what can be presented as the logical conclusion. We can do little more than speculate about the use to which those who developed the argument put it. Perhaps it simply turned an accusation to good account: "your messiah

was crucified and therefore accursed"; "yes, but we are thereby delivered from being cursed." In any case, they seem not to have seen the argument as leading to the conclusion that the law should not be kept.

4. Paul does not employ or even refer to the argument in Romans or in Philippians when he recounts his own rejection of the law. If it truly stood behind that rejection, he has concealed the fact.

5. Finally, Gal. 3:13 is not actually an argument against righteousness by the law. It explains why Christians who were under its curse (apparently even the Gentiles not actually covered by 3:10) are so no longer. The *argument* is that faith blesses (3:9) and that the law curses (3:10). The explanation in 3:13 is not developed as an argument against accepting or obeying the law. That must be drawn out by implication, but no one seems to have drawn the implication.

Thus it would seem that, while the cross was doubtless a stumbling block to Jews, Gal. 3:13 does not provide the reason which lies behind Paul's position. The plausibility of the explanation which is based on it may indicate that Paul missed the opportunity to make use of a good argument. To repeat the last point, he does not actually use it as an argument against the requirement to keep the law.

What, then, can be said on the basis of Galatians 3 about the motive that lies behind Paul's view? It seems that in Gal. 3:10–12 — indeed, in 3:6–18 — we do not have an explicit statement of the reason for which Paul held that no one is righteoused by the law. We see, rather, Paul's skill in Jewish exegetical argument. He "proves" by Scripture that accepting the law leads to a curse, that righteousness is by faith, that it is available for the Gentiles, and that the law is not by faith. These diverse statements are not reasons, they are arguments. They have, however, a discernible common ground: they are based on Paul's view of God's plan of salvation. He can argue from Scripture precisely because he considers that he is discussing God's eternal plan, clearly laid out in the Abraham story and thus stated in the law itself. The full and final revelation of this plan may be recent (cf. Gal. 1:16; 3:23–25), but the plan is not. The Scripture saw *in advance* that God would righteous the Gentiles by faith and proclaimed that message *in advance* to Abraham (Gal. 3:8, putting emphasis on the prefix *pro-*). In Gal. 3:10–12, in other words, Paul states, with scriptural proof, what he considers to be the facts of God's plan of salvation: righteousness is by faith and includes the Gentiles; the law curses.

That Paul's viewpoint is that of God's eternal plan of salvation is seen even more clearly in Gal. 3.15–26, where the law and faith are assigned their places in the history of salvation.[50] Abraham's inheritance has nothing to do with the law (3:15–18); the law has another purpose than salvation (3:19–24); in giving the law God intended to lead up to salvation through Christ (3:22, 24).[51] With regard to righteousness by the law the "punch line" seems to be 3:21: righteousness *cannot* be by the law; no law has been given which can make alive.

Thus the whole thrust of the argument is that righteousness was never, in God's plan, intended to be by the law. This helps us see that the problem with the law is not that it cannot be fulfilled. Paul has a view of God's intention which excludes righteousness by the law; his position is dogmatic.[52] It lies ready at hand to conclude that his revised view of the law in God's plan springs from his conviction that salvation is through the death of Christ (Gal. 2:21). In the midst of a sometimes bewildering series of arguments, quotations, and appeals, there seem to be two sentences in Galatians in which Paul states unambiguously not only what his position is (which is never in doubt), but *why* he holds it. These statements are the last two cited. Put in propositional terms, they say this: God sent Christ; he did so in order to offer righteousness; this would have been pointless if righteousness were already available by the law (2:21); the law was not given to bring righteousness (3:21). That the positive statement about righteousness through Christ grounds the negative one about the law seems to me self-evident.

Galatians 5:3

One of the reasons for emphasizing the word "all" in the quotation of Deut. 27:26 in Gal. 3:10 is that Paul returns to the point in Gal. 5:3: "I testify again to everyone who is circumcised that he is obligated to do the whole law."[53] On the understanding proposed here, this shows that, although Paul quoted Deut. 27:26 for the connection of "curse" and *nomos*, he did not forget that it said "all." He makes use of the fact that accepting circumcision implies accepting the whole law, however, not to argue that the law should not be accepted *because* all of it *cannot* be kept, but as a kind of threat: if you start it *must* all be kept. To make this support the view that Paul argues against the law because it is impossible to keep all of it quantitatively, one must make a long list of assumptions about Paul's and the Galatians' presuppositions about the law: one must keep it all; one cannot do so; there is no forgiveness of transgression; therefore accepting the law necessarily leads to being cursed. The middle terms of this thought-sequence are never stated by Paul, and this sequence of views cannot be found in contemporary Jewish literature.[54] The sequence of thought sounds plausible, but it does not appear to be Paul's,[55] nor that of any form of contemporary Judaism.

27

This brings us to a general consideration which has a significant bearing on the understanding of the source of Paul's view of the law. Hübner thinks that Paul's argument is governed not by his Christian convictions (Gal. 2:21), but by his Pharisaic view of the law. He is able to argue that the burden of Paul's opposition to the law in Galatians falls on human inability to fulfill all of it because he depicts Paul as a Shammaite who thought that the law must be observed without exception.[56] The argument in Galatians is, then, between the former Shammaite Paul and Hillelite opponents, who merely required that obedience outweigh disobedience. But this explanation will not withstand scrutiny. All the rabbis whose views are known to us took the position that all the law must be accepted. This was not only a Shammaite position. No rabbi took the position that obedience must be perfect.[57] Pharisees and rabbis of all schools and all periods strongly believed in repentance and other means of atonement in the case of transgression. From the Jewish point of view, the position which Hübner attributes to Paul is unheard of. Even in Qumran, where perfection of way was stressed, allowance was made for transgression and atonement. The requirement of virtually perfect obedience in 4 Ezra makes the work stand out as unique in Jewish literature of the period — and that requirement is entirely unattested before 70 C.E.

It is equally un-Jewish to think that the law is too difficult to be fulfilled. As Philo put it, "the commandments are not too huge and heavy for the strength of those to whom they will apply . . ." (*De Praemiis et Poenis [On Rewards and Punishments]* 80). But this is not only Philo's view; it is standard in Jewish literature.

It would, in short, be extraordinarily un-Pharisaic and even un-Jewish of Paul to insist that obedience of the law, once undertaken, must be perfect. Such a position would directly imply that the means of atonement specified in Scripture itself were of no avail. Appeal to Paul's pre-Christian views lends no support to the position that the weight of Paul's argument in Galatians 3 rests on the word "all" in 3:10, or to the position that Paul came to his negative stance on righteousness by the law because it cannot be adequately fulfilled. Paul's Pharisaic past counts heavily against both positions. The common Jewish (including Pharisaic, to the degree that it can be known) view on the matters under discussion here would be this: the law is not too difficult to be satisfactorily fulfilled; nevertheless more or less everybody sins at some time or other (see above); but God has appointed means of atonement which are available to all. Now, to have Paul's argument stem from his pre-Christian views about the law, one must have him deny two of these points. He must hold that the law is too hard to do adequately and that there is no atonement. Yet it is granted on all hands that, in the extant correspondence, he never states either view explicitly. Hübner and others must hold that the view that the law cannot be fulfilled is presupposed by Gal. 3:10 and 5:3 as something too obvious to need explicit statement. But for this to hold good as an explanation, they would also have to maintain that Paul, while arguing on the basis of his Jewish suppositions, also presupposes that atonement is not possible. My argument is that none of this would have been obvious to someone of Paul's background. In fact, it would be unheard of.

To return directly to Gal. 5:3: beyond observing that it does not say that it is impossible to do the whole law and that for that reason it should not be kept, one can only hazard a guess as to the force of the threat that accepting circumcision would require keeping the whole law. There is good reason to think that, although observing the law was not burdensome to Jews, it appeared onerous and inconvenient to Gentiles. Paul's opponents may have adopted a policy of gradualism, requiring first some of the major commandments (circumcision, food, days), a policy which was probably not unique among Jewish missionaries.[58] Paul may very well simply have been reminding his converts that, if they accepted circumcision, the consequence would be that they would have to begin living their lives according to a new set of rules for daily living.[59]

Romans 3—4 and 9—11

We have observed that Galatians 3 is an argument to the effect that Gentiles who enter the people of God must do so on the basis of faith alone and that the law must not be a condition of their admission. It is striking that Paul applies this same principle to Jews. The reason for saying that application to Jews is striking is that it does not proceed from traditional Jewish messianic expectations, at least as far as we can now determine them. We have previously noted the fairly widespread Jewish view that Gentiles would join the people of God in the "messianic" period.[60] But it should be noted that in the passages which reflect this view "the people of God" is constituted by "Israel according to the flesh."[61] Gentiles might be expected to join Israel, but it appears to be a Christian innovation to claim that the people of God are, in effect, a third entity[62] which must be entered by Jew and Christian alike on the same ground.[63]

We cannot say with certainty that this is a Pauline innovation, since in Gal. 2:15f. Paul claims that Peter agrees. At any rate, it is in that passage that we first meet the view, passionately embraced by Paul, that Jew and Gentile alike are righteoused only[64] by faith in Christ. The theme is developed in Romans.

In the opening chapters of Romans Paul is arguing a different case from that of Galatians, despite the similarities between Romans 4 and Galatians 3. In Romans the argument concerns the equal standing of Jew and Gentile — both are under the power of sin — and the identical ground on which they change that status — faith in Jesus Christ. Thus while I do not disagree with the general view that the theme of Romans is announced in 1:16, I would put the emphasis more on the second part of the verse ("to all who faith, the Jew first and also the Greek") than on the phrase "the righteousness of God."[65] Several turns of phrase indicate that the brunt of the argument is in favor of the equality of Gentiles and against the assumption of Jewish privilege. Thus Paul asks in 3:9 whether Jews are better off than Gentiles (to which the answer is negative), in 3:29 whether God is the God of Jews only (no, also of Gentiles), and in 4:9 whether the blessing mentioned in Psalm 32 is for the circumcised alone (no, but also for the uncircumcised). The situation of the Jews is stated: they too are under sin and can be righteoused only by faith in Christ; but the Jews become the main topic only in Romans 9 — 11. In Romans 1 — 4, even taking into account 2:17-29, Paul's view is focused on the Gentiles.

Romans 3 and 4 and 9:30 — 10:13 are the principal passages on which is based the view that Paul's argument against the law was that keeping it leads to boasting and self-estrangement. This was for Rudolf Bultmann the key to understanding Paul's attitude towards the law,[66] and Hübner has recently defended this understanding. Hübner, however, restricts this reason for Paul's rejecting the law to Romans, having argued that Paul opposed the law in Galatians because it could not be satisfactorily fulfilled. In his view the argument in Galatians is "quantitative," in Romans "qualitative."[67]

The attempt to understand Paul's argument against righteousness by the law in Romans raises the questions of the occasion of the letter, its addressees, and its subject matter. There are debates about such questions with regard to Galatians, although there I think that the answers are straightforward. When we ask about the occasion and addressees of Romans, however, we enter one of the more controverted topics of recent New Testament research, and the controversy is based on very real problems. The basic question is this: does Paul have in view problems in Rome about which he has some information, or is the setting of Romans to be understood in the context of Paul's own ministry, with the controversies in Galatia and Corinth behind him and the meeting with the Jerusalem apostles before him? A second, though related, problem is whether he sees himself as debating with non-Christian Jews, or whether his arguments about the law are still directed, at least in his own mind, to other Christians.[68] The dialogue character of Romans is generally recognized,[69] but with whom does Paul see himself as in dialogue?

I am on the whole persuaded by those who, following the lead of T. W. Manson, view Romans as primarily coming out of Paul's own situation.[70] It is especially telling that in the long debate about Jew and Gentile in Romans 1 – 11 there is no direct reference to problems in the community in Rome.[71] This could conceivably reflect only Paul's reticence to speak directly to problems in a church which he did not found, and the possibility that he knows about them and addresses them indirectly cannot be completely excluded. It seems best, however, to view Romans as being Paul's reflection on the problem of Jew and Gentile in the light of his past difficulty in Galatia and the coming encounter in Jerusalem. He is concerned that the Romans may have heard that his position on the law leads to antinomianism, or even that he himself is antinomian (Rom. 6:1, 15; cf. 3:8). He doubtless wanted to clarify his position on the law in view of his impending visit, but the clarification is of a position which we have already met in Galatians. Thus his letter sometimes repeats themes from Galatians, but more often refines them and shifts the emphasis. That his eye is in part fixed on the coming meeting with the Jerusalem apostles is clear in Rom. 15:30f., and the desire for intercessory prayer before he meets the "unbelievers" and the "saints" in Rome is probably one of the principal motives behind the writing of the letter.[72]

We shall later offer some summary remarks on the relationship of Romans to Galatians. Here, however, it is necessary to note one distinct difference. In Galatians the polemic had to do with the entry of Gentiles into the people of God, and the status of Jews and Gentiles prior to or without faith was referred to in a confusing way (e.g. Gal. 3:23 – 4:10).[73] In Romans, on the other hand, Paul strives to state what he perceives to be the plight of Jews and Gentiles without faith in a way that distinguishes between them, while still concluding that their status, whether prior to faith or in the Christian community, is the same (Rom. 1:18 – 3:9; 4:11f.). This change of focus leads him to discuss in detail, for the only time in his extant correspondence,[74] the situation of "Israel according to the flesh" (Romans 9 – 11),[75] and he also attempts a much fuller account of the role of the law in God's plan than appears in Galatians. All this gives a somewhat different slant to his discussions about the law from the one which we met in Galatians. This "different slant," however, will be especially visible when we take up the question of why God gave the law (chapter 2). We shall first of all investigate the passages in which Paul says that righteousness is not by works of law.

Romans 3:27 — 4:25. It is this passage which, perhaps more than any other, has served as the foundation stone for those who think that Paul opposed the law because following it leads to pride. In 3:27 Paul says that "faith" excludes "boasting," and it is common to regard "boasting" as being "boasting in one's own meritorious achievement." Thus, for example, J. Christiaan Beker describes the boasting which Paul attacks as the Jews' "proud self-awareness of their moral stature and achievement." He sees that "boast" in 3:27 picks up the use of the word in 2:17, 23, but thinks that 3:27 presses Paul's attack further. In 3:27 Paul criticizes not just immoral behavior (as in 2:23), but shows that the fault of the Jew is that he transgresses the will of God "by his very attempt to be moral."[76]

Hübner shows himself to be much more aware of the degree to which this way of reading Paul may be questioned.[77] He recognizes that neither in Galatians nor in the Corinthian correspondence is there any evidence that Paul defines the Christian life as denying boasting.[78] Viewed on their own, the first three chapters of Romans do not reflect such a view.[79] There Paul criticizes improper behavior, not boasting in one's own fulfillment of the law. In the light of Romans 4, however, Hübner says, it becomes clear that the phrase "law of works" in 3:27 means the perverted use of the law: works-righteousness.[80] He understands Paul's discussion of Abraham thus: He was a sinner in two ways. In the first place, he did not fulfill the work which would produce righteousness (arguing that this may be inferred from 3:9ff.), while in the second place he *wanted* to be righteoused by works. Because of his faith, God forgave him for both (4:7).[81] Thus in interpreting this section, Hübner agrees with Bultmann's general understanding of Paul's criticism of the law.[82]

Hübner can then reconcile Rom. 1:18 — 3:26, especially 2:17–19, with the rest of Romans by proposing that there is a difference between righteousness by the law (which is permitted by 1:18 — 3:26) and "works-righteousness" (which is excluded by 3:27ff.). There is no conflict between the two sections.[83] Distinguishing between the perverted use of the law and the law rightly done also enables him to understand "the law of faith" in 3:27 as the Mosaic law.[84] In the same vein, as we shall see, he is of the view that it is only the misused law that comes to an end (Rom. 10:4).[85]

I must confess that I disagree with almost evey aspect of this interpretation. Rather than taking up the various aspects of Hübner's view one by one, however, I wish to follow the policy thus far adhered to of concentrating the discussion on the text before us.

We should first of all note what is widely acknowledged, that the term "boasting" in Rom. 3:27 picks up the same term in 2:17, 23.[86] There the term referred to the assumption of special status on the part of the Jews. Is there any reason to interpret the term differently in 3:27? The argument of the immediately succeeding verses tells against any change. Paul proceeds to argue that God is the God of Gentiles as well as of Jews (3:29) and that he righteouses the uncircumcised and the circumcised on the same basis, faith (3:30). The argument, in other words, is in favor of equal status and against privilege — especially against boasting in privileged status.[87] The *nomos* which is the means by which such boasting is excluded is "faith" — hardly "the law when practiced in the right spirit," but faith in the atoning death of Jesus, which Paul has just said is available to *all without distinction* (3:21–25). It is faith in Jesus Christ, which is available to *all*, which excludes boasting in privileged status. Thus *nomos* in 3:27 is correctly translated "principle." On this reading, 3:27–30 fit perfectly into the context of the entire preceding discussion regarding the status of Jew and Gentile: they are equal.

In Romans 4 Abraham is brought forward to prove Paul's point. "If Abraham had been righteoused by works, he would have had a boast, but not before God" (4:2). I see here no hint of the view that Abraham *tried* to be righteoused before God by works,[88] and certainly not of the view that the effort to merit righteousness by following the law is what constitutes human sin and is why Paul objects to the law. Paul's argument is a scriptural-factual one: Abraham was righteoused, it was not by works, and he could not boast. Paul will subsequently point out that Abraham had not even been circumcised (4:10). For the present, however, Gen. 15:6 remains the scriptural proof. Abraham was not righteoused by works since Gen. 15:6 says that his faith led to his being reckoned righteous. This sets Abraham up as a paradigmatic type[89] which shows how God righteouses: it is by faith; it has always been by faith; that is how God works. We can paraphrase 4:2f. thus: Abraham was not righteoused by works, since Scripture explicitly says that righteousness was reckoned to him because of faith. Had he been righteoused by works, he could have boasted, but even so not before God, since, again, Scripture says that God righteoused him because of faith.

The quotation of Gen. 15:6 in Rom. 4:3 answers both halves of 4:2. It shows that Abraham was not in fact righteoused by works, and also that in any case works would not count towards righteousness, since God counts only faith.

In attempting to understand the use of Abraham in 4:2 we should note the conclusions which Paul himself draws. The case of Abraham proves that God will deal with the uncircumcised on the same ground as he deals with the circumcised (4:9–12). The thrust of the argument is in favor of what Paul regards as a soteriological fact, a fact which is stated in 4:13 in so many words: the promise to Abraham and his offspring was connected not with law but with faith. Especially telling is 4:14: If those who are "of the law" are Abraham's heirs, faith is empty. Here it is clear that the denial of the law as a means to righteousness is directed against privileged status, not against boasting in meritorious achievement. The target of the argument is the same from 3:27 to 4:25: Jews who do not have faith in Christ. If one looks only at the phrase "law of works" (3:27) and the participle "the one working" (4:4)[90] it may appear, as Hübner proposes, that what Paul attacks is achievement. But one must note the other terms which characterize those whom Paul criticizes: "Jews" (3:29); "the circumcision" (3:30; 4:9, 12); those "of the law" (4:14, 16) — all phrases which focus on status, not religious attitude or behavior. What I have called Paul's "scriptural-factual" position comes out especially clearly in the conclusion of the chapter. Scripture, he says in effect, was very carefully worded to say that Abraham's faith is what was counted towards righteousness. This shows that those who have faith in the God who raised Jesus will have righteousness (4:22f.).

Thus two interrelated themes dominate Rom. 3:27 – 4:25: (1) God righteouses Jew and Gentile on the same ground, faith, and his action is in no way dependent on obedience to the law, nor is the promise restricted to those who are "of the law" (3:29f.; 4:9–14; 4:16). (2) The case of Abraham proves the point. Abraham was righteoused by faith; this had nothing to do with the law (4:2–4; 4:10f.; 4:13; 4:16f.). Underlying both these interrelated themes is a view of God's intention. The case of Abraham shows the way God acts. Righteousness comes by faith because of God's intention to have the promise include all Abraham's descendants, namely, all who have faith and not just those who are "of the law," the Jews (4:16). The statement in Genesis that Abraham's faith is what was reckoned for righteousness is to be applied in the present, and God's intention and the basis on which he righteouses have never changed (4:23f.).

The main lines of Paul's argument are thus clear. The continuation of 3:27 in vv. 29f. shows that the main point is that Jew and Gentile are to be included on the same basis, and similarly the use made of the Abraham story in 4:9–25 shows that Paul is primarily interested in the status of the Gentiles, in denying that those who are "of the law" (Jews) are privileged, and in asserting that God righteouses in the present on the same basis as in the past. Rom. 3:29f. and 4:9–25 seem to show beyond dispute that the thrust of the argument is not against misusing the law by boasting about fulfilling it. But what about 4:4? Does that verse not show that Paul was against claiming the "reward" as if God owed it and in favor of accepting righteousness as a gracious gift? It does indeed. Other passages show that Paul was against boasting in anything other than the cross of Christ (Gal. 6:14; cf. the criticisms of Gentile boasting in Rom. 11:17–20 and of human boasting in 1 Cor. 1:26–31); and that he favored relying on the grace of God for righteousness is also beyond doubt (so also Rom. 3:24). There is here, however, no indication that Paul thought that the law had failed *because* keeping it leads to the wrong attitude or that his opposition to boasting *accounts* for his saying that righteousness is not by law. The unbroken argument of Rom. 3:27 — 4:25 concerns not the attitude of self-righteousness, but God's plan of salvation, which is stated clearly in the Abraham story and which is now made available to those who have faith in Christ, without distinction.

We have concentrated thus far on the question of whether or not the objection to righteousness by law in 3:27 — 4:25 is based on the supposed attitude of self-righteousness which obeying the law produces, since that is the argument which has come to the fore in recent scholarly discussion. We should note, however, that Romans 4 follows 1:18 — 3:26, where Paul argues that everyone transgresses. In Romans 5 also, as we have already noted, Paul says that everyone has sinned. It might therefore be proposed that what really stands behind Paul's objection to righteousness by law in this section is the universal fact of transgression.

That is, in fact, the sequence of Paul's argument: Gentiles sin according to the law "written on their hearts" (Rom. 2:15), Jews sin according to the law as given to Moses (2:21–24), all are under sin (3:9), all have sinned (3:23), and righteousness is by faith (3:24). Similarly in chapter 5: all sinned (5:12), all are condemned by Adam's trespass (5:18f.), all (or many) gain righteousness through Christ (5:18f.). Thus Paul unquestionably appeals to universal sinfulness as an argument. Yet it is apparent that the argument is based on the conclusion, rather than the conclusion on the argument. The statements of universal sinfulness are remarkably inconsistent. As we shall show in detail in the appendix to chapter 3, Rom. 1:18 — 2:29 is not actually a consistent or even successful argument in favor of universal transgression. Romans 2 repeatedly holds out the possibility of righteousness by the law as a real one. Further, the statements of Romans 2 and Romans 5 are not harmonious. Romans 2 argues that the same law judges everyone; Rom. 5:12–14 that, during the period from Adam to Moses, sin led to death even without the law. Paul then inconsistently says that law is required for sin to be counted, but that it was counted anyway. Transgression led to condemnation even between Adam and Moses (5:14, 18). The diversity and inconsistency of the statements of universal transgression, especially the fact that it is both associated with the law and said to have been the human condition apart from law, lead to the conclusion that the difficulty of fulfilling the law is not the basis for the view that righteousness is by faith. Paul's argument has the appearance of being an inductive and empirical one, but it is evident that the various statements of human transgression are arguments in favor of a position to which Paul came on some other ground. Rom. 1:18 — 2:29 and chapter 5 do not lead to the conclusion that the basis of Paul's view was human inability to fulfill the law.[91]

Romans 9:30 — 10:13. Paul's argument in Romans 9 — 11, as far as it concerns the law, is also based on his view of the facts of soteriology. For the purpose of the present discussion we shall consider only Rom. 9:30–10:13.

This passage, or part of it, at first blush offers the best proof that Paul's argument against the law is really against a legalistic way of observing it. Further, the passage has been taken to prove that Paul accuses Judaism, or at least non-Christian Jews, of legalism. This understanding can be grounded on one plausible reading of 9:30–32a and emphasizing *tēn idian* in 10:3.

The translation of 9:30f. constitutes a well-known difficulty. Translated more or less literally, the passage says this: "Gentiles, though they did not seek righteousness, attained righteousness, namely righteousness on the basis of faith. But Israel, though pursuing a law of righteousness, did not reach law." The problem is the last clause. Precisely what is Israel's fault? That they did not reach righteousness by the law, or that they did not succeed in fulfilling the law? The koine text-type substituted "law of righteousness" for "law" and thus solved the problem, and many scholars interpret the passage by arguing that "of righteousness" or "that law" should be understood.[92] In this case "righteousness" is the understood object of the final verb.

C. E. B. Cranfield has argued strongly against improving the meaning by supplying a word to modify the final "law."[93] If one were to accept this point, and if 9:30–32a were not followed by 9:30b — 10:13, his understanding of a difficult passage would be the best available: some Gentiles who did not pursue righteousness nevertheless received it, explicitly the righteousness based on faith. But Israel, pursuing a law which would lead to righteousness, did not succeed in *fulfilling* the law. Why? Because they pursued it as if it were based not on faith but on works. According to this understanding of the verse, the argument is that had Israel pursued the law *in a different way*,[94] not as external deeds to be done to establish self-righteousness, but in reliance on the gift of God, fulfilling the law would have produced righteousness — apart from Christ.

The first, although relatively minor difficulty with Cranfield's interpretation is the understanding of the verb *ephthasen*, ordinarily translated "reach" or "attain," to mean "fulfill."[95] The principal difficulty, however, is that the rest of Paul's argument in the section stands against it.

We should first of all observe that Rom. 9:30–33 is the beginning of a discussion which concludes in 10:21. While there is no sharp break between the preceding "remnant" passage and 9:30, the question "what then shall we say" does mark the beginning of a new turn to the argument. Johannes Munck, for example, regarded 9:30 — 10:21 as the central section of chapters 9 — 11. The section "serves to explain the way of salvation opened by God in Christ — justification by faith — and to make it clear that God never tires of issuing the call to salvation, a call that includes Israel."[96] Numerous other scholars have pointed out the connection of 9:30–33 with what follows.[97] Without trying to decide in detail the structure of the passage, we need only make the point that the interpretation of 9:30–32a needs to make sense within the context of what follows.

The immediate sequel clarifies Paul's statement that Israel sought their goal not by faith but by works: they stumbled on the stumbling stone which God ("I" in the conflated quotation of 9:33) placed in Zion. Had they believed in him they would not have been put to shame (9:33b). The simplest interpretation of the meaning of the quotation, and the one generally accepted, is probably correct: the "stumbling-stone" is Christ, and those who believe in him are not put to shame.[98] The explanation of "not by faith but by works," then, is "they did not believe in Christ," not "they incorrectly tried for righteousness and by trying achieved only self-righteousness." Israel's failure is not that they do not obey the law in the correct way, but that they do not have faith in Christ.[99]

This line of argument continues. Israel is at fault not for the manner in which the goal was sought — zealously, and Paul approves of zeal in the sense of "fervor"[100] — but because the goal was through ignorance perceived wrongly. They did not know about God's righteousness and sought their own (10:3). The contrast between their own righteousness and God's is explained by v. 4: Christ is the end of the law, so that there might be righteousness for *all* who have faith. Here Paul repeats one of the main themes of Romans 3 — 4, that God's righteousness is, through Christ, available on the basis on faith to all on equal footing. If God's righteousness is the righteousness which is by faith in Christ and which is available to Gentile as well as Jew, then the Jewish righteousness which was zealously sought is the righteousness available to the Jew *alone* on the basis of observing the law.[101] *"Their own righteousness," in other words, means "that righteousness which the Jews alone are privileged to obtain" rather than "self-righteousness which consists in individuals' presenting their merits as a claim upon God."* The argument is christological and is oriented around the principle of equality of Jew and Gentile.

Rom. 10:1–3 have, to be sure, been understood to confirm the view that Paul's objection to the law is that it leads to self-righteousness. Thus, in commenting on "zeal," Herman Ridderbos comments: "Zeal for the law can altogether alienate man from God, and has precisely the effect of making him a sinner."[102] "Their own" is interpreted thus: "It is already fundamentally sinful to wish to insure oneself righteousness and life; indeed this is the human sin par excellence."[103] Beker has an equally generalized paraphrase of Paul's meaning:

> Although I am "confessionally" and publicly zealously engaged in attending to God and my neighbor, I am secretly striving for my own righteousness (Rom. 10:3). The person under the law is, from the perspective of the lordship of Christ, the *homo incurvatus in se* (Luther).[104]

I must confess that I find this sort of interpretation bewildering. Paul does not say anything which remotely approaches this individualized and generalized interpretation of the passage. He does not equate "zeal" with "sin," but rather concedes that it is a credit to the Jews, who despite it pursue the wrong goal. *Tēn idian* in 10:3 is unmistakably "their own" righteousness, as we remarked above, not "my own." The contrast with "their own" righteousness, which is available by law, is "the righteousness of God," apparently "true" righteousness,[105] which has two characteristics: it comes by faith and it is available to *all* (10:4).[106] "Their own" righteousness, then, is not characterized as being self-righteousness, but rather as being the righteousness which is limited to followers of the law.[107]

Rom. 10:4 has, perhaps, received as much attention as any single verse in Paul. Most of the debate has centered around *telos*, which may mean either "goal" or "end." Either interpretation can be supported by other passages in Paul. Paul's view that Christians are no longer under the law (Rom. 6:15; 7:4; Gal. 2:19) could easily result in his saying that the law is at an end. That the law had the function of holding people in bondage *so that* they could be saved by faith (Gal. 3:23f.) could just as easily lead to the statement that Christ was the goal towards which the law pointed. Further to complicate the issue, we may observe that these two interpretations of *telos* in 10:4 are not mutually exclusive. Christ could simultaneously terminate the law (for Christians) and fulfill its intent.

I am inclined toward the view that *telos* in 10:4 means primarily end, but this question is not decisive for understanding the general argument. In any case the distinctive characteristic of the righteousness brought by Christ is made clear in the closing words of the verse, "to *all* who *faith.*" To understand Paul's precise meaning it is important, however, to understand the force of the phrase *eis dikaiosynēn*, "unto righteousness."[108] The phrase is not a purpose clause, which Paul elsewhere uses when he tries to state the relationship between the law on the one hand and faith and righteousness on the other (Rom. 5:20f.; Gal. 3:22, 24).[109]

The closest parallel is Rom. 3:22, "the righteousness of God through faith in Christ for all who faith" *(eis pantas tous pisteuontas).* This verse, despite the similarity, does not solve the problem of *eis dikaiosynēn* in 10:4. In 3:21 *eis pantas* is governed by *dikaiosynē.* Paul is discussing God's righteousness, which is "for all who faith." The antecedent of *eis dikaiosynēn* in 10:4, however, is by no means clear. Some would connect it directly with *telos.* Thus Paul Meyer, who understands *telos* to be "goal," translates "intent of law . . . to lead to righteousness for everyone who believes." His paraphrase of the verse as a whole is this: "For the intent and goal of the law, to lead to righteousness for everyone who believes, is (nothing different from) Christ."[110] Franz Mussner also connects *eis dikaiosynēn* directly with *telos,* but he understands *telos* to mean "end." He translates, "Christus (ist) des Gesetzes Ende zur Gerechtigkeit für jeden, der glaubt."[111] In Mussner's view this means that Christ is the end of the law for the righteousness of those who believe, while the possibility remains open that Israel, without having faith, will be righteous by the law. Christ is the end of the law with regard to righteousness for Christians, but not necessarily for Jews.[112]

Neither lexical study nor considerations of grammar and syntax result in unquestionable results. Scholars will continue to interpret this verse in accordance with their general understanding of the law and righteousness in Paul and in conformity with their construction of the immediate context. The most that can be accomplished here is to indicate the reading of the verse which is adopted and the reasons for the choice of that reading. In the first place, it seems probable that *eis dikaiosynēn* is final or consecutive, "with a view to" or "resulting in." Several passages can be adduced to support this interpretation of *eis:* Rom. 5:18, *eis katakrima, eis dikaiōsin zoēs;* Phil. 1:19, *eis sōtērian;* Rom. 10:1, *eis sōtērian;* 10:10, *eis dikaiōsynēn, eis sōtērian.*[113] Second, it is unlikely that *eis dikaiosynēn* modifies only *telos* or *nomou* (the latter would mean that Christ is the end of the law as a way of righteousness, but not in other respects).[114] Käsemann and others are to be followed in understanding the phrase which begins with *eis dikaiosynēn* to modify the entire preceding clause.[115] Thus the reading is this: Christ is the end of the law; the result is that righteousness is available to all who faith. Translating *telos* as "goal" would not greatly alter the meaning.[116] The weight falls on the statement that the consequence or result of Christ's coming is that righteousness is available to *all* who *faith.*

C. K. Barrett adopts this understanding of the syntax, but he puts the accent on righteousness: "The key to the present passage is to be found in the words 'by realizing righteousness' (literally, 'unto righteousness' — 'unto' expressing purpose, or goal). Christ is the end of the law, with a view not to anarchy but to righteousness."[117] The context, however, seems to require putting the emphasis on "all" and "faith." The discussion begins with "Israel" and "Gentiles" (Rom. 9:30f.) and continues by denying that Israel's "own" righteousness is the same as "the righteousness of God" (10:3). Paul will continue by contrasting "the righteousness which is based on law" with "the righteousness which is based on faith" (10:5f.). Thus the point at issue is not "righteousness versus anarchy" but "righteousness for all by faith" versus "righteousness for the Jews by law."

Some, we have seen, find in Rom. 10:4 a distinction with regard to *how* the law is observed (Christ ends legalism, the law as perverted by self-righteousness, not the law as such),[118] or with regard to those for whom the law is at an end (Christ ends the law only for "those who faith," not necessarily for Jews, who may still hope to be righteous by the law).[119] Paul's own distinction, however, is stated in what should be unmistakable terms in 10:5f.: there is a righteousness by law and there is a righteousness by faith. Hübner reads even this verse as meaning that the contrast is between two ways of observing the law. Rom. 10:5, in his view, says that Moses correctly stated that the law, when not perverted by legalistic self-achievement, leads to life.[120] But the more natural reading of the verse yields much better sense: there is a righteousness based on law, concerning which Moses wrote, "the one who does [it] shall live by it" (Lev. 18:5). But Scripture, Paul continues, shows that there is another righteousness, which is near in the "word of faith which we preach." When one confesses Christ as Lord and faiths in his heart that God raised him from the dead, *then* he will be saved (10:9f.). This is proved by another Scripture: "*Everyone (pas) who faiths* in him will not be put to shame" (10:11). The climax of the immediate argument is then reached: There is *no distinction* between

Jew and Greek. He is the Lord of *all (pas)*; his riches are for *all (pas)* who call on him; *everyone (pas)* who calls on the name of the Lord will be saved (10:12f.). That is, Moses was incorrect when he wrote that everyone who fulfills the law will "live." There is another righteousness, based on faith, available to all without distinction, and it is this righteousness which saves. The fourfold repetition of *pas* (all or everyone), the phrase "without distinction," and the explicit contrast between "righteousness by law" and "righteousness by faith" show without ambiguity the thrust of the argument. We may summarize it, beginning with 10:2: The Jews have been ignorant of the righteousness of God. They sought it zealously, but misunderstood it. They pursued "their own" righteousness, that which is by law. Christ is the end of the law, and the consequence is that righteousness is available to all on the basis of faith. Although Moses said that those who are righteous by the law would live, Scripture itself shows that real righteousness is by faith and leads to salvation for all who faith, without distinction.

Recently, a discussion has arisen as to whether or not Paul connects faith exclusively with Christ. His thought, it has been proposed, may have been theocentric rather than christocentric.[121] "Faith" in Rom. 10:9 is "faith that God raised him from the dead," but this may imply more "faith in God" than "faith in Christ."[122] The "Lord" of 10:12f. may be God rather than Christ. Romans 4 may be cited to support the theocentric meaning of "faith" in Paul.[123] Vv. 16f. are especially striking: "those who share the faith of Abraham," which is explicitly said to have been in God. It is noteworthy that, in a phrase similar to that of 10:9, Paul in 4:24 characterizes faith as "faith in him who raised from the dead Jesus our Lord."

I think that Rom. 9:30 — 10:13 is on the whole christocentric. The fact that the Jews "did not submit to God's righteousness" is grounded by the statement that "Christ is the end of the law." That is, God's righteousness is defined by reference to Christ. The "word of faith which we preach" includes Christ; the confession is that "Jesus is Lord" (10:8f.). The christological content of the preaching which leads to faith is reaffirmed in 10:17.

It is probably a mistake, however, to play off against each other "theocentric" and "christocentric" interpretations of Paul. It is doubtful that Paul could have made a clear distinction between "faith in the God who reveals himself in Christ" and "faith in Christ."[124] In his treatment of Abraham, he does not speculate on whether or not anyone had "the faith of Abraham" between Abraham's own day and the coming of Christ. Abraham, as we noted above, is a paradigmatic type.[125] What is said about him applies to "us" (Rom. 4:23), and there is no generalization. "Faith" may be "faith in the God who raised Jesus" (Rom. 4:24; 10:9) or "faith in Christ" (10:17:

41

faith comes by the preaching of Christ), apparently with no alteration in meaning. Modern theology is rightly concerned with the distinction, but it is perhaps asking too much to look to Paul for the solution to this particular problem.

The entire line of argument from Rom. 9:30 to 10:13 should now be clear. We may state it in the form of three propositions: (1) Israel has failed because, being ignorant of the righteousness of God, they sought the righteousness which is available only to those who do the law; (2) the righteousness of God is available to all on an equal basis; (3) that basis is faith in Christ.[126] These points are so clear, and they have so little to do with Israel's manner of observing the law, or even Israel's success in fulfilling the law, that they allow us confidently to grasp the intended meaning of 9:31. The meaning is that Israel did not *attain* (a better translation of *ephthasen* than fulfill)[127] the one thing that would produce true righteousness. "The one thing" Paul enigmatically calls *nomos*. Even if one supplies "that" before *nomos* ("that law," namely, the "law of righteousness" mentioned in the previous clause) or the phrase "of righteousness" after *nomos*,[128] it must still be said that Paul did not say precisely what he meant. The context requires the last clause of 9:31 to be more general than *nomos* allows. Paul immediately specifies what Israel did not attain: the righteousness of God which comes by faith in Christ. To use *nomos* when one means "righteousness by faith" is certainly curious, and Cranfield's broadside against scholars who want to change what Paul wrote so that it agrees with what he thought is certainly understandable.[129] Paul probably repeated the word *nomos* because it had just occurred and it seemed to make a balanced phrase.[130] One can perhaps observe that this would not be the only instance in which the desire for a balanced antithesis led Paul to an almost incomprehensible combination of words. Rom. 8:10 is a case in point.[131] Despite the difficulties of 9:31, however, the thrust of the passage is clear, and it seems to leave no room for the position that Paul opposed the law on the grounds that no one is able to fulfill it or on the gounds that Jews sought to fulfill it in the wrong way. Paul is discussing what he regards as a soteriological fact. His hope for Israel is that they be saved, but he states with emphasis the only ground of salvation: faith in Christ, which is available to all without distinction (10:11–13) and which excludes the law as a way to "righteousness."

Before leaving Romans, we should ask whether or not, in Romans 3 − 4 and 9 − 10, the passages in which Paul discussed "righteousness by faith, not by law," the topic is "admission to the body of those who will be saved," as it was in Galatians. Romans does not have the polemical edge of Galatians, where Paul was combating the imposition of another admission requirement on his Gentile converts. In Romans 3 — 4 the discussion is not couched so explicitly in terms of membership in the people of God as it is in Galatians. The general flow of the argument from Romans 3 to 5, however, shows that the topic is how to escape the universal power of sin (3:9) and how to gain eternal life (5:21). The general setting of the discussion of righteousness by faith, in other words, is the transfer from one state to another. In the passage on Abraham, Paul naturally puts some of his argument in terms of belonging to a group: by faith one becomes a descendant or heir of Abraham (4:13f.). Much of the terminology, however, describes not the condition of attaining membership in a group, but the ground on which one attains the correct relationship to God (e.g. 4:2).

That "righteousness by faith, not by law" still has to do with transfer to, or membership in, the body of those who will be saved is clearer in Romans 9 — 10. One of the topics of chapter 9 is "who belongs to Israel?" (9:6), and Paul's view is that there is not a one-to-one correlation of "Israel" with the physical descendants of Abraham (9:7f.). "My people" (9:25) are those whom God has called, whether from Israel or from among the Gentiles (9:24). In this context, the question of who has righteousness, and on what basis it is attained, is to be seen as a question of membership in the people of God. This question, in turn, bears directly on salvation, which is named as the topic in 10:1 and as the result of faith in 10:13. Thus we conclude that "righteousness by faith, not by law" remains in Romans Paul's principle when discussing membership in the body of those who will be saved.

Philippians 3:9

For the sake of completeness we should take some account of Phil. 3:9, where the terms righteousness, law, and faith occur. We shall return to Philippians 3 in chapter 4 below, and here only one or two observations are necessary. In the first place, we must note that this is not a passage in which Paul says that "righteousness is not by law." Even more clearly than in Rom. 9:30 — 10:13 he distinguishes two righteousnesses — one by law, the other by faith. The distinction is clearer here than in Rom. 10:4–6 because in Phil. 3:9 the obvious meaning is that Paul himself had righteousness by the law, while in Rom. 10:3 it is said that the Jews sought that righteousness, without the explicit statement that they found it but that it turned out to be the wrong righteousness,[132] which is what Paul says of himself in Phil. 3:6, 9. As will be seen in chapter 4 below, I regard this passage as extremely revealing for Paul's overall view of the law. Here we may make the limited point that the passage lends support neither to the view that Paul regarded the law as impossible to fulfill, nor to the view that he regarded fulfilling it as wrong because it leads to self-righteousness.

The passage, to be sure, has been generally interpreted as supporting the second view — in fact it is one of the bases of that view.[133] The phrase "my righteousness" *(emēn dikaiosynēn)* in 3:9 is understood as "my individual righteousness, based on the merit achieved by the performance of good deeds, which leads to boasting." This reading requires a conflation of Phil. 3:9 with Rom. 3:27; 4:2 ("boasting"), the understanding of "boasting" as "boasting in one's individual performance" *(Sich-Ruhmen)*[134] rather than "boasting in the special status of Israel," and the supplying of two views which Paul does not express: (1) righteousness by law is a meritorious achievement which allows one to demand reward from God and is thus a denial of grace; (2) such righteousness is self-evidently a bad thing. There goes with this remarkable reading the assumption, either implicit or explicit, that Paul accused Judaism of leading to this regrettable state of affairs.[135] The conflation of Phil. 3:3–11 with Rom. 3:27 and 4:2 is aided by the reference to "confidence in the flesh" in Phil. 3:3f.[136] Further, Paul says that his former confidence in the flesh was partly in status (circumcised, Israelite, Benjaminite) and partly in accomplishment (zealous and blameless). Thus it can be made to appear that Paul accused Judaism, with himself as the paradigmatic example, of the attitude of boastful self-righteousness.

This line of interpretation probably appears all the more convincing because of two judgments: opposition to self-righteousness is part and parcel of the Christian faith and therefore Paul must have expressed it; Jewish literature itself reveals Judaism as a religion of legalistic self-righteousness;[137] therefore when Paul speaks of his confidence in his former life he must have had that attitude in mind.

Yet the traditional interpretation is not confirmed by a simple reading of the text. Paul does not say that boasting in status and achievement was wrong because boasting is the wrong attitude, but that he boasted in things that *were gain.* They *became loss* because, in his black and white world, there is no second best. His criticism of his own former life is not that he was guilty of the attitudinal sin of self-righteousness, but that he put confidence in something other than faith in Jesus Christ.

Thus "my own righteousness" in Phil. 3:9 is indeed, as is commonly said, the same as "their own righteousness" in Rom. 10:3. It is not, however, what is thought of today as "self-righteousness." It is the righteousness which comes by law, which is therefore the peculiar result of being an observant

44

Jew, which is *in and of itself a good thing* ("zeal," Rom. 10:2; "gain," Phil. 3:7), but which is shown to be "wrong" ("loss," Phil. 3:7f.) by the revelation of "God's righteousness," which comes by faith in Christ.

In the light of Rom. 10:4–6 and especially Phil. 3:9, we also gain an important insight into Paul's use of the *dik*-root. In the other passages Paul says that no one is righteoused by doing the law; in these two passages he distinguishes between two righteousnesses, the righteousness of the law and the righteousness of or from God which comes by faith in Christ. It seems fair to conclude that the statements to the effect that righteousness is not by law mean that *real* righteousness is not by law. I think that the explanation of Paul's usage is simple. He knows that the most common term in Judaism for the *maintenance* of correct status is "righteous." Philippians 3 also shows that he is prepared to grant that observant Jews — he is the paradigm — have such righteousness. In the terms appropriate to Judaism, one is put in the covenant by the gracious election of God; one stays in it by observing the law and atoning for transgression; such a person is "righteous by the law." Paul, however, uses the passive form of *dikaioun* to mean "be transferred from the state of sin to the new life of Christ." Those who make that transfer have "the righteousness of God." Thus he can say, as he says in Galatians and in some passages in Romans, that no one is "righteoused" by law (his distinctive use of the passive verb), but he can also say that those who have the righteousness which comes by observing the law (the common Jewish meaning) do not have the righteousness of God — that is, true righteousness.

Paul also thought, as we said above and as will become especially clear in chapter 3 below, that Christians should behave in the correct way in order to maintain their new status. He ordinarily does not use the *dik*-root for such behavior, but rather a variety of terms, many drawn from the purity language of the Bible, such as "blameless."[138]

Conclusion: Not by Law

We are now ready to see what conclusions can be drawn from the passages in which Paul says that one cannot be righteoused by law. The first conclusion is to confirm the opening observation. The topic is how one transfers from the state of sin and condemnation to the state which is the pre-condition of end-time salvation.[139] Since Paul thought of those who would be saved as constituting a group, which he calls by various terms, I have called the topic "how to enter the body of those who would be saved." What Paul says on this topic, as it touches the law, is "not by means of observing the law."

45

Thus the topic is, in effect, soteriology, although one should always respect Paul's own reservation of the *sōzō/sōtēr* root for final salvation.[140] Romans 3 – 4, to repeat, is part of a discussion of escape from the power of sin and attainment of eternal life (3:9; 5:20). In 4:13 the promise to Abraham is that he would inherit "the world," where "the world" almost certainly means, in Jewish terminology, "the world to come." The soteriological significance of "righteoused by faith, not by law" is explicitly stated in Romans 9 – 10, where *sōtēria* appears in 10:1, 10 and *sōzō* in 10:9. Galatians is remarkable for the relative absence of end-time language, but the ruling topic of chapter 3 is how to become a descendant of Abraham, and the reason for discussing this is the unspoken assumption that the true descendants of Abraham will be saved. That the assumed goal in mind is salvation is seen in 5:5: the "hope of righteousness" most likely refers to the final judgment. The soteriological context is also evident in Philippians 3, especially v. 11.

With regard to the identity of those against whom Paul says "not by works of law," we have seen that the slashing attack of Galatians refers not to Judaism on its own terms, but to a Christian position. Nevertheless, Paul applies the principle to Judaism also, first in Gal. 2:15f., then more fully in Romans 3 – 4; 9 – 11. The application to Judaism, however, is not against a supposed Jewish position that enough good works earn righteousness. In the phrase "not by works of law" the emphasis is not on *works* abstractly conceived but on *law*, that is, the Mosaic law. The argument is that one need not be Jewish to be "righteous" and is thus against the standard Jewish view that accepting and living by the law is a sign and condition of favored status. *This is both the position which, independently of Paul, we can know to have characterized Judaism*[141] *and the position which Paul attacks.*[142]

In other terms, Paul's "not by works of law" shows that he had come to hold a different view of God's plan of salvation from that of non-Christian Judaism. It was never, he argues, God's intention that one should accept the law in order to become one of the elect. Though fully evident now that Christ has come, God's intention to save on the basis of faith, not the law, was previously announced in Scripture.[143] The case is made above all by Abraham, who was chosen without accepting the law. *This is, in effect, an attack on the traditional understanding of the covenant and election,* according to which accepting the law signified acceptance of the covenant.

With regard to the final question — *why* Paul said "not by works of law" — our first conclusions are negative. It was not because the law cannot be followed, nor because following it leads to legalism, self-righteousness and self-estrangement. Most of Paul's arguments are based on Scripture, but we can hardly think that simply by reading the Scripture he came to the view that obedience to the commandments contained in it is not the prerequisite for righteousness. We see, rather, that he arrived at a position which led him to read Scripture and to understand God's intention in a new light.[144]

In the passages considered thus far we have seen two principles dominating Paul's discussions. One I have called that of God's plan of salvation or the facts of soteriology. It is that God intended that salvation be by faith; thus by definition it is not by law. Further, this discussion is connected with faith in Christ,[145] so that one may equally well call the principle that of christology. The other main concern is that the Gentiles are to be saved on the same basis as the Jews. Thus the Jewish law as such is excluded as a means of entry. Interestingly enough, this can also be called a revised view of God's plan of salvation: God intended that the Gentiles should come in and that the law and election, the points of Jewish privilege, should not count with regard to salvation (e.g., Rom. 3:1-9). Obviously these two points form a tight unity: God intended that *all* be saved on the basis of *faith*. Scripture predicted that the *Gentiles* should receive the inheritance of Abraham on the basis of *faith* (Gal. 3:8); the death of Christ was for the purpose of making salvation available on the basis of faith (Rom. 3:26, *eis to*), and explicitly for the inclusion of the Gentiles on that basis (Gal. 3:13f., *hina*); the law itself was given with the end in view that salvation would be by faith apart from law (Gal. 3:22, 24, *hina*).[146]

This gives us another way of defining Paul's "attack" on the law — more precisely, what he found inadequate in it. I said just above that it is the notion of Jewish privilege and the idea of election which he attacks, and I have elsewhere written that his real attack on Judaism is against the idea of the covenant and that what he finds wrong in Judaism is that it lacks Christ.[147] Perhaps putting the matter in terms of God's plan of salvation formulates those ideas in a more precise and more understandable way. What is wrong with the law, and thus with Judaism, is that it does not provide for God's ultimate purpose, that of saving the entire world through faith in Christ, and without the privilege accorded to Jews through the promises, the covenants, and the law.[148]

Thus far, then, we have found this answer to the question of why Paul said "not by works of law": God intended that entry to the body of the saved be available to all on the basis of faith in Christ. This answer can be separated out into two: Christology and the status of the Gentiles,[149] but the fundamental unity of Paul's revised outlook must be stressed.

The answer to our question has two limitations which should be noted. It is, in the first place, an answer which takes into account a limited number of passages in which Paul discusses the law, those in which he says that no one is righteoused by doing the law and those in which he contrasts righteousness by the law with God's righteousness. These are not the only passages in which Paul finds "fault" with the law, and thus it is not certain that we have succeeded in adequately explaining what Paul found wrong with the law, and consequently with Judaism. Secondly, we have thus far remained in the realm of exegetical explanation. The twofold reason which we have seen for Paul's rejection of righteousness by the law may itself be derived from factors which have not yet become visible. There may be, that is, more than one level of explanation for Paul's attitude toward the law.

Despite these limitations, something has been achieved. We have seen, at least thus far, a limited rejection of the law. The attack on righteousness by the law is against making acceptance of the law a condition of membership in the body of those who will be saved. The reasons for his position which are thus far visible can be immediately connected with one of his primary convictions: salvation is available to all on the same basis, faith.

NOTES

1. In reading Rudolf Bultmann "one gets the impression that zeal for the law is more damaging than transgression": Heikki Räisänen, "Legalism and Salvation by the Law," in *Die Paulinische Literatur und Theologie* (Aarhus: Forlaget Aros, 1980), p. 68.

2. Three positions on why Paul said "not by law" will receive little or no attention here: (1) It was a standard Jewish view that the law ceases with the messianic era (Schweitzer, Schoeps); (2) Romans 7 shows that Paul had become frustrated in his attempt to find righteousness under the law and therefore denounced it (many scholars, especially of an earlier period); (3) Paul had an apocalyptic view of the law as a monolithic totality and could thus dismiss it *it toto* (Wilckens). On these see E. P. Sanders, *Paul and Palestinian Judaism* (Philadelphia: Fortress Press, 1977), pp. 478–80 and notes (hereafter cited as PPJ). The second explanation continues to be brought forward and will be briefly reconsidered on pp. 76f. and n. 33.

3. Hans Hübner, *Das Gesetz bei Paulus*, 2d. ed. (Göttingen: Vandenhoeck & Ruprecht, 1980).

4. In reviewing Betz's commentary on Galatians, Davies challenges the view that the converts were pagan Gentiles (W. D. Davies's, review of *Galatians* by Hans Dieter Betz, RSR 7 [1981]: 312–14). The question is discussed in detail in the second part of the present work.

5. Most scholars agree that the opposing missionaries introduced such Biblical themes as sonship to Abraham. See, for example, Jost Eckert, *Die urchristliche Verkündigung im Streit zwischen Paulus und seinen Gegnern nach dem Galaterbrief* (Regensburg: F. Pustet, 1971), pp. 76, 105; Hübner, *Gesetz*, pp. 17f. A few have doubts: Brendan Byrne, *"Sons of God"—"Seed of Abraham"* (Rome: Biblical Institute Press, 1979), pp. 148f.

6. Most scholars agree that the opposing missionaries were Christian. Note Paul's

description of their message as "a different gospel" (Gal. 1:6) and his accusation that his opponents wish to escape being persecuted for the cross of Christ (6:12). In addition, his appeals to the defeat of the "false brethren" in Jerusalem and to the agreement with Peter and James have point only if the dispute is an inner-Christian one. For the history of research see Heinrich Schlier, *Der Brief an die Galater*, 5th ed. (Göttingen: Vandenhoeck & Ruprecht, 1971), pp. 19–24; Franz Mussner, *Der Galaterbrief*, Freiburg: Herder, 1974), pp. 11–29 (with a detailed summary of positions); Hans Dieter Betz, *Galatians*, (Philadelphia: Fortress Press 1979), pp. 4–9; Eckert, *Verkündigung*, pp. 1–18.

Munck made it a main thesis in his attack on the Tübingen school that "the Judaizing opponents in Galatians are Gentile Christians" (Johannes Munck, *Paul and the Salvation of Mankind* (Atlanta: John Knox Press, 1977), pp. 87f. The principal evidence is the present participle *hoi peritemnomenoi* in 6:13. So also H. J. Schoeps, *Paul* (Philadelphia: Westminster Press, 1961), p. 65; Peter Richardson, *Israel in the Apostolic Church* (New York: Cambridge University Press, 1969), pp. 84–97. Cf. Pierre Bonnard, *L'Epitre de Saint Paul aux Galâtes*, 2d. ed. (Neuchâtel and Paris: Delachaux & Niestlé, 1972), pp. 2–5, 13: the opponents were certainly Christians, probably of Hellenistic Jewish origin or former pagans who had proselytized before embracing Christianity. George Howard (*Crisis in Galatia*, [New York: Cambridge University Press, 1979], pp. 17–19) takes full account of the present participle but nevertheless concludes that the opponents were probably Jewish Christians; see generally his chapter 1. He proposes that they may not have known that Paul had reached agreement with the "pillars."

Some have attempted to describe the situation of the opposing missionaries more precisely. Thus, for example, Robert Jewett ("The Agitators and the Galatian Congregation," *NTS* 17 [1970–71]: 198–212) proposed that they were acting under "zealotic" pressure from non-Christian Jews. This view seems to be accepted by W. D. Davies in "Paul: From the Semitic Point of View," *Cambridge History of Judaism II* (forthcoming).

For the present purpose, it is the position of the opponents, not their precise identity, which is important. Here only one other scholarly proposal need be mentioned. Some have argued that Paul faced a "second front" in Galatia and that chapter 5 is his response to libertines. I follow the majority as seeing the paraenesis in chap. 5 against the background of Paul's own denial of the law in chaps. 3 and 4. The last two chapters of Galatians presuppose the same polemical situation as the first four. Note the references to the law in 5:14, 18, 23; 6:2. On all this see Eckert, *Verkündigung*, pp. 15–18 (literature), 64–71 (reply), 149f.

7. I am grateful to J. Louis Martyn for several discussions on the occasion and purpose of Galatians and on the position of the opposing missionaries.

8. "Jewish Christians" here include Paul. On the Jewish expectation see J. Jeremias, *Jesus' Promise to the Nations* (Philadelphia: Fortress Press; London: SCM Press, 1982), p. 61. It should be added that another Jewish view is attested: that the Gentiles would be destroyed. So 1QM; Jub. 22:20f. and elsewhere.

Many scholars have emphasized the eschatological setting of Paul's work and his view of the mission to the Gentiles. Thus Schoeps (*Paul*, p. 219): "Throughout his life the same prophetic promises were the impelling force behind this activity, the promise that in the Messianic age the nations would join Israel in the worship of its God . . ." (citing Zeph. 3:9). Munck especially emphasized the eschatological setting of the mission to the Gentiles, as well as Paul's reversal of the traditional scheme in Romans 9 – 11. See his *Christ and Israel* (Philadelphia: Fortress Press, 1967), pp. 11f. (citing Isa. 2:2–4 and Mic. 4:1–4); *Paul*, pp. 123, 255–58, 276f., 303–5. See also Ernst Käsemann, *Commentary on Romans* ET (Grand Rapids: Wm. B. Eerdmans, 1980), pp. 307, 312. The principal evidence is supplied by Romans 9 – 11, especially Paul's struggling with the reversal of the traditional scheme (so that the inclusion of the Gentiles precedes the full salvation of Israel) in 11:13–26. See further Part Two below.

Drane does not agree with the statement that all Jewish Christians whose views are known favored the mission to the Gentiles, disagreeing only as to the conditions on which Gentiles should be admitted. "On any account of the history of the earliest church, one of the most difficult questions for the Christians of the first generation was to decide whether the Christian faith was to be just a sect of Judaism, and whether therefore their preaching should be restricted to Jews, or whether the message was intended for Gentiles also" (J. W. Drane, *Paul: Libertine or Legalist?* [London: SPCK, 1975], p. 24). He has in view Matt. 10:5ff., which does indeed raise the question. The difficulty is in finding the *Sitz im Leben* of that passage. In any case, as far as the evidence of Galatians goes, the alternative is not "either a sect of Judaism" or "the Gentile mission," but "the Gentile mission without requiring the law" or "the mission to the Gentiles while requiring full proselytization."

9. Isa. 56:6–8 does give *halakah* (circumcision and Sabbath), but the passage is not cited in Paul's letters, and we cannot know whether or not it was used against him.

10. We need not here discuss the question of whether some Jews in the first century allowed proselytization without circumcision. On this see recently Neil J. McEleney, "Conversion, Circumcision and the Law," *NTS* 20 (1974): 319–41, esp. pp. 328–33; Peder Borgen, "Observations on the Theme 'Paul and Philo': Paul's preaching of circumcision in Galatia (Gal. 5:11) and debates on circumcision in Philo," in *Die Paulinische Literatur und Theologie* (Aarhus: Forlaget Aros, 1980), p. 88; Larry Schiffman, "At the Crossroads: Tannaitic Perspectives on the Jewish-Christian Schism," in *Jewish and Christian Self-Definition*, vol. 2, *Aspects of Judaism in the Graeco-Roman Period* (Philadelphia: Fortress Press; London: SCM Press, 1981), p. 127 and the note on p. 342; Eckert, *Verkündigung*, pp. 53–8. The rival missionaries in Galatia obviously took the view that circumcision was required.

11. Munck argued otherwise: the Jewish Christians (other than Paul) did not oppose the mission to the Gentiles (*Paul*, p. 119), but rather they "neither thought about nor laid down regulations for the admission of Gentiles into the Church." They presumed "that Israel's conversion would result in the saving of Gentiles" (p. 130; cf. pp. 255–58). It is clear in Gal. 2:3f., however, that the coming of Titus to Jerusalem forced the matter to the attention of the Jerusalem Christians (even if nothing else did); and the fact that emissaries came from James (Gal. 2:12) shows that some in Jerusalem were thinking about the consequences of the Gentile mission, even if for their own part they were prepared to leave it to others.

12. Cf. the discussion of the "third race" in Part Two below.

13. See, for example, F. F. Bruce, *Paul: Apostle of the Heart Set Free* (Grand Rapids: Wm. B. Eerdmans, 1977), pp. 176f.; Peter Richardson, "Pauline Incon-

sistency: I Corinthians 9:19–23 and Galatians 2:11–14," *NTS* 26 (1980): 347–62, esp. 348, 360f.

14. This point is well made by Bultmann in *TDNT* 6: 203–19. Cf. *PPJ*, pp. 441 n. 54, 445.

15. The formula quoted in Rom. 10:9 (*pisteuein hoti*), for example, is to be distinguished from Paul's characteristic usage.

16. H. Räisänen, in an article with which the present essay is in close agreement ("Legalism and Salvation by the Law"), poses the very interesting question of why Paul set up the law as a means of salvation only in order to knock it down (p. 77). His answer gives a convincing account of part of Paul's history (pp. 78–82). I would, however, pose the problem differently. Neither side sees the law as a possible means of salvation in the sense of producing sufficient *merit*. Paul's opponents take the standard Jewish view that to enter into the Biblical promises one has to accept the Biblical condition: the law of Moses. On doing the law as the *condition* of salvation, but not as earning it, see *PPJ*, index, s.v. obedience.

17. Cf. Lloyd Gaston, "Paul and the Torah," in *Anti-Semitism and the Foundations of Christianity* (New York: Paulist Press, 1979), p. 56: "It is remarkable that in the endless discussions of Paul's understanding of the law, few would have asked what a first century Jew would have thought of the law *as it related to Gentiles.*" He then, however, discusses the rabbinic concepts of "the righteous among the nations of the world," the Noachian Commandments, etc. One must be still more precise. In Rom. 2:14 the question of "righteous Gentiles" comes up, but the question of how much of the law Gentiles must do in order to be righteous *by the law's own standards* is not the principal question in Galatians (see on 3:10 and 5:3, discussed immediately below). The question is a Gentile one, but it is the question of circumcision and admission.

18. Or of "Pharisaic soteriology." See e.g., Betz, *Galatians*, p. 116 (on 2:16); modified on p. 146 (on 3:12): "not only against Judaism in general, but also against the Galatians' expectation, introduced by the anti-Pauline opposition." Hübner holds that the argument is against Judaism as Paul understood it, leaving open the possibility that he misunderstood it. (See, e.g., "Identitätsverlust und paulinische Theologie," *KuD* 24 [1978]: 183.) The distinction is irrelevant if the argument is not against Judaism. On Galatians 3 as against Jews as such see also G. Wagner, "Pour comprendre l'apôtre Paul," *Lumière et Vie* 27 (1978): 5–20; Ferdinand Hahn, "Das Gesetzesverständnis im Römer und Galaterbrief," *ZNW* 67 (1976–77): 51f. (following an excellent discussion of aspects of the law in Romans, Hahn curiously says that Galatians deals almost exclusively with Judaism); Ulrich Luz, *Das Geschichtsverständnis des Paulus* (Munich: Chr. Kaiser, 1968), p. 219 (Galatians is the earliest letter to confront Judaism). Among relatively recent treatments, that of Herman Ridderbos is remarkable for its lack of attention to occasion and context (*Paul: An Outline of His Theology* [Grand Rapids: Wm. B. Eerdmans, 1975]). He maintains with absolute consistency that Paul's discussions of the law are directed against Judaism. See pp. 131–43; 151; 170; 178. There is no treatment of the position of Paul's opponents in Galatia, and Paul is depicted as attacking Jewish legalistic works—righteousness, salvation by meritorious deeds, etc. (esp. pp. 131–53).

That the opponents in Galatia are Jewish Christians, not Jews, has been especially emphasized by Franz Mussner, who also sees the theological implications of the distinction. See *Der Galaterbrief*, pp. 11–29; "Theologische 'Wiedergutmachung.' Am Beispiel der Auslegung des Galaterbriefes," *Freiburger Rundbrief* 26 (1974): 7–11. Richardson (*Israel*, p. 91) points out that the discussion of the law in Galatians, though offensive to Jews, is against opponents within Christianity (Richardson views the opponents as Gentile Christians): "it is not a polemic directed against those who by birth are under that mantle."

19. Note Hübner's view, discussed below. Cf. Betz, *Galatians*, p. 117; Ridderbos in the preceding note.

20. So also Ulrich Wilckens, "Über Abfassungsweck und Aufbau des Römerbriefs," in *Rechtfertigung als Freiheit: Paulusstudien* (Neukirchen-Vluyn: Neukirchener Verlag, 1974), p. 132: the argument of the opponents in Galatians is that "the Gentiles must first of all accomplish the fundamental presupposition of full membership in the Church of God, namely, belonging to Israel."

Cf. W. D. Davies, "Paul and the People of Israel," *NTS* 24 (1977): 10: "Even when [in Galatians] he most forcefully presents the doctrine of justification by faith, Paul . . . was essentially concerned with establishing who constitute the true people of God"; so also Davies, in his review of Betz's *Galatians*, p. 317; "Paul: From the Semitic Point of View": the struggle over the law, as well as the doctrine of justification by faith, has to do with "the central question as to who constituted 'Israel,' the people of God."

In a paper presented at the meeting of the Society of Biblical Literature in December 1981, Robert Gundry argued that, from Paul's point of view, the question in Galatians is how one *stays* in, not how one gets in. There is a sense in which that is entirely correct. Those who accept the law will be cut off from Christ (Gal. 5:4). But that does not change the fact that the argument is about a membership requirement: how to be righteoused or how to be a true descendant of Abraham. Paul argues that the Galatian Christians already have that status and must not accept the law, represented by circumcision, in order truly to be "in." Accepting another membership requirement besides faith in Christ means rejecting the one which, in Paul's view, really counts.

21. I have previously discussed Gal. 3:10–12 in "On the Question of Fulfilling the Law in Paul and Rabbinic Judaism," in *Donum Gentilicium: New Testament Studies in Honour of David Daube* (Oxford: At the Clarendon Press, 1978), pp. 103–26. The present discussion somewhat alters and appreciably expands the view taken there. It is also exegetically distinct in confining the discussion to Galatians rather than combining Galatians and Romans.

The principal recent proponent of the view which is being opposed is Hans Hübner. See "Gal. 3, 10 und die Herkunft des Paulus," *KuD* 19 (1973): 215–31 (commented on in *PPJ*, p. 138 n. 61); "Das Ganze und das eine Gesetz," *KuD* 21 (1975): 239–56; "Identitätsverlust"; *Gesetz*, pp. 19f.; "Pauli Theologiae Proprium," *NTS* 26 (1980): 445–73. Hübner's principal points are that Galatians 3, and 3:10 in particular, opposes an understanding of human existence and that the accent falls on the word "all" in Gal. 3:10: Paul opposes the view that human existence is based on the quantity of fulfillment.

22. In favor of this view (because it is impossible to do all of it), besides Hübner, one may cite recently Mussner, *Galaterbrief*, p. 226. Georg Eichholz (*Die Theologie des Paulus im Umriss* [Neukirchen-Vluyn: Neukirchener Verlag, 1972], p. 247) also

emphasizes the word "all." Bonnard (*Galâtes*, p. 67) notes that some stress "all," some "curse." He prefers the latter. One may compare here the position of Ulrich Wilckens ("Was heisst bei Paulus: 'Aus Werken des Gesetzes wird kein Mensch gerecht?'" in *Rechtfertigung als Freiheit: Paulusstudien*, pp. 77–109). He sees the argument of Gal. 3:10–12 to run as follows: no one can do *all* the law (v. 10); *therefore* righteousness is no longer by the law but by faith (v. 11); for only one who does *all* the law will earn life by it (v. 12) (p. 92). It follows that the principle "not by works of law" applies to sinners; but everyone is a sinner; therefore *sinners* (= all) can be righteoused only by faith in Christ (p. 94). Cf. p. 84 (Romans 1 – 3, 7); pp. 97f. (Rom. 4:1–8); pp. 101f. (Rom. 9:30 – 10:13); p. 103 (Philippians 3); and the conclusion: it is actual sin which makes righteousness by works of law impossible (p. 104). As will be seen, I interpret all these passages differently.

23. The construct of the quotation from Hab. 2:4 in Gal. 3:11 continues to be debated, some holding that *ek pisteōs* modifies *zēsetai* rather than *ho dikaios*. Thus, for example, A. T. Hanson, *Studies in Paul's Technique and Theology* (London: SPCK, 1974), pp. 41f.: the construct of *ek pisteōs* as modifying *zēsetai* is confirmed by 3:12 "'live by them'" (a quotation of Lev. 18:5). Hanson finds the intended contrast to be between living by faith and living by the law. Similarly H. C. C. Cavallin, "'The Righteous Shall Live by Faith.' A Decisive Argument for the Traditional Interpretation," *ST* 32 (1978):33–43.

There is no doubt that Paul thought that one should live by faith rather than by the law. In the present passage, however, the precise argument contrasts being righteous by faith with being righteous by the law. The view of Hanson and Cavallin requires the reader to skip Paul's own interpretive remarks about the meaning of Hab. 2:4 and Lev. 18:5. The most natural reading is to understand Paul's own preface "no one is righteoused by law" to be the opposite of the quotation from Hab. 2:4. The meaning of Lev. 18:5 in Gal. 3:12 is discussed immediately below.

24. Paul's quotation in Gal. 3:8 agrees with Gen. 18:18 except for *en soi*, where it agrees with Gen. 12:3 (18:18 has *en autōi*). Barnabas Lindars (*New Testament Apologetic* [London: SCM Press, 1961], p. 225) puts the emphasis the other way: the quotation is based on Gen. 12:3, but the term *ethnē* is from 18:18. Lindars thinks that Paul must have had Gen. 12:3 in mind, since, in his view, Paul's argument requires that the promise to Abraham had been made before Gen. 15:6. That, however, does not seem to be Paul's point. The *pro*-verbs in Gal. 3:8 mean "before the present revelation of the gospel" rather than "before Gen. 15:6."

We should note that the terms "blessing" and "Gentiles" are connected with Abraham in Gen. 22:18; and in 17:5, 6, Abraham is said to be the father of many nations (*ethnē*, Gentiles). Gen. 18:18 suited Paul's argument best.

25. Paul's argument proves the case to those who are convinced by proof-texts. I hesitate to draw inferences about the education of Paul's readers from the subtlety of Paul's arguments, as does Betz (*Galatians*, p. 2). Paul may have argued according to his own education and that of his opponents, not that of his readers. Did they know how clever he had been? In any case, he almost certainly argued in the way approved in Pharisaic circles, as, we must presume, did his opponents. On proof-texting, see Ellis Rivkin, *A Hidden Revolution* (Nashville: Abingdon Press, 1978), pp. 273f. On the Jewishness of Paul's arguments, and the implication of that, see more fully below, pp. 182f. and notes.

26. The same argument applies against Schlier's view that the emphasis is on *poiein* (*Brief an die Galater*, p. 132).

27. For a good example, see Hübner, "Proprium," p. 462.

28. So also Betz, *Galatians*, p. 144 ("he states his conclusions first"; the meaning "is simply that exclusion from 'blessing' (cf. 6:16) equals 'curse'"); Schlier, *Der Brief an die Galater*, pp. 132f. ("Die Schriftstelle soll vielmehr nur bekräftigen, *dass* die Gesetzesleute unter dem Fluch stehen").

29. I leave aside here the relationship of the proof-text in 3:6 to the argument as a whole.

30. The force of the quotation of Lev. 18:5 in Gal. 3:12 is much debated. Hübner regards my view that Paul uses the verse to prove that the law does not rest on faith as "an interesting variant" ("Proprium," p. 461). But the interesting variant is Paul's own statement of what he intends to prove by quoting the verse! In Hübner's interpretation Lev. 18:5 goes together with Deut. 27:26 and shows that, when writing Galatians, Paul thought that in theory "life" could result from "doing," though factually this is not so, since no one can do *all*. That is, Paul quotes Lev. 18:5 in order to agree with it theoretically, while he quotes Deut. 27:26 to show that the theory cannot be carried out in practice (Hübner, *Gesetz*, pp. 19f.; "Proprium," pp. 461f.). I can only repeat that we should discover Paul's meaning in his own statements as to what each citation proves. He himself says that Lev. 18:5 proves that "the law does not rest on faith." Bonnard correctly observes that the point is that "the law *has nothing in common* with faith" (*Galates*, p. 68). So also Joseph Tyson, "'Works of Law' in Galatians," *JBL* 92 (1973):428; F. F. Bruce, "The Curse of the Law," in *Paul and Paulinism* (London: SPCK, 1982), pp. 27–36, here p. 29.

In addition to Hübner, other scholars also understand Paul to agree that one who did the law would live, provided that the law were perfectly fulfilled: Lindars, *Apologetic*, p. 229; Byrne, "*Sons of God,*" p. 152; Ridderbos, *Paul*, p. 134.

31. On Gal. 3:11f., cf. Tyson, "'Works of Law' in Galatians," p. 428: "The quotation from Habakkuk is intended to show that God intends man to live on the basis of faith; that from Leviticus makes it clear that the law does not provide such a basis."

32. Cf. Eckert, *Verkündigung*, p. 79.

33. Betz's analysis of the structure is slightly different. See the outline in *Galatians*, p. 19. He takes the assertions of 3:8–9, 3:10, 3:11, 3:12, and 3:13 to be five successive arguments, whereas I would subordinate 3:10–13 to 3:8. For the present purpose, however, the difference is not substantial, since we agree on the force of 3:10. Hübner, without a literary analysis to substantiate the point, states that 3:10, and particularly "all," is of decisive weight in the argument ("Proprium," p. 462).

34. For the same conclusion, based on different arguments, see Betz, *Galatians*, pp. 145f.

Some still argue that Paul here opposes not accepting the law as such, but only a *manner* of observing it: legalism. Thus, e.g., D. P. Fuller, "Paul and 'the Works of the Law'," *Westminster Theological Journal* 38 (1975):28–42. I find no trace of such a view in Galatians.

35. This is the reading required by Hübner's view that the emphasis falls on 3:10, and especially on the word "all," and that Paul's objection to the law is that quantitatively one cannot fulfill enough of it.

36. Cf. A. van Dülmen, *Die Theologie des Gesetzes bei Paulus* (Stuttgart: Verlag

Katholisches Bibelwerk, 1968), pp. 31–35; E. P. Sanders, "On the Question of Fulfilling the Law." Note Ulrich Luz's very careful statement of the relationship between 3:10 and 3:11: Gal. 3:10, which presupposes that no one fulfills the law, is itself grounded by the following verse. Paul is thinking christologically (Luz, *Das Geschichtsverständnis des Paulus*, pp. 149–51).

37. Heikki Räisänen, "Paul's Theological Difficulties with the Law," in *Studia Biblica 1978*, vol. 3 (Sheffield: JSOT Press, 1980), p. 308.

38. Note also the phrase "compel to be circumcised" in 6:12, also echoing 2:14. Gal. 6:14 echoes 2:20.

39. Paul had his own dilemma with regard to observance of the law, as 1 Cor. 9:20f. makes clear. Cf. Richardson, "Pauline Inconsistency."

40. Räisänen, "Paul's Theological Difficulties," pp. 308–10.

41. See the index in *PPJ*, p. 626, s.v. "Sin, as transgression."

42. Sanhedrin 101a. For the present purpose it does not matter whether or not the story is apocryphal.

43. Below, pp. 35f.

44. J. Christiaan Beker, *Paul the Apostle* (Philadelphia: Fortress Press, 1980), p. 187. Similarly earlier Albert Schweitzer, *The Mysticism of Paul the Apostle* (New York: Henry Holt, 1931), pp. 72f. Beker drags in other passages by force. Thus Rom. 6:10 ("the death he died, he died to sin") "means that Christ satisfied the righteous requirement of the law (Rom. 8:4)" (Beker, p. 186). This does violence to both passages.

45. A. E. Harvey, *Jesus and the Constraints of History* (Philadelphia: Westminster Press, 1982), p. 22; cf. Morna D. Hooker, "Paul and 'Covenantal Nomism,'" in *Paul and Paulinism* (London: SPCK, 1982), pp. 47–56, here p. 55.

46. So Beker, *Paul the Apostle*, pp. 143ff., 182–84, 191f., 202. This explanation of persecution is questioned below, pp. 191f. and nn. 76, 77.

47. Harvey (*Jesus and the Constraints of History*) argues that Paul's statement requires Jesus actually to have been condemned by the law. But it is very dubious that either Paul or those who developed the argument which he reflects were thinking about the causes which historically led to Jesus' death. We have an argument and a counter argument based on a turn of phrase in Scripture, and it requires only one historical fact—that Jesus was crucified.

48. For a sound evaluation of the matter, see Peter Stuhlmacher, "Das Ende des Gesetzes," *ZTK* 64 (1967): 33f.

49. See Beker, *Paul the Apostle*, p. 187.

50. One might call Paul's view that of *Heilsgeschichte* rather than "God's plan of salvation" if *Heilsgeschichte* could be understood not to mean "development." Paul, in common with his contemporaries, thought that God's intention was always the same. Käsemann's argument against understanding Paul in terms of *Heilsgeschichte* is primarily against attributing to Paul the notion of development in God's dealing with humanity (*Romans*, pp. 254, 264, 273). Keck would like to retain the term "salvation history" in the sense of God's intention, not God's developing intention (Leander Keck, *Paul and his Letters*, [Philadelphia: Fortress Press, 1979], pp. 66–69).

51. Gal. 3:19–24 is discussed more fully in chapter 2.

52. Cf. Hahn, "Gesetzesverständnis," p. 55: "That there is no righteousness by

the law is for Paul not merely a statement based on experience, but much more is declared within the Old Testament itself by Hab. 2:4. . . ."

53. See Hübner, *Gesetz*, p. 22.

54. Cf. n. 41 above. Even in the DSS, where perfection is urged, provision for atonement is made (*PPJ*, pp. 284–87; 298, 298–305). The view that one must keep the law perfectly but that very few do (not that no one does) is found in 4 Ezra, but this is atypical (as well as being distinctly post-70) (*PPJ*, pp. 415, 427f.).

55. On supplying the assumption that it is impossible to keep all the law, see the discussion in Schlier, *Der Brief an die Galater*, pp. 132f. and n. 1 to 133. Schlier correctly opposes supplementing Paul's statement.

56. Hübner, "Herkunft"; apparently accepted by Beker, *Paul the Apostle*, pp. 43f., 52f.

57. Hübner (ibid.) misreads Sifra Qedoshim pereq 8.3 as saying that proselytes must successfully do all the law. The point is rather that they must accept it all. See *PPJ*, p. 138 n. 61.

58. One of the points in the famous story about Hillel and the would-be pros- elyte (Shabbath 31a) is that the details of keeping the law should be introduced or arrived at gradually. See David Daube, *The New Testament and Rabbinic Judaism* (London: University of London, Athlone Press, 1973), pp. 336f. So also the later instructions for admitting a proselyte: at the time of baptism they acquaint him with some light and some heavy commandments (Yebamoth 47a). Proselytes were expected to accept the whole law (T. Demai 2.5), but the rabbis seem to have been aware that presenting it all at once would be burdensome. If the rival missionaries were following a policy of gradualism, the threat in Gal. 5:3 would be Paul's counter to it.

Eckert (*Verkündigung*, p. 41) considers the possibility proposed here, that Paul's opponents were employing the tactic of gradualism, but rejects it in favor of the view that in 5:3 Paul presupposes that the Galatians will recognize that keeping all the law is impossible.

59. Howard (*Crisis*, p. 16) does not see Gal. 5:3 as intended to frighten the Gala- tians with the difficulty of keeping a law foreign to them. He argues that the em- phasis falls on the word *opheiletēs* and that the threat is that one who accepts cir- cumcision comes under bondage to the law and thus to sin.

60. Above, n. 8. It should be noted that in the passages in view there is not necessarily an individual messiah.

61. See e.g. Tob. 3:3, 13 ("you who are the sons of Israel"); Ps. Sol. 17.32 ("under his yoke," *viz* the law); SibOr III.702–20.

62. See Part Two below.

63. This paragraph states as succinctly as possible my position on Paul's Christology over against that of W. D. Davies. He argues, in effect, that the key to Paul's thought is Jewish messianic expectation. (See the modified restatement of his view, against my earlier criticism, in *Paul and Rabbinic Judaism*, 4th ed. [Philadelphia: Fortress Press, 1980], p. xxxiv.) I do not disagree with him on whether or not Paul's work falls into a general context produced by that expectation (see ibid.). That is cer- tainly the case: Paul thought that the end was at hand and that it was time for the Gentiles to enter the people of God. If asked, he would doubtless also have agreed that Jesus was the Jewish messiah. But at this point Jewish messianic expectation

stops explaining the positions which characterize his letters and which make his views different from those of other Jewish Christians who also thought that Jesus was the messiah. Christ is, for Paul, universal Lord: he is as much Gentile savior as Jewish savior. The Jews as such are not already in the new creation. They must enter. They have no advantage over Gentiles with regard to admission. This is why I think it to be accurate to speak of "conversion" (see Davies's criticism, ibid., p. xxxvi; below, Part Two).

64. Paul does not use the word "only," but most interpreters correctly supply it. This view has been challenged by Eugene Boring in a paper as yet unpublished. He makes the correct point that, in addition to the passages which depict the destruction of non-believers (e.g. Phil. 3:18–21), there are others which envisage universal salvation (e.g. 1 Cor. 15:22; Rom. 5:18). One does not decide Paul's "true" view by counting passages. The two sorts of statements, Boring explains, spring from two images — that of judgment, in which there must be "losers" if there are "winners," and that of sovereignty, in which all are joined under the victorious Christ. It seems to me that his explanation of the two figures is basically correct. I would put it this way: when Paul thought of those who reject the gospel, he considered them "lost" or "being destroyed" (see 2 Cor. 2:16; 4:3). When he thought of God's intention and the greatness of his mercy, he would say that all would be saved (1 Cor. 15:22; 15:28; Rom. 11:32, 11:36).

I am not of the view, however, that it is impossible to discover Paul's view behind different ways of speaking. As I have argued before and am attempting to demonstrate in the course of this essay, Paul's view of the law depends more on the exclusivism of his Christology than on anything else. The conclusion of Galatians 3 seems to imply very distinctly an "only": it is those who faith in Christ who are the seed of Abraham (3:29), not those who are of the law, who are under a curse and enslaved (3:10, 23).

Paul's view becomes clearest when he comes to concrete cases. Unless I entirely misread Romans 9–11, he is anguished about his own people lest they not convert — the word is not too strong — and thus be saved (Rom. 9:2; 10:1).

65. *PPJ*, pp. 488f. and notes. So also Richardson, *Israel*, pp. 134–37: the theme of equal access for Jew and Gentile on the basis of faith "stands over the whole letter."

66. As Räisänen correctly points out ("Legalism and Salvation by the Law," p. 68), the key texts for Bultmann were Rom. 3:27; 4:2ff.; 7:7ff.; 10:2–3; Phil. 3:4ff. In the last two the emphasis is on "own." See Rudolf Bultmann, *Theology of the New Testament*, vol. 1 (New York: Charles Scribner's Sons, 1951–1955), pp. 264–67.

67. Hübner, *Gesetz*.

68. Some of the most important articles are collected by Karl P. Donfried in *The Romans Debate* (Minneapolis: Augsburg Publishing House, 1977). See also the discussion by Dieter Zeller, *Juden and Heiden in der Mission des Paulus. Studien zür Römerbrief*, 2d. ed. (Stuttgart: Verlag Katholisches Bibelwerk, 1976), pp. 42f., 75f., 285f. See n. 70 below.

69. Rudolf Bultmann, *Der Stil der paulinischen Predigt und die kynisch-stoische Diatribe*, (Göttingen: Vandenhoeck & Ruprecht, 1910); Robin Scroggs, "Paul as Rhetorician: Two Homilies in Romans 1–11," in *Jews, Greeks and Christians* (Leiden: E. J. Brill, 1976), pp. 271–98. There is an excellent brief evaluation and correction of aspects of Bultmann's view by Abraham J. Malherbe, ΜΗ ΓΕΝΟΙΤΟ

in the Diatribe and Paul," *HTR* 73 (1980):231–40. Malherbe also refers to a Yale Ph.D. thesis by Stanley K. Stowers, *A Critical Reassessment of Paul and the Diatribe* (Chico, Calif.: Scholar's Press, 1982).

70. T. W. Manson, "St. Paul's Letter to the Romans — and Others," *BJRL* 21 (1948): 224–40. It is not necessary to follow Manson in thinking that Romans was prepared by Paul himself in two recensions, one of which was intended to be used as a circular letter, in order to adopt his view on its setting in Paul's own ministry. For this general position, see also Munck, *Paul*, pp. 66; 197–200 ("Romans is essentially a summing-up of the point of view that Paul had reached during the long struggle that begins in 1 Corinthians and Philippians 3" [p. 199]); Jacob Jervell, "The Letter to Jerusalem," in *The Romans Debate* (Minneapolis: Augsburg Publishing House, 1977), pp. 61–74 (Romans 1 – 11 is Paul's defense speech in Jerusalem, written for himself; the letter is written to Rome in order to solicit the Romans' intercession); Jack Suggs, "'The Word is Near You': Romans 10:6–10 within the Purpose of the Letter," in *Christian History and Interpretation* (New York: Cambridge University Press, 1967), pp. 289–312; Günther Bornkamm, "Der Römerbrief als Testament des Paulus," in *Geschichte und Glaube*, vol. 2 (Munich: Chr. Kaiser, 1971), pp. 120–39; *PPJ*, p. 488; Udo Borse, "Die geschichtliche und theologische Einordnung des Römerbriefes," *BZ* 16 (1972): 70–83. The fullest and, in my judgment, best statement of the position is that of Wilckens, "Über Abfassungszweck und Aufbau des Römerbrief." Wilckens allows that Paul has heard of tension between Jewish and Gentile Christians in Rome (p. 124), but he does not regard the Roman situation as foremost. The contents of the letter are determined primarily by the approaching debate in Jerusalem. Nevertheless it is not precisely a "letter to Jerusalem" (Jervell). It is directed to the Roman community because Paul desires their intercessory prayer (Wilckens, pp. 128, 138f.).

Beker's objection to this view, that it dissipates "the contingency of the letter" and leads to reading Romans as an abstract theological treatise (*Paul the Apostle*, pp. 61f., 69), is off target. Having a different view of the occasion of Romans from Beker's is by no means the same as turning it into a timeless theological treatise. Beker's own view — that Romans is addressed both to the problems of Roman Christianity and to non-Christian Jewish objectors to Paul's message (pp. 69f., 74–86) — is unconvincing. Thus Beker says that Romans is a reply to such "Jewish questions" as "What is the function of the Torah and circumcision?" (p. 77). These questions, however, arise most naturally from Paul's mission to the Gentiles: if God has provided for their salvation apart from law and circumcision, what is the function of these signs of Israel's covenant with God?

71. Wilckens, "Abfassungszweck," p. 126.

72. Ibid., p. 128: "The intercession of the Romans is for Paul a matter of the most realistic efficacy, precisely as real as the hoped-for prayer of thanksgiving of the Jerusalemites."

73. See below, pp. 68f.

74. Compare the much briefer reference in 2 Cor. 3:14f.

75. It is doubtless this fact which leads Beker to regard Romans as a dialogue with Judaism and as reflecting Paul's own debates with the synagogue (above, n. 70; see especially Beker, *Paul the Apostle*, p. 86). But even when, in chaps. 9 – 11, Paul takes up the status of non-believing Israel directly, he does so in the third per-

son. The only people directly addressed are Gentile Christians (11:13–24). The rhetorical address to Jews in 2:17 is probably based on traditional material (see below, pp. 123–35). The perceived addressee of Rom. 7:1 cannot be precisely determined. At any rate, despite this disagreement with regard to the understood dialogue partner, all parties to the dispute would agree that Judaism as such is discussed in Romans. Cf. Zeller, *Juden und Heiden*, pp. 42f.

76. Beker, *Paul the Apostle*, pp. 81–83.

77. See Hübner, *Gesetz*, pp. 96, 102 and nn. 86, 87, and 102. Hübner sees the debate as being chiefly between the Bultmannian position on the one hand (n. 66 above) and that of Ulrich Wilckens on the other (Wilckens, "Was heisst bei Paulus: 'Aus Werken des Gesetzes wird kein Mensch gerecht?'").

For arguments against reading this passage in particular, or Paul in general, as opposing the law because fulfilling it leads to boasting, see especially Räisänen, "Legalism and Salvation by the Law," pp. 68–72 (on p. 72 he correctly objects to an ambiguity in my previous position, which I hope will be corrected here).

Cf. van Dülmen, *Theologie des Gesetzes*, p. 87 (not "works and faith," but Mosaic law and faith); Karl Hoheisel, *Das antike Judentum in christlicher Sicht* (Wiesbaden: O. Harrassowitz, 1978), p. 200: ἰδία δικαιοσύνη "hat aber nicht das geringste mit 'Selbstgerechtigkeit' . . . zu tun."

78. Hübner, *Gesetz*, pp. 81–93.

79. Ibid., pp. 93–99.

80. Ibid., p. 99 (4:2 disqualifies works-righteousness); cf. 101f. To an appreciable degree, however, Hübner seems to think that the phrase "*nomos* of works" in 3:27 in and of itself shows that Paul is opposed to the law only when it becomes a law which permits self-achievement (p. 96).

81. Ibid., p. 101. I cannot see that Abraham is directly in mind in Rom. 3:9–20, or even in 4:7, but this point is not crucial.

82. See Hübner, *Gesetz*, p. 102.

83. Ibid., pp. 102f.

84. See above, Introduction, n. 26.

85. Hübner, *Gesetz*, p. 118.

86. So Wilckens, "Was heisst bei Paulus," p. 94; "Abfassungszweck," p. 151; Räisänen, "Legalism and Salvation by the Law," p. 70; cf. Hoheisel, *Das antike Judentum*, p. 201; van Dülmen, *Theologie des Gesetzes*, p. 86.

87. See especially George Howard, "Romans 3:21–31 and the Inclusion of the Gentiles," *HTR* 63 (1970): 233: the verses 3:27–30 "go together and argue for one thing, i.e., the inclusion of the Gentiles." Similarly p. 232: "The idea of justification by faith as a polemic against works of merit dominates Christian theology of the modern period. It is for this reason that [3:28] so often does not appear to relate to verse 27 before it or verse 29 and 30 after it. These verses all allude to the inclusion of the Gentiles; the modern understanding of justification by faith does not."

88. See Räisänen, "Legalism and Salvation by the Law," p. 70 n. 43: "Note that Paul does *not* say that had Abraham *tried* to be justified by works, then his attitude would have been that of one who boasts." Also Howard, *Crisis in Galatia*, p. 56: "Paul concedes the possibility that Abraham has a boast on the basis of his works, he only denies that he has a boast before God." My reading is slightly different: Abraham did not have a boast before either man or God on the basis of works,

since he was not in fact righteoused by works, since Gen. 15:6 says otherwise. *Even had he been* righteoused by works, he could not have boasted before God, since God righteouses by faith. In any case, Räisänen, Howard, and I agree that there is nothing in the passage about wanting to be righteoused by works (against Hübner, above, n. 81), and certainly nothing about the attitude of self-righteousness.

89. On Abraham as a type see Leonhard Goppelt, *Typos* (Gütersloh: Gerd Mohn, 1939), pp. 164–69; Hanson, *Studies in Paul's Technique and Theology*, p. 79 (though one doubts that Paul's argument is actually that Abraham represents "a universalism that had always been potentially accessible." The only application is to "us" [4:24]); Luz, *Geschichtsverständnis*, p. 181 (Abraham is an example of righteousness by faith, but he is isolated from prior and subsequent history). Stuhlmacher calls Paul's use of Abraham "paradigmatically historical" ("Interpretation von Römer 11:25–32," in *Probleme biblischer Theologie* [Munich: Chr. Kaiser, 1971], p. 563).

90. Hübner, *Gesetz*, pp. 96, 101f.

91. Cf. *PPJ*, pp. 474f.

92. Thus, for example, Stuhlmacher, "Das Gesetz als Thema biblischer Theologie," *ZTK* 75 (1978): 276 ("this law"); Hahn, "Das Gesetzesverständnis," p. 50 (this *nomos dikaiosynēs*); Käsemann, *Romans*, p. 277 ("did not advance to such a law"), (in *An die Römer* [Tübingen: J. C. B. Mohr (Paul Siebeck), 1974], p. 267, the translation is "drang jedoch zu [solchem] Gesetz nicht vor"); Wilckens, "Abfassungszweck," p. 163 (paraphrases, Israel did not reach its goal, righteousness); Richardson, *Israel*, p. 133 ("Israel was pursuing, but they did not attain what they sought").

93. C. E. B. Cranfield, *The Epistle to the Romans*, vol. 2 (Edinburgh: T. & T. Clark, 1979), pp. 504–6.

94. Ibid., p. 509. So also C. K. Barrett, "Romans 9:30 – 10:21," in *Essays on Paul* (Philadelphia: Westminster Press, 1982), p. 143.

95. Note the translation of the RSV, "did not succeed in fulfilling that law." On *ephthasen*, see C. H. Dodd's discussion of Matt. 12:28; Luke 11:20: *The Parables of the Kingdom*, rev. ed. (London: William Collins Sons, 1961), p. 29. On the difference between Cranfield's interpretation and his own translation, see n. 127 below.

96. Munck, *Christ and Israel*, pp. 78f. I cannot follow Munck in considering that 9:30 – 10:4 refers to the earthly life of Jesus and that 10:5-21 refers to Paul's present situation.

97. Cf. Zeller, *Juden und Heiden*, p. 122: 9:30 is "enigmatic," but 9:30-33 are a prelude to chap. 10. Luz (*Geschichtsverständnis*, p. 31) proposes a very strict correlation between 9:30-33 and 10:1-3, describing them as parallel. Both point to Christ as the decisive point in determining if people gain righteousness.

98. Paul Meyer has offered an alternative to this understanding of 9:32b-33 (see "Romans 10:4 and the End of the Law," in *The Divine Helmsman* [New York: KTAV, 1980], p. 64). The stumbling-stone is the Torah, which misleads (cf. Romans 7). "Believe in him" refers to faith in God, and Paul's argument is theocentric rather than christocentric. To find Christ in 9:33, Meyer urges, "one must . . . simply read Paul as anticipating here his mention of Christ in 10:4." He has pointed out to me in a letter than *pisteuein epi* (in the quotation in v. 33) is not Paul's regular usage, and urged that the use of *pisteuein* may not have yet been frozen so that it refers only to faith in Christ, a point supported by Rom. 4:16f. and 10:9b. I fully agree with the observations about *pisteuein* in general and *pisteuein epi* in particular,

but the simplest reading of the present passage is that "stone" is the antecedent of *autōi* and that both refer to Christ. It is awkward, as Meyer acknowledges, to have the intended referent of *lithon* and *autōi* change.

99. Räisänen, "Legalism and Salvation by the Law," p. 71.

100. Cf. 2 Cor. 9:2.

101. Cf. van Dülmen, *Theologie des Gesetzes*, p. 127.

102. Ridderbos, *Paul*, p. 139.

103. Ibid., p. 142.

104. Beker, *Paul the Apostle*, p. 247. Cf. p. 106.

105. On the two righteousnesses, see further below, pp. 43–45.

106. Cf. Howard, *Crisis*, p. 76.

107. Cf. Gaston, "Paul and the Torah," p. 66: "Their own" "does not mean that individual Jews attempted to justify themselves by their own actions in defiance of the God of the covenant, but that Israel as a whole interpreted the righteousness of God as establishing the status of righteousness for Israel alone, excluding the Gentiles." Also George Howard, "Christ the End of the Law: The Meaning of Romans 10:4ff.," *JBL* 88 (1969):336: "Their own righteousness" is their "collective righteousness, to the exclusion of Gentiles."

108. Several scholars have pointed out that the interpretation of the verse depends more on the understanding of *eis dikaiosynēn* than of *telos*. See C. K. Barrett, *A Commentary on the Epistle to the Romans* (New York: Harper & Row, 1957), pp. 197f.; Richard Longenecker, *Paul: Apostle of Liberty* (New York: Harper & Row, 1964), pp. 144–53; Meyer, "Romans 10:4 and the End of the Law," p. 61, where several renderings of *eis dikaiosynēn* are given.

109. On the use of purpose clauses, see below, p. 66.

110. Meyer, "Romans 10:4 and the End of the Law," p. 68. It seems unnecessarily awkward to make *telos* the subject of the sentence and *Christos* the predicate nominative.

111. "Christ is the end of the law unto righteousness for all who believe." See Mussner, "'Christus [ist] des Gesetzes Ende zur Gerechtigkeit für jeden, der glaubt' (Rom 10, 4)", in *Paulus — Apostat oder Apostel* (Regensburg, 1977), pp. 31–44.

112. Ibid., pp. 40–44.

113. See C. F. D. Moule, *An Idiom Book of New Testament Greek*, 2d ed. (New York: Cambridge University Press, 1959) p. 70. Moule himself translates "Christ is an end to legalism for the attainment of righteousness," prefacing the translation with "perhaps."

114. Cf. Bultmann, *Theology*, vol. 1, p. 341. Cranfield (*Romans*, vol. 2, pp. 519f. and n. 2) notes that some take 10:4 to mean the end of the law as a means of attaining righteousness, but he rightly points out that in that case *eis dikaiosynēn* should have directly followed *nomou*. This construct also makes it difficult to connect "to all who believe" with "unto righteousness."

115. Käsemann, *Romans*, p. 283.

116. Thus Cranfield (*Romans*, vol. 2, pp. 519f.), who reads *telos* as goal but who understands *eis* as consecutive and as beginning a phrase which modifies the entire preceding clause, translates, "If Christ is the goal of the law, it follows that a status of righteousness is available to every one who believes." Although I disagree with Cranfield's view of Rom. 9:30 — 10:13, and with his general understanding of Paul's

view of the law (namely, that Paul opposed only the legalistic misuse of the law),
I think that his translation of 10:4 is in accord with the syntax and the context.

117. Barrett, *Romans*, pp. 197f.

118. Moule (n. 113); Hübner (*Gesetz*, pp. 118, 129). Cf. Longenecker (*Paul*, pp.
144–153): Paul distinguishes the law as the standard and judgment of God (which
he approves) from the law as a contractual obligation (which he abrogates).

119. Mussner, n. 111 above.

120. The view hinted at in *Gesetz*, p. 93, was spelled out more fully by Hübner
in "Der theologische Umgang des Paulus mit dem Alten Testament in Römerbrief,"
a paper presented to the Seminar on the Use of the Old Testament in the New, SNTS,
1980.

121. For this position as it applies to Romans 4 and 9 — 11, see especially Meyer,
"Romans 10:4 and the End of the Law," pp. 59–78, esp. pp. 67f. I am also indebted
for an understanding of this point to an exchange of correspondence with Professor
Meyer. Beker, though he emphasizes Paul's theocentricity, has not, as far as I have
noted, used Romans 4 and 9 — 10 to make the case (see *Paul the Apostle*, esp. pp.
362–67).

122. Since Rom. 10:9 is almost certainly an inherited formula, one may question
whether or not it should be used to determine Paul's "own" thought. In the present
case he cites the formula almost as another proof-text in the midst of a series of
proofs-texts from Scripture. (For the introductory *hoti*, cf. Gal. 3:11.) We may ask
here, as we asked above (pp. 21f.), if one best interprets Paul by interpreting the precise wording of material which he quotes. Since our principal interest is the law, rather
than whether or not "faith" is always to be understood to be christologically determined, I let the point pass for the present.

123. Meyer, "Romans 10:4 and the End of the Law," p. 68.

124. Faith is equated with the coming of Christ in Gal. 3:23f., but this need not
be determinative for Romans. The present argument is that "faith in God" and "faith
in Christ" are not truly distinguished in Romans.

125. Above, n. 89. It seems to me to be a mistake to read Romans 4 as implying
the continuous, or at least sporadic, existence of people of faith between Abraham
and Christ. David (4:6) is not cited as a second historical person who also had faith,
but rather a psalm (traditionally attributed to David) is quoted which pronounces
a blessing on those who have faith. Abraham is immediately returned to (4:9), and
he continues to be employed in a typological way.

126. On the thrust of Rom. 9:30 — 10:21, see also Eichholz, *Paulus*, pp. 223f.:
Israel's fault is refusing the gospel of faith in Christ.

127. Cranfield (*Romans*, vol. 2, p. 503) correctly translates *ephthasen* "attained,"
although he then interprets this to mean that Israel is guilty "because it has failed
to obey its own law" (p. 505).

128. Above, n. 92, especially Richardson's paraphrase.

129. Cranfield, *Romans*, vol. 2, pp. 507f. Cranfield also, however, takes "of
righteousness" to be understood after "law" in v. 31.

130. I spent some months thinking that perhaps here Paul plays on the word
nomos, as he does in Rom. 3:27 ("*nomos* of faith") and 8:2 ("*nomos* of the Spirit
of life"), and that the word in 9:31b thus means "principle." Further reflection,
however, aided by a helpful exchange with Professor Stuhlmacher, has persuaded

me that in Rom. 9:31 the shift in meaning is not deliberate. The verse will remain difficult, but the best solution seems to be that Paul wanted to achieve a striking turn of phrase.

131. Note Bultmann's explanation of Rom. 8:10 and 1 Cor. 6:17: the apparent difficulties "are due to their pointed, rhetorical formulation" (*Theology*, vol. 1, p. 208).

132. I believe that the best reading of Rom. 10:5 is that the Jews might have righteousness by doing the law, but that one does not "live" thereby. The point need not, however, be pressed, and Phil. 3:6-9 remains the only passage in which Paul unambiguously says that there is *a* righteousness which is actually obtainable by law.

133. Bultmann, *Theology*, vol. 1, pp. 266f.

134. I take the term from Hübner, *Gesetz*, pp. 93–104. Hübner, however, noting that Philippians is difficult to date (p. 105) leaves it largely out of account. The conflation of "my righteousness" in Philippians with "boasting" in Romans is evident in Bultmann, *Theology*, vol. 1, p. 267.

135. See *PPJ*, pp. 2–6; 549–51.

136. See Rudolf Bultmann, "Romans 7 and the Anthropology of Paul," in *Existence and Faith: Shorter Writings of Rudolf Bultmann*, (Cleveland and New York: World Publishing Co., Meridian Books, 1960), pp. 147–57.

137. *PPJ*, *passim*, esp. pp. 419–23, 426f., 550.

138. On this distinction between purity terms for behavior and *dik-* terms for transfer, see *PPJ*, esp. pp. 544–46; on each set of terms: *PPJ*, pp. 450–53 (behavior); 470–72, 493–95 (*dik-*). See now Michael Newton, "The Concept of Purity at Qumran and in the Letters of Paul," (Ph.D. diss.; Hamilton, Ontario: McMaster University, 1980). The distinction is not absolute. In 1 Cor. 6:11 purity terminology joins the *dik-* root in describing the transfer from the pagan to the Christian life.

139. In Philippians 3 Paul does not use one of the passive forms of *dikaioun*, and the verb which indicates the transfer from one state to another is *kerdēsō*, "gain." "In Christ" he has "righteousness from God," but righteousness here is still not used to describe the behavior appropriate to remaining in Christ, but rather what is gained by the transfer.

140. This is a common observation in Pauline studies; see *PPJ*, pp. 449f. and notes. The point is repeated here because one reviewer missed the distinction between the present transfer to the body of those who will be saved and future salvation itself, making it a major criticism of *PPJ* that I discussed soteriology as a major topic in Paul's letters, while Paul used *sōtēria* and *sōzō* infrequently.

141. See, for example, the discussion of the relation of the covenant to the commandments in *PPJ*, pp. 81–84, and the summary, pp. 419–22.

142. Some reviewers of *PPJ* have inquired why I did not accept Paul's criticism of Judaism as evidence for the characteristics of Judaism (e.g., W. Horbury's review in *Expository Times* 96 (1979): 116–18). I hope to make it clear that, in my view, Paul's criticism of Judaism, rightly understood, does correspond to Judaism as revealed in its own literature. This is the significance of my previous argument that Paul's true attack concerns the adequacy of the Jewish covenant (or the concept of national election): "Fulfilling the Law," p. 124; *PPJ*, pp. 551f. Beker (*Paul the Apostle*, pp. 87f.) accepts this view, including the term "covenantal nomism," for the Judaism which Paul rejects.

143. Besides the *pro-* verbs of Gal. 3:8 (above, p. 26), note also Rom. 1:2; 15:4. Cf. Stuhlmacher, "Erwägungen zum Problem von Gegenwart," pp. 434f.

144. Thus Paul's use of Scripture is more than clever proof-texting, which I may have inadvertently suggested in *PPJ*. See Davies's criticism in *Paul and Rabbinic Judaism*, p. xxxv. Paul continued to see Scripture as revealing God's will, but he had a revised understanding of the one, and consequently a new reading of the other. We shall return to the question of "law" and "Scripture" in the conclusion to this essay.

145. See above, at n. 121.

146. On the purpose clauses in Gal. 3:22, 24, see further below, p. 66.

147. N. 142 above. Cf. also John Townsend, "The Gospel of John and the Jews," in *Anti-Semitism and the Foundations of Christianity* (New York: Paulist Press, 1979), pp. 72–97, here p. 75: Romans 4; Galatians 3 – 4 and Phil. 3:2–11 are arguments that "Jewish election had become meaningless."

148. I believe that Professor Caird and I are basically in agreement: see his review of *PPJ* in *JTS* 29 (1978):538–43, esp. 542. His formulation is this: "If Paul was indeed brought up in Judaism as Sanders understands it, believing that God treats the elect with mercy and outsiders with strict justice, then small wonder if his conversion opened his eyes to the enormity of thus impugning the impartiality of God." I believe that Caird did not see the intended force of my saying that Paul objected to the law (and Judaism) on the basis of the Gentile question and the traditional understanding of the covenant.

149. *PPJ*, p. 497.

2

The Purpose of the Law

In both Galatians and Romans, after Paul has asserted that no one is righteoused by the law, he asks why the law was given. This is the question of Gal. 3:19, and the same question is implied in Rom. 3:20; 4:15; 5:20; 7:7, 13. This sequence (no one is righteoused by works of the law; why was the law given? or, what is its function?) shows the thoroughly Jewish character of Paul's presuppositions: God gave the law; he must have done so for a purpose.[1] Our selection of these passages as dealing with the function of the law, or its role in *Heilsgeschichte*, appears not to be controversial.[2] It remains a difficult problem, however, to understand them and to discover their relationship to other things that Paul says about the law. In the following discussion we shall focus on two related problems in Paul's treatment of the role of the law in God's plan of salvation: whether or not he always gives it the same role and how he relates being under the law to other human conditions prior to Christ. We shall also see that Rom. 7:7 — 8:8 raises the question of whether or not Paul's thought about the law is subject to a fundamentally different explanation from the one thus far offered.

Galatians 3:19—4:7

Paul's question in 3:19, *ti oun ho nomos*, is triggered by the statement in 3:18 that the inheritance (in this context, the inheritance which promises salvation) does not come by law. The question is literally "what, then, is the law?," but the context shows that the phrase is intended primarily to ask "why, then, was the law given?"[3] Following the denial of the law's positive role in the history of salvation (3:15–18), the natural question is "what was the function of the law, since it does not save?" That this is the question uppermost in Paul's mind is also evident from the subsequent answer. It was given because of transgressions, and temporarily (3:19); it consigned all things to sin (3:22); it kept "us" in restraint (3:23); it was our custodian (3:24); it can be compared to the guardians of a minor (4:2, 5). These statements show clearly enough that Paul is discussing the role of the law in *Heilsgeschichte*, and thus they demonstrate that in asking *ti oun ho nomos* Paul meant to ask, no matter what problems later grammarians throw in his way, "what was the purpose behind the giving of the law?"

Yet, although the intended question is clear, aspects of the answer are difficult. Difficulty, even tortuousness, marks the principal passages in which Paul replies to the implied question of why God gave the law. The reason for the difficulty in responding to the question is obvious enough: as we said above, he was Jewish; he thought that whatever happened was in accord with divine providence; the law, then, could not be opposed to God's will; yet the law does not provide for salvation.

In general terms, Paul's way out of this dilemma was to connect the law with sin and to assign it a negative place in God's plan of salvation.[4] This point stands out in sharpest relief when we note the statements of God's positive intention. The Scripture consigned all things to sin *so that* the "promise" would be given on the basis of faith in Christ (Gal. 3:22); the law was our pedagogue until Christ, *so that* we would be righteoused by faith (3:24).[5] The result is that the way in which one becomes a descendant of Abraham, and thus heir of the promise given to him, is belonging to Christ (3:29). In these sentences Paul states what he believes God's intention to be, as the purpose clauses make evident. The Scripture (or law),[6] by "locking up" "all things" (or "us"), functioned as part of the divine purpose, so that God's plan to give the promise (or righteousness) on the basis of faith in Christ would be fulfilled.

The way in which the law does this is less clear. The law, Paul says, was added (after the promise of the inheritance was given) "because of transgressions" (*tōn parabaseōn charin*, 3:19). In 3:22 he says that the law "imprisoned all things under sin," in 3:23 that we were confined under law before faith came, imprisoned unto the revelation of the coming faith, and in 3:24 that the law was our pedagogue. It is difficult to determine whether or not these four statements about the function of the law are synonymous. In and of itself "on account of transgressions" can mean either "to produce transgressions" or "to deal with transgressions." The simplest reading of 3:19a is that the law deals with transgressions until the coming of Christ ("the seed").[7] It would also be possible to understand the law as pedagogue in 3:24 as a temporary schoolmaster which constrains.[8] The image of the custodian is worked out in 4:1–7, and here the import of the image becomes clearer. Those who are under guardians are "no better than slaves." The law as pedagogue, then, is more an enslaver than a protector. Thus it is understandable that many scholars view the phrase "on account of transgressions" in 3:19 as meaning "for the sake of producing transgressions."

This reading need not depend entirely on interpreting Gal. 3:19 in the light of Rom. 5:20,[9] but can be derived from the enslaving character of the pedagogue (as interpreted by Gal. 4:2) and from the phrase "imprisoned under sin" in 3:22.

It does not seem necessary for the present purpose, however, to decide whether or not the statements that the law was given "on account of transgressions," that it "locked up all things under sin," that "we were confined under the law," and that "the law was our pedagogue" are in precise agreement with one another. The general line of argument is in each case clear. The constraining *or* enslaving force of the law lasted until the coming of faith (3:19; cf. 4:4f.), and in fact the law was given for the purpose of leading up to righteousness by faith, even though negatively (3:22, 24).[10]

Hans Hübner has attempted to smooth the line of Paul's argument by distinguishing between the "immanent intention" of the law, the intention of the angels who gave it, and the intention of God.[11] The intention of the law itself, he argues, is stated in Gal. 3:12: those who do the law live by it.[12] Gal. 3:19–21a states the intention of the angels who gave the law: to provoke sin (as he reads *tōn parabaseōn charin*). God's intention is reflected in 3:22: he uses the evil action of the angels and turns it to his own goal. The advantage of Hübner's position is twofold. On the one hand it gives full weight to Gal. 3:19, where Paul attributes the giving of the law to angels, through a mediator, thus denying that God gave it. On the other, it eliminates self-contradiction from Paul's letter, since in other passages he talks about how the law carries out God's intention. Paul's argument, as reconstructed by Hübner, would be this: the law itself intends to save those who do it (though that is impossible); the angels who actually gave the law, however, intended to provoke sin and thus vanquish humanity; God redeemed the situation by providing for the salvation of all those whom the law condemned.

I do not, however, find Hübner's position persuasive. I have already argued that in Gal. 3:12 Paul cites Lev. 18:5 not to agree that the law gives life in theory, but rather to prove that the law does not rest on faith.[13] There are strong a priori reasons for not reading Gal. 3:19 as representing a position which Paul consciously worked out and systematically held. We would have to suppose that, when he wrote Galatians, Paul was prepared to deny what he had been taught and believed all his life, that God gave the law; that he structured the argument of Galatians 3 around the premise that God did not give the law, but rather "saved" the situation after it was given; that he reverted to the view that God gave the law when he wrote Romans; and that he had even changed his mind about who gave the law when he wrote the Corinthian correspondence, which most scholars date at approximately the same time as Galatians.[14] All this, it seems, makes Hübner's position unlikely. There is another consideration, however, which is even more telling. The debate about Abraham is conducted on the assumption that the law reveals the true way to righteousness, and thus God's own intention.[15] This assumption characterizes not only Gal. 3:6–18, but also 4:21–31, where Paul cites "the law" to prove his own case.[16]

It is much better to read Galatians 3 as showing the depth of Paul's dilemma, a dilemma which reappears in Romans, although there it is handled somewhat differently. We have already characterized that dilemma: he believed that God gave the law, but he also believed that salvation is through faith in Christ and that the law served only to condemn. The denial that God gave the law (3:19) is a thrust against the law in the heat of debate. It does not represent an actual change of mind which is systematically carried through.[17] Thus the main line of Paul's argument is that God always intended to save by faith, apart from law. God gave the law, but he gave it in order that it would condemn all and thus prepare negatively for redemption on the basis of faith (3:22, 24, the purpose clauses conveying God's intention). The law was not given to make alive (3:21).

One of the most striking features of Paul's argument is that he puts everyone, whether Jew or Gentile, in the same situation. This is best explained by hypothesizing that he thought backwards, from solution to plight, and that his thinking in this, as in many respects, was governed by the overriding conviction that salvation is through Christ. Since Christ came to save all, all needed salvation.[18] The fact that Paul can equate the status of Jew and Gentile is explicable on this hypothesis and is simultaneously the best proof that Paul did not begin by analyzing the human condition. This is a point which is crucial for our final understanding of the role of the law in Paul's thought, and we shall return to it.

The equation of the status of Gentile and Jew first appears in Gal. 2:15f., where Paul states that even Jews, who are *not* Gentile sinners, are righteoused only (*ean mē*) through faith in Jesus Christ. This is an extremely revealing statement. It shows that Paul is not working with a traditional messianism, according to which "righteous" Jews are already members of the people of God.[19] It also shows that he knows full well that observant Jews are not in fact sinners by the biblical standard. Thirdly, it indicates the ground on which the plight of Jews and Gentiles is equated: all need faith in Christ.

When Paul turns to the plight, however, his statements would make a systematist shudder. Christ, he says, redeemed "us" — apparently whether

Jew or Gentile—from the curse of the law (Gal. 3:13).[20] This line is continued in Gal. 3:19—4:10. Scripture puts "all things" under sin (3:22). "We" were confined under the law (3:23); the law was "our" pedagogue (3:24), from which "we" have been released (3:25). Then, even more astonishingly, he writes, "Thus also we, when we were children, were enslaved under the *stoicheia tou kosmou*" (4:3).[21] God's son redeemed those "under the law," so that "we" might also be sons (4:4f.). Thus "you" are an heir (4:7). "You" were enslaved to nondivine deities (4:8). If you accept the *law*, you return to slavery under the *stoicheia* (4:9). The case is proved by the observance of special times (4:10).

The actual situation, of course, is that Jews were under the law, while pagans were under "beings" which are not actually gods. How, then, can Paul say that "we" were under the law and—with emphasis on the pronoun *hēmeis*—that *"we"* were slaves of the *stoicheia*? In order to make sense of this extraordinary sequence of statements, some scholars have proposed that Paul regarded the law as one of the *stoicheia* or that he thought of the angels of 3:19 as among the "beings" of 4:8.[22] But the parallel does not hold at the level of explicit conceptualization. The *stoicheia* of 4:3, 9 are the same as the beings of 4:8 (thus 4:8f.: you were enslaved to beings, how can you turn back to the *stoicheia*?). In 4:3-5, however, the *stoicheia* are paralleled with the law (we were enslaved to the *stoicheia*, but through his son God redeemed those under the law, so that we might receive adoption as sons). Paul cannot be thinking here in terms of explicit identification. Although paralleled with both, the *stoicheia* cannot simultaneously be the law and the beings (= the angels) who gave it. The point of the parallel between the *stoicheia* and the law is perceived when one focuses on Paul's conviction that the plight of Jew and Gentile must be the same, since Christ saves all on the same basis. The common denominator is bondage and the equation of law and *stoicheia* is material.[23] Thus Paul can go back and forth from "we" to "you" and also from pagan deities to the law. Everyone needs to be liberated from bondage by Christ. The argument that being under the law is the same as being under the *stoicheia* is driven home by the statement that both require the observation of special times: accepting the law is materially the same as resuming worship of beings which are not gods (4:10).

Before leaving this section of Galatians, we should note another way in which Paul connects being under the law with other statements of the human condition prior to Christ, one which becomes a major theme in Romans. In assigning the law a negative role in God's plan of salvation, he can speak of the human condition prior to the coming of Christ as both "under sin" (Gal. 3:22) and "under law" (3:23). In Gal. 4:21–31 there is a parallel between being under the law and being born "according to the flesh," and the parallel is repeated in other terms in 5:16–18 (note Spirit/flesh in 5:16f. and Spirit/law in 5:18). These parallels do not establish the identity of "the law" with either "sin" or "flesh," just as the parallel between the law and the *stoicheia* in 4:3–5 does not mean that the two are identical. We do, however, see a tendency of his thought: he tended to think in black and white terms.[24] Since the law does not secure the inheritance promised to Abraham, it is paralleled with, though not made the same as, sin, the power of evil, and pagan deities.

Romans: The Purpose of the Law and
Its Relationship with the Flesh,
Sin, and Death

We began this chapter by noting that in both Galatians and Romans, after asserting that righteousness does not come by obeying the law, Paul assigns it another role in God's plan. In Romans he does not ask the explicit question "why did God give the law?," but he does respond to it. In fact, he now regards the fact that the law has a negative role as establishing the statement that righteousness is not by the law. Thus he writes that by works of law no one will be righteoused before God, *since (gar)* through the law comes knowledge of sin (Rom. 3:20). Rom. 4:15 is similar, although this time the righteousness terminology is replaced by "inheritance": those who are "of the law" are not heirs, *since (gar)* the law brings about wrath. In Rom. 5:20 the statement that "law entered in order to increase the trespass" follows the statement that "by one man's obedience many will be made righteous." The continuation in 5:21 makes it even clearer that Paul is discussing God's plan of salvation, for there God's ultimate purpose is stated: "in order that (*hina*) just as sin reigned in death, thus also grace would reign through righteousness unto eternal life. . . ." Just as in Gal. 3:22, 24, the purpose clauses in Rom. 5:20f. are significant: the ultimate purpose of God's action was to prepare for salvation; the law was given in order to increase the trespass, with the intent that grace would ultimately reign.

We should observe that these three statements are not synonymous, although they may be complementary.[25] The present purpose is best served, however, not by trying to find a precise connection between bringing sin to knowledge and "increasing the trespass," but rather by repeating the basic observation that in all three passages the law plays a negative role in salvation history.

The statements about the law in Rom. 3:20; 4:15; and 5:20f. probably struck the initial readers of Romans as being at least a little surprising.

J. A. T. Robinson has noted that there is no immediate argument or explanation. Rom. 3:20 is "dogmatic (almost axiomatic)." "It is the first of a series of unargued statements on the subject of the law which he does not take up and justify till chapter 7." Robinson characterizes Rom. 5:20 as "another *obiter dictum*."[26] It would appear that the connection between the law and sin which we have seen in Galatians had, by the time Paul wrote Romans, become so customary to him that he could, at least in the early chapters, simply assert it without explanation. We have an advantage over the original readers of Romans. We have Galatians, and, if it is read first, the three short passages in Romans in which the law is connected with sin do not seem so surprising. It now remains, however, to see just how Paul works out the relationship between the law and sin in Romans 7.

The role assigned to the law in Rom. 5:20 ("in order to increase the trespass") is echoed in one clause in 7:13 ("in order that through the commandment sin might become sinful beyond measure"), while 3:20 ("through the law comes knowledge of sin") finds a partial counterpart in another clause in 7:13 ("in order that sin might appear [as such]"). A relationship between the law and the knowledge of sin is also stated in Rom. 7:7 ("I did not know sin except through the law"). Despite these similarities with what has gone before, the passages in Romans 7 are quite different. The purpose clauses of 7:13, unlike those of Gal. 3:22, 24; Rom. 5:20f., do not indicate that God has turned the knowledge of sin, or its increase, to good account. In fact, the active agent that produces sin is not God, nor even the law, but sin itself. Rom. 7:7 – 8:8 exhibits such a marked difference from the other passages in which Paul attempts to formulate the relationship between the law and God's plan of salvation that it requires us to rethink what we have thus far posited as being Paul's view. In order to get perspective on the problem, we should consider what Paul says about the law and sin after the statement that law "increases the trespass" (5:20) and before the statement that sin, not God, employed the law (7:7–13).

In Romans 6 Paul describes the pre-Christian human state as bondage to sin which can be escaped by sharing Christ's death (esp. 6:5–11). In 6:14 he writes that "sin will have no dominion over you, since you are not under law but under grace." At this particular point Paul does not explain why not being under the law means that one is not under sin, but is rather under grace. The verse appears to point back to 5:20f., where grace is also depicted as the counter to sin, which is increased by the law. In 6:14, however, sin appears more as a power than as "trespass" (5:20), which is quite in keeping with the overall theme of Romans 6: sin is a power to which one dies (6:10f.) and, more important, it is a power to which one may yield one's members and as such is placed in direct opposition to God, almost as an equivalent power (6:13, "do not yield your members to sin . . . but yield yourselves to God"). Being under law is then made parallel to being under sin: sin does not rule those who are not under the law (6:14), but "we" are not under the law, but rather under grace (6:15). In the subsequent verses sin appears as the enslaving power which is the opposite of righteousness, rather than directly of God (6:16–18).

The law is mentioned again in 7:1–6. The analogy which Paul employs in 7:2f. is, as is well known, imperfect. The point, however, is directly stated in 7:4–6: you have died to the law through Christ; you belong to another, Christ. The law here is spoken of as if it were the power opposite Christ. Paul continues by paralleling it with "the flesh": "while we were living in the *flesh*. . . . But now we are discharged from the *law*, dead to that which held us captive."

Throughout, Paul describes the human plight prior to Christ as bondage, slavery to a power which opposes God. The pre-Christian state is described as slavery to sin (6:6, 17, 20), as being in the flesh (7:5), and as being under the law (6:14f.; 7:6). Paul, to be sure, does not say that the law *is* sin or *is* the flesh. Rom. 7:5 itself makes a distinction: those who are in the flesh have their sinful passions aroused by the law. Nevertheless, those who are under sin are also under the law; those who are in the flesh are under the law; and the escape from sin and the flesh involves escape from the law.

This is reminiscent of the parallel in Galatians between being under the law and being under the *stoicheia*. Just as in Galatians, the law is part and parcel of the *universal* human condition apart from Christ. Thus we note also in Rom. 6:1–7:6 an oscillation between "you" and "we." "You" are not under the law (6:14); "we" are not under the law (6:15); "you" were slaves of sin (6:20); "you" have died to the law (7:4); "we" were in the flesh (7:5); "we" are discharged from the law (7:6). It is not possible to divide the pronouns up, "you" referring to Gentiles and "we" to Jews; all were previously under sin, all were in the flesh, all were under the law. Although Paul has shown in Gal. 2:15 that he knew the standard distinction between being a Gentile "sinner" and a righteous Jew, his general tendency, in evidence in Rom. 6:1 – 7:4 as well as in Gal. 3:19 – 4:10, was to universalize the human plight. All were under sin and in need of redemption; all were under the law.

In connecting the law with the universal human plight, Paul says things a good deal worse about it than that it does not righteous: it crops up, rather, on the bad side of the dividing line between those under sin and those under Christ. This is the case in Galatians 3 and 4, but in Romans 6 and the first verses of Romans 7 the law appears in still worse light. Sin is virtually personified as the opponent of God, and all who are enslaved by sin are under the law. Sin is not, in Romans 6, the instrument of God, used in order to hold all captive *so that* he could save all on the basis of faith. It has independent status and is not subject to God's control. In Romans 6 and the first part of Romans 7 Paul retains his earlier connection of sin and the law. He comes close to equating the law with sin; but, since sin is now an alien power outside God's will, he must explicitly deny the implied equation.[27] I think that it is the virtual dualism of Romans 6 and 7:1–6 which leads to the discussion of the law and sin in 7:7–25. We turn now directly to that discussion.[28]

We earlier said that Paul was in a dilemma, since he thought, as a good Jew, that God gave the law, while he also was convinced, on the basis of the revelation of Christ to him, that the law could not produce righteousness. We saw that he responded to the dilemma by giving the law a negative role in God's plan of salvation. It produces sin, *so that* salvation would be on the basis of faith. The dilemma, in other words, remained difficult but manageable as long as sin was given a place *within* God's plan of salvation. But when, as happens in Romans 6, sin is depicted as a power to which humans may give their allegiance, which can be escaped only by death, and which is thus not entirely subordinate to God's purpose — it cannot be utilized, but must be escaped by dying — the dilemma requires a different solution. *The law could no longer be said to produce sin or to multiply transgression as part of God's overall plan*, since *the realm of sin is now considered entirely outside that plan.* God will, in Paul's view, defeat sin, but that requires the sending of the Son (8:3). Individuals can escape sin, but only by death (6:11). God does not, however, "call the shots" within the sphere of sin.

Paul responded to this version of his dilemma in a way that is somewhat surprising. At first he did not sever the former connection between the law and sin, but he had to have another explanation of how they are related than their common subordination to the saving will of God. Thus in Rom. 7:7–13 Paul still holds (1) that God gave the law; (2) that the law and sin are connected. But here the relationships among the law, God's will, and sin change: the law is good, it was even given "unto life" (7:10), but it was used by the power alien to God — not by God himself, but by sin (7:8, 11, 13). That produced a situation *contrary* to the will of God. Thus there is an alteration in Paul's view of the relationship between sin and God's intention (God does not, as in Gal. 3:22, 24 intend bondage to sin), and between God's will and the law (he gave the law to save, an intention which was frustrated, rather than with the intent to condemn). These changes seem to be required by the new role given to sin: it is now an active agent which employs the law against the purpose of God. It is almost (not quite) needless to say that sin does not pervert the intention of the law by causing people to fulfill it in the wrong way, thus producing legalism. The law, rather, is the agent of sin because it condemns and thus provokes transgression. Sin, through the commandment, teaches what it is to covet; the law condemns covetousness, and consequently the one who covets (7:7–11); and the law is thus the agent of sin.

In 7:7–13, then, God does not intentionally give the law to condemn *so that* he can subsequently save on the basis of faith; rather he gives the law in order that it should be obeyed.[29] But sin grasps the law away from God. It uses it to promote transgression (7:8, 11, 13), and the result is that the law kills (7:10f.). In 7:7–13 the law is still connected to sin, but sin is not attributed to God's will.

This, at least, is one line of thought. It is important to note that there is another one.[30] The problem is the flesh in the sense of human nature.[31] Humans are fleshly (7:14), governed by a principle which causes them to act against the good which the law commands (7:15–23).[32] In this section, which is prepared for by 7:10, God wills the good, which is represented by the law. The individual knows what is good and tries to do it, but is *prevented* by "another law." This is somewhat different from saying that sin uses the law itself to *provoke* transgression. Rather, there is *another* law, a law of sin (7:23), which is indeed simply sin itself (7:17, 20), which prevents one from fulfilling God's law. Here Paul breaks the positive connection between the law and sin.

Rom. 7:7–13 is connected with the discussions of law and sin in Galatians and earlier in Romans because the law is said to *lead to* transgression. This line is not developed, however, in 7:14–23, where the law simply requires what is good, but humans are depicted as unable to fulfill it because of sin and the flesh. It is primarily the second depiction of the human plight for which Paul offers a "solution" in 8:1–8. Those in Christ are set free from this entire situation. The law did not carry with it the power to enable people to fulfill it (8:3, presumably because they are fleshly, 7:14). That lack, however, has now been overcome by God, who has done what the law (which he himself gave) could not do. God sent his son, and through his death he condemned "sin in the flesh." The purpose was to enable what the law requires to be fulfilled in those who walk according to the Spirit (8:3f.). Those who live by the Spirit fulfill the law; those who remain in the flesh are unable to do so (8:7f.).

According to what I have called a second line of thought, which dominates what is said about the law and sin from Rom. 7:14 to 8:8, the law does not even provoke sin. Its "fault," rather, is that it does not bear within itself the power to enable people to observe it. Only those who are in Christ, who have the Spirit, can do that. But is that a fault with the law? The human plight, without Christ, is so hopeless in this section that one wonders what happened to the doctrine that the creation was good. Those who see here a profound analysis of why the law is not an answer to the plight of humanity may miss the criticism of God the creator and giver of the law which can easily be derived from Rom. 7:10 and 7:14–25. Paul, to be sure, does not derive such a criticism. His intention is to conclude by praising God for offering the possibility of redemption through Christ, not to criticize him for creating humans who, being fleshly, are sold under sin, nor even to criticize him for not sending a law strong enough to do the job in the first place.

We have seen three different ways in which Paul states the interconnections among God's will, the law, and sin. The majority statement, that of Gal. 3:22–24 and Rom. 5:20f. (apparently also echoed in Rom. 3:20; 4:15), subordinates the law and sin, with which it is positively connected, to God's will. This view can be diagrammed thus:

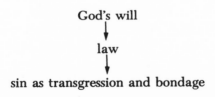

The view of Rom. 7:7–13, that the law is employed by sin to produce transgression against God's will, would be represented in this way:

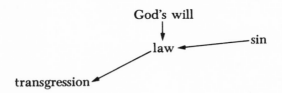

Finally, the position of Rom. 7:14–25, which breaks the positive connection between the law and transgression, leads to this chart:

I think that the shifts indicated by these diagrams, and some of the other complexities of Paul's various statements about the law, can be understood if we think of them as arising from an organic development with a momentum towards more and more negative statements until there is a recoil in Romans 7, a recoil which produces other problems. Paul's problems with the law do not *start* with Romans 7. It is the continuing theological problem of how to hold together both his native belief that God gave the law and his new conviction that salvation is only by faith in Christ (which leads him to give the law a negative role) which largely accounts for the torment and passion which are so marked in Romans 7.

Many will object to this proposal and will still wish to look to Romans 7 as offering *the* explanation of Paul's rejection of the law. I shall give first some account of possible objections, then indicate why I think that alternative views are not satisfactory and why the proposal made here offers a better explanation of a difficult chapter.

The anguished character of Romans 7 naturally makes us look for its explanation as close to experience as we can. Some will find the explanation in Paul's own autobiography — his own frustration at being unable to do what the law commands. Thus, for example, J. Christiaan Beker views the chapter as at least in part autobiographical and as reflecting a secret dissatisfaction with the law, one hidden perhaps even from himself, prior to Paul's conversion.[33] Others, persuaded by the obvious and telling exegetical arguments against the autobiographical explanation, find the torment to arise as Paul surveys the human scene from the standpoint of one who is in Christ — that is, from his anthropology.[34] Paul Meyer, for example, sees Romans 7 as revealing the chief reason behind Paul's rejection of righteousness by the law, and attempts to find a way of doing justice to the existential character of the chapter while still not describing it as autobiographical:

> It was after all not only Paul's discovery of the *justificatio impii*, of God's vindication of the sinner (and hence of the irreconcilable contradiction between that death and justification through the law, Gal. 2:21), but also, and perhaps for himself personally more importantly, this experience, interpreted in the light of the cross, of the power of sin to convert even his delight in the Torah into captivity (7:22–23) that raised to the level of an axiom in Paul's mind the conviction that no person's standing before God could be secured by observance of the law. . . .[35]

Let me first grant that there are some things about the history of Paul's attitude toward the law that we simply cannot know. We cannot discover whether or not Paul harbored a latent resentment of the law which he has disguised and which was perhaps hidden even from himself (Beker), nor can we exclude the possibility that in retrospect, in light of the Christ event, Paul saw his own previous efforts to obey the law as perverted by sin (Meyer). I think that one can say that Rom. 7:14–25 hardly reveals Paul's full thought about the "sorry plight of the Jew."[36] In other passages Paul shows that he knows full well that Jews were capable of doing what the law required, and he himself is a prime example. Our understanding of Romans 7 is thus partly determined by our understanding of other passages, such as Gal. 2:15f. and Philippians 3. But now let me turn to the arguments against seeing Romans 7 as *springing from* an anthropological/existential analysis of the hopeless state of humanity as it struggles to obey God without accepting Christ. We may summarize them under two headings: (1) the focus and subject matter of the chapter; (2) the consistency and chronology of Paul's thought.

The precise subject is neither "why is it that the law does not righteous?," nor "what is the human condition to which God has responded by sending his son?" (although the second question does arise, as we shall shortly note). The precise topic is "what is the relationship between the law and sin?" That is the question which the discussion in Rom. 6:5 – 7:6 has made insistent, and this question is closely connected to the implied further one, "why, then, did God give the law, since it is connected in some way or other with sin?" The point in making this distinction is that it enables us more clearly to see that, in Romans 7, the discussion is focused on God (particularly the divine purpose), the law, and sin, and on the relationships among them, and not primarily on the human condition for its own sake. Now, of course, Paul does say a fair bit in the chapter about the human condition as it is affected by, or responds to, God's law, as well as about the connection between sin and being human. But here we must note that what Paul says on these topics is not consistent with what he says elsewhere, nor do his comments about the human condition in Romans 7 appear to be the *source* of his other statements about the law, sin, and humanity. This leads us to the questions of consistency and chronology.

Most readers of Paul seem to take the view that in Romans 7 he has finally told us what he really thought and why he thought it. Having disguised his actual view of the relationship among the law, the human condition, and God's will in Galatians and the first chapters of Romans, he finally divulges "what he really thought" in Romans 7, and that turns out to have an existential-anthropological core which fortunately corresponds to modern anthropocentrism; and thus Paul becomes fully comprehensible. He returns to his deceptive way of talking in Romans 9 – 11, where again (as in Galatians 3, for example, and Romans 4) he assumes the point of view of God's dealing with the world — that is, a theocentric view which asks just what God has been doing in the history of Israel and what the final outcome of his dealing with humanity, both Jew and Greek, will be.

It seems to me unlikely that Paul kept concealed so long and so well the actual source of his own thought about the law, while writing about it and trying in various ways to explain how God had intended to use it. If the anthropological and existential analysis which many find in Romans 7 were the foundation on the basis of which he thought about the law, sin, and humanity, it should have surfaced in Galatians. Further, one might expect it to crop up somewhere else: if not in Romans 3, then in Romans 4; if not in Romans 4, then in 9 — 10; if not there, then in Philippians 3.

Naturally those who see Romans 7 as the central and definitive passage for understanding Paul's view of the law do see its point of view as cropping up elsewhere, especially in Romans 1:18 — 2:29 and Romans 9:30 — 10:13.[37] They view those passages as presenting from the point of view of humanity or from the point of view of the Jew the human inability to obey the law which is existentially described in Rom 7:14–25. But in fact the three passages present quite different arguments. Romans 9:30 — 10:13 argues that Jews while pursuing righteousness by the law have not found God's righteousness, of which the defining characteristics are that it comes by faith and is for all equally. Romans 1:18 — 2:29, as we shall see below, argues that everyone has been guilty of heinous sins, while holding out simultaneously the possibility that some may be righteous by the law. The argument of Rom. 7:14–25 is quite distinct: it is that humanity without Christ cannot fulfill the law at all. It is worth observing that in none of these passages does Paul argue that the law is too hard to be fulfilled adequately.

Rom. 7:14–25, then, does not express existentially a view which Paul consistently maintains elsewhere. Its extreme presentation of human inability is unique in the Pauline corpus. The point which is most nearly consistent throughout Paul's diverse discussions of the law, as well as chronologically prior, is that God has intended all along not to save on the basis of the law, but on the basis of faith, and thus to save all on the same ground.[38] This created a theological problem (one which is, in a sense, autobiographical, since Paul was Jewish) of considerable proportion. He was in a situation which required him to cast off, to deny, God's principal redemptive activities in the past: the election and the law. That he desperately wanted to find room for them is clear, for example, in Rom. 9:4–6; but it is equally clear that he could not have them still count for salvation. Here was a theological problem of the first order of magnitude: What was God up to before Christ? What was the point of the law? How can one hold together the history of Israel (including the law) with God's intention to save all by Christ?

These were real problems, and it seems to me far more likely that Paul was driven to passionate expression by them than that the cause of his torment was *Angst* within his own psyche or his analysis of the existential plight of humanity. These may be the real problems for moderns, but I doubt that they were for Paul.

To summarize this objection to the anthropological interpretation: Romans 7 comes at the end of repeated attempts to explain the purpose of the law in God's plan; its focus is on the interconnections among law, sin, and God's intention; it represents a development of what Paul says on these matters, a development that appears to be the result of the virtual dualism of Romans 6; the inconsistency of explanation of the purpose of the law makes it unlikely that Romans 7 is to be put at the center of an attempt to understand Paul and the law; the passion of expression is more likely to be explained as resulting from an acute theological problem than from an analysis of the human plight. I should add that it is in no way remarkable that a Jew of the ancient world would have been moved to passion when history or beliefs raised challenges to the view that God is constant and fair. For this last point, one may call to mind Job and 4 Ezra, in both of which theology and experience combine to call into question precisely the same aspects of God's dealing with humanity.

Just as the problem which touches off Romans 7 is directly expressed in the rhetorical question of 7:7, "is the law sin?" (that is, what is the relationship between the two?), so the overriding concern of the chapter is expressed in the question of 7:13: "Did that which is good, then, bring death to me?" There lurks not very far behind that question the criticism of God to which we earlier pointed. How could God, who all along intended to save on the basis of faith, have given a law which does not save, which first produces and then condemns sin, or which at best does not help? Worse, as we have seen, when he reaches Romans 7 Paul has just put the law on the side of death, sin, and the flesh. He then recoils from the potential denial that God acted for the good: it is not God's fault, nor the law's, but sin's. As he shifts the responsibility for transgression away from the good law given by God, he attributes it first to sin's use of the law and then to the sin which pervades what is fleshly and prevents it from obeying God's law. In this second shift an "existential" element does enter ("I do not do what I want," and the like). After he shifts the responsibility from God to the power of sin which pervades those whom God created, he shows that this new description of the human plight itself can move him to compassionate sympathy. What starts out as an agonizing theological problem (God's intention in giving the law, which leads to condemnation) quite readily becomes the human problem of how to escape from the enslavement to sin which either employs the law itself or prevents humans from obeying it ("who will deliver me?" 7:24).

We must note (and here we pursue further the questions of the consistency and rigor of Paul's theological analysis) that, in recoiling from attributing transgression and thus condemnation to the law (the question posed in 7:13), he goes to another extreme. He retracts the positive connection between sin, God's will, and the law, a connection which is otherwise made whenever he asks about the function of the law. This finally puts the law on the side of good (where it naturally belongs, since God gave it) and exonerates God. Yet Paul now runs into other difficulties. He thinks in black and white terms, as we have already said, and now he overstates human inability to fulfill the law as well as Christian success in doing what it requires. The fleshly human is incapable of doing anything which the law commands (7:15–23). Only Christians are able to fulfill the requirement of the law, and they do so perfectly, while those in the flesh "cannot please God" by submitting to his law (8:3–8). This extreme position runs contrary to his own experience both as Pharisee and apostle (Gal. 2:15f.; Philippians 3; 1 Corinthians passim).

There is another difficulty. He is led to make a contrast between God and the law in Rom. 8:3. The law is God's law (7:25), it was given for life (7:10), yet God must launch a rescue operation apart from law (8:3). God's first effort, it would appear, was a failure, and he had to redeem his own failure by sending his son. Paul, to be sure, does not say that it was God's failure: "the law" could not do what was necessary. But God gave the law.

In escaping one way of accounting for God's action, a way which was obviously not entirely satisfactory (the law was given by God with the purpose of producing sin, so that he could save on the basis of faith), Paul states the relationship between God, the law, and sin in a way which creates another problem: God gave the law to be obeyed, but humans are entirely unable to do so; therefore he had to launch a second effort.

Thus we see the depth of Paul's dilemma as he tried to hold both that God gave the law but that salvation is only through faith in Christ. I think that the dilemma itself it partly responsible for the passion and anguish of Romans 7.

It seems wise not to look for Paul's "real" point of view within the tortured explanations of the relationship between the law and sin.[39] We must back away from strict exegesis of Romans 7 to understand Paul's thought. He was absolutely convinced that God sent Christ to save all humanity on the same basis, and therefore apart from law. He had already, when we reach the passages here under consideration, argued extensively that righteousness does not come by keeping the law. Yet he thought that God gave the law. He attempted to hold these convictions together in different ways. Each attempt springs from the same central convictions and is, in that sense, part of a coherent line of thought. But in and of themselves the attempts are not harmonious. We do learn from them: we learn that the problem remained real for him, since he kept searching for a formulation which was satisfactory. We learn more about what his underlying convictions were. Perhaps most important, we learn that he did not begin his thinking about sin and redemption by analyzing the human condition, nor by analyzing the effect of the law on those who sought to obey it. Had he done so we should doubtless find more consistency. What is consistent in Paul's description of the human plight, as I wrote elsewhere, is the assertion of its universality.[40] Similarly, what is consistent in his treatment of the law is the assertion that it does not righteous and that God saves another way. Paul can say that that is the case because God always planned it that way — the majority statement — or because the fleshly nature of humanity makes obedience to the law impossible (Rom. 7:14–25), or because sin uses the law to provoke transgression, which leads to death (7:7–13). It is the conclusion which is consistent, not the treatment of the law: all are condemned; all can be saved by God through Christ.

All Are Under the Law / Christians Die
to the Law

We have touched on a group of statements about the law which seems to arise from Paul's attempts to answer the question of why God gave the law, but which, on the other hand, goes beyond that category. In explaining why God gave the law, Paul connects the law in various ways with sin, and he puts all humanity under sin and thus also under the law.

Some, to be sure, read either Galatians or Romans, or both, as saying that only Jews are under the law. Thus Ferdinand Hahn, whose discussions of the law in Romans is perceptive and carefully nuanced, seems to miss the degree to which Galatians also puts all under the law. He sees Gal. 2:16a,c and 3:22 as pointing toward the theme as it is worked out in Romans, but thinks that Paul does not explicitly bring all under the law in Galatians.[41] This seems to overlook the significance of the use of "we" and "you" in Gal.

3:23 — 4:9 which we discussed above (pp. 68f.). Most scholars also, as we noted, correctly see the "us" of 3:13 as including both Jew and Gentile.[42]

Friedrich-Wilhelm Marquardt and Markus Barth have also argued that Paul puts only Jews under the law. Marquardt notes the statement in Rom. 7:1 that Paul speaks "to those who know the law" and concludes that the "you" of 7:4 and the "we" of 7:6 refer only to Jewish Christians.[43] Barth seems to make systematic the distinction of Rom. 2:12 (some sin under the law; some sin without the law), which he applies to Gal. 2:15 (which he reads as "we [are] sinners of Jewish origin, not of heathen descent"); 2 Cor. 3:6, Rom. 5:12–14; 4:15; and 7:10f.[44]

There is no doubt that, at one level, Paul was quite conscious of the fact that Jews but not Gentiles were under the law. This appears not only in Rom. 2:12, but also in such a passage as 1 Cor. 6:9–11, where he says that at least some of his converts had been guilty of idolatry. Yet he generally writes on the basis of Jewish presuppositions. In writing to a church which was probably mixed, but which he calls Gentile (e.g. Rom. 1:13f.), he nevertheless speaks about Abraham "our forefather" (Rom. 4:1; cf. 1 Cor. 10:1; the Israelites, "our fathers," are used to prove that former pagans should not commit idolatry). We shall later take note of the Jewish character of many of Paul's arguments (pp. 182f.). With regard to the human plight, he could conceivably have offered another formulation. Thus, for example, he could have conformed the Jewish situation to the pagan one by saying that Jews had made an idol of the law. He kept the Jewish perspective and made the Gentile problem fit it, with virtually no explanation of how former idolaters were "under the law." The explanation on the basis of natural law in Romans 2 is striking because it is not otherwise employed. The full ambiguity of Paul's way of describing the human plight comes to expression in Rom. 3:19: "We know that whatever the law says it speaks to *those who are under the law*, so that *every mouth* may be stopped, and *the whole world* may be held accountable to God. For *no human being* will be righteoused in his sight by works of the law. . . ." He offers no explanation of how what the law says to those under it (the Jews) also applies to "the whole world."[45]

This gives us one more way of seeing the degree to which Paul's thought about sin and redemption is not based on a systematic, empirical account of the human condition. One often reads that Paul "demonstrates" that all are under sin. He does not, however, "demonstrate" it — not even in Rom. 1:18 — 2:29, as we shall see — he asserts it. Since God sent Christ to save humanity, and to do so on a common basis, all are in the same situation, under sin (e.g., Rom. 3:9). God had given the law before the coming of

Christ. It does not save; therefore it is connected with sin, the common condition of everyone, and thus everyone, before Christ, was under the law.

Paul views all Christians, whether Jew or Gentile, as having died to the law. It is part of the old world order, just as are sin and the flesh, and it must be escaped (die to sin, esp. Rom. 6:5–11; Christians are no longer in the flesh, Rom. 7:5, 9; Christians die to the law or are freed from it, Rom. 6:14f.; 7:4, 6). The law is different from sin and the flesh, however, because it is an agent of death, probably because of its power to condemn: it kills (2 Cor. 3:6; cf. Rom. 7:9–13).[46] It is probably for this reason that Paul can say both that he died to the law and that he did so through the law (Gal. 2.19), although the formulation is difficult. It seems to agree more with his general view of escape from the powers hostile to God to say that Christians die through Christ (Rom. 7:4).

These passages show that, whether or not the word *telos* in Rom. 10:4 means "end," Paul could think of the law as at an end, at least for Christians.[47] While this point is before us, and even before we offer a more detailed analysis of Paul's positive statements about the law, we should consider how it is that Paul can say both that Christians die to the law and that the law is to be upheld (Rom. 3:21) and fulfilled (Rom. 8:4; 13:8–10). We shall focus on the negative thrust.

When Paul says that the law kills or that Christians die to the law, the statements include all the law.[48] He does not distinguish between the ritual law (to which one dies) and the moral law (which remains).[49] Nor does he distinguish between the law as abused through self-righteousness and the law as fulfilled in the right spirit.[50] It is not a precise statement of Paul's view to say that one dies to only one function of the law. Many have seen the "end of the law" (whether indicated by Rom. 10:4 or by the statements that Christians die to the law) as meaning that one dies to the law as a system of salvation. It is only that aspect of the law which has come to an end since Christ.[51]

We should note, however, the strength of this explanation. It takes account of both Paul's positive and negative statements about the law. This is Rudolf Bultmann's formulation:

> Christ is the end of the Law so far as it claimed to be the way to salvation or was understood by man as the means to establishing "his own righteousness," *for so far as it contains God's demand, it retains it validity.*[52]

Ernst Käsemann puts it this way:

> The obedience of faith abrogates the law as a mediator of salvation, sees through the perversion of understanding it as a principle of achievement, and

in eschatological retrospect restores to the divine gift the character of the original will of God.[53]

Herman Ridderbos quite succinctly stated the same view: works of law are good "where meritoriousness is not in question."[54]

The explanation which is proposed here has, as is natural, a surface similarity to that of Bultmann. The similarity is natural, since every reader of Paul must see that sometimes he says that the law is, for Christians at least, at an end, while at other times he urges fulfillment of it. I propose that the negative statements arise from the discussion of membership requirements, first of all for Gentiles and then also for Jews. The positive statements arise from questions of behavior within the Christian community. How does this differ from distinguishing between the law as a way to salvation and the law as God's demand? In two ways: (1) Accepting the law as a membership requirement was not urged by Paul's opponents because they favored self-salvation, nor does Paul deny it on the grounds that pride in achievement would be the result. The traditional formulation misstates the point at issue. (2) The traditional formulation implies that Paul had consciously in mind two different functions or "uses" of the law. This does not seem to be correct. It is not that he saw that the law, *if* pursued for self-gain, would kill, but *if* followed in faith would lead to fulfillment of the will of God. Rather, when he was asked, as it were, the question of what was the necessary and sufficient condition for membership in the body of Christ, he said "not the law." When he asked about its function, which it had to have, since God gave it, he was led by painful steps to connect it with sin and death and to make it one of the enslaving elements to which Christians die. When, however, he thought about behavior, he responded, "fulfill the law."

The virtual equation of the law with sin and the flesh in some passages (e.g. Rom. 6:14; 7:4–6; Gal. 5:16–18) is not part of a harmonious view of the law which held in balance its destructive and its productive power, depending on human response.[55] It arises, rather, most immediately from Paul's assigning the law a negative role in God's plan of salvation, an assignment which itself arose from his view that righteousness is only by faith in Christ and that God must have given the law with *that* righteousness, and not some other, ultimately in view. Paul's most extreme negative statements, in other words, can be understood if we think of them as arising organically at the end of a chain of thought which begins with the assertion that righteousness is by faith and not by law. The sequence is not that of logical necessity, but it is "organic" because each step arises from the preceding one. It is noteworthy that each step in the series is progressively more negative: from "the law does not righteous" to "the law produces transgression" to "the law itself is one of the powers to which Christians must die, along with sin and the flesh." Finally, in Romans 7, Paul attempts to pull back; but then, as we have noted, he encounters other problems, either of having the law be used by a power other than God, or of having to separate the law from God.

The point will perhaps be clearer if we consider Paul's view of God's plan. Paul did not think that when God gave the law he also permitted its "abuse," and that only human misuse of it for self-righteous ends was wrong. Paul, I think, viewed God as being more sovereign than that. God must have planned what in fact resulted.[56] If the law condemns, God gave it *in order* that he might subsequently save on the basis of faith. It is paradoxical, perhaps ironic, that it was Paul's attempt to hold together God's will and the negative function which his exclusivist christology led him to assign the law which finally pushed him into *disassociating* the result of God's giving the law from his will. The disassociation takes place in two different ways in Romans 7: God willed that the law be followed so as to lead to life, but sin used the commandment to provoke transgressions; God willed that the law be followed — the same premise — but humanity, being fleshly, proved utterly incapable of doing so. In one case sin uses the law against the will of God; in the other God's will is ineffective because of the weakness of the created order. This "saves" God by putting his will on the side of good, instead of depicting him as intending to produce sin when he gave the law.[57] Paul here separates "God's will" from "what actually happened." In Paul's world, this last position is the most surprising: that God failed; that his original intention in giving the law was not achieved. It is noteworthy that "God's will" and "what happened" are reconnected again in Rom. 11.32: "God has consigned all to disobedience, *in order that* he could have mercy on all."

We here see how persistently Paul attributed to God a changeless plan. At the end of a series of not entirely successful attempts to combine his convictions about God's will, salvation by Christ and not by law, and the divine origin of the law, he virtually denies the last in favor of the first two. God's will to save by Christ is changeless, and it is reasserted at the end of numerous attempts to combine all three points, even though this requires distinguishing what God does from what the law could not do (Rom. 8:3).

The complexities of Paul's positions on the law, then, are partly to be explained as reflecting a development of thought which has a momentum toward more and more negative statements. Paul attempts to reverse the momentum in Romans 7, but other problems arise. Further, the negative thrust, which connects God's will and sin, reappears in Rom. 11:32.

There is another way in which we can explain how Paul could say so many different things about the law – including, this time, the most positive statements. All Paul's statements cannot be harmonized into a logical whole,[58] but each one can be understood as coming from the application of different of his central convictions to diverse problems. When his virtual equation of the law and sin forces him to ask directly if they are identical (Rom. 7:7), the answer is inevitable, given his native convictions about the law, God, and the changelessness of God's will. The same point can be made about each of his statements about the law in turn, but the various statements cannot be held together by the formulations of Bultmann and Käsemann, trenchantly though they are put.

The inadequacy of the Bultmannian explanation can be demonstrated in another way. When Paul does unmistakably talk about the law as at an end, he does not say that it is at an end in only one respect, and especially not as a way of salvation. When he uses the "until" formulation in Gal. 3:23f., he has in mind the law as a pedagogue which held all things under constraint. In this passage, and indeed throughout Galatians, Paul's argument is that the law was *never* intended by God to be a means of righteousness. It is not only *lately* that it has come to an end as such. Similarly, in Romans 6 and 7, Christians are not said to die to the law as a way of salvation, but to the law, the whole law; and it is conceived as an enslaving power, not as a potential means of righteousness.

In all these passages the law is thought of as all of one piece. It does not provide for righteousness, it was given by God, it is connected with sin, one dies to it – in no case is there a distinction within the law, nor are there distinctions between different functions of the law. This is also the case in Rom. 7:14–25. The "law of God" is the whole law, all of which is good, none of which can be fulfilled by fleshly humans.

NOTES

1. Rudolf Bultmann, *Theology of the New Testament*, vol. 1 (New York: Charles Scribner's Sons, 1951–1955), p. 263: according to Paul's concept of God, "whatever factually is or happens, is or happens according to divine plan." Cf. H. J. Schoeps, *Paul, The Theology of the Apostle in the Light of Jewish Religious History* (Philadelphia: Westminster Press, 1961), p. 231: "Paul sees all earthly happenings as cohering with the continuity of a concrete divine plan of action."

2. Cf. Ulrich Luz, *Das Geschichtsverständnis des Paulus* (Munich: Chr. Kaiser, 1968), pp. 186–93. Luz notes that the question of the law's meaning arises only in historical contexts, citing Gal. 3:19; Rom. 3:20; 4:15; 5:20; 9:30–33. He also discusses the different nuances of these passages. J. Christiaan Beker, *Paul the Apostle* (Philadelphia: Fortress Press, 1980), p. 243 states that the role of the law in salva-

tion history is discussed in Rom. 7:13; 5:20; 11:32, Gal. 3:19 – 4:24. We should note that Rom. 11:32 does not mention the law, although it is indirectly related to Paul's statements on the function of the law via the "all" statement.

3. On the grammar and the meaning of *ti oun*, see E. deWitt Burton, *The Epistle to the Galatians* (Edinburgh: T. & T. Clark, 1921), p. 187. Note especially Andrea van Dülmen, *Die Theologie des Gesetzes bei Paulus* (Stuttgart: Verlag Katholisches Bibelwerk, 1968), p. 39: "was ist das Gesetz? Zu welchem Zweck ist es gegeben? Welche Rolle spielt es im Heilsplan Gottes?"; cf. Franz Mussner, *Der Galaterbrief* (Freiburg: Herder, 1974), p. 245; Heinrich Schlier, *Der Brief an die Galater*, 5th ed. (Göttingen: Vandenhoeck & Ruprecht, 1971), p. 151; H. D. Betz, *Galatians* (Philadelphia: Fortress Press, 1979), p. 162, who takes the question to be "what is the law?" The passages which Betz cites in n. 10, p. 162, as also asking "the question" do not seem to be true parallels. They ask other questions, such as why the law was given in the desert and why God gave the laws regarding clean and unclean. See also Jost Eckert, *De urchristliche Verkündigung im Streit zwischen Paulus und seinen Gegnern nach dem Galaterbrief* (Regensburg: F. Pustet, 1971), p. 81. Eckert states that Paul asks about the quality of the law and also about its *heilsgeschichtlich* significance. If the question is "what is the law?" the answer is that it is something given by angels. This answer itself, however, blends into the response to the implied question about its function in God's plan.

4. Cf. Eckert, *Verkündigung*, pp. 109f.

5. "Would be given" and "would be righteoused" are better translations than "might be." "Might be" usually implies doubt or uncertainty. The verbs are subjunctive in Greek because the conjunction *hina* (in order that) requires the subjunctive. Paul does not intend to express any doubt as to whether or not the promise and righteousness come by faith.

6. We shall discuss "law" and "Scripture" in the conclusion to Part One. Here we note only that the terms in 3:22 and 3:24 seem synonymous. David Lull, in his review essay on Betz's commentary on Galatians, indicates that he would make a distinction in Galatians 3 between "the Jewish law" and "the Scripture" (*Perkins Journal* 34 [1981]: 44–46). I can see no basis for the assertions that the book of the law (Gal. 3:10) and "the Scripture" (3:22) are intended by Paul to refer to two different entities. We return to "law" and "Scripture" in the conclusion.

7. Thus, for example, Leander Keck, *Paul and his Letters* (Philadelphia: Fortress Press, 1979), p. 74.

8. Lull, for example (n. 6 above), sees the pedagogue as "teaching what to do and not to do and . . . giving rewards for obedience and punishing transgressions."

9. Cf. Eckert, *Verkündigung*, p. 82: "on account of transgressions" means "to increase sin," appealing to Rom. 5:20; 7:7; see also Betz, *Galatians*, pp. 165.

10. So, e.g., Burton, *Galatians*, pp. 196f., 201.

11. Hans Hübner, *Das Gesetz bei Paulus*, 2d. ed. (Göttingen: Vandenhoeck & Ruprecht, 1980), pp. 27–33.

12. Cf. ibid., p. 40: the law in Gal. 3:12 is not regarded as deceptive. It actually could give life if one could keep it completely.

13. Above, chapter 1, at n. 30.

14. Throughout the Corinthian correspondence the Scripture is cited in Paul's usual manner, as indicating the will or word of God. See, e.g., 1 Cor. 1:19,

31; 14:21; 2 Cor. 6:2; 6:16–18 (I assume the authenticity of the passage, though not that the present location is original); 8:15; 9:9; 10:17. On the relative dating of Galatians and the Corinthian correspondence, see Hübner, *Gesetz*, p. 91; p. 157 n. 47.

15. Against Hübner's view that the law has an immanent intention distinct from God's, see Heikki Räisänen, *Paul and the Law*, (forthcoming publication). Note also Luz, *Geschichtsverständnis*, p. 224: Paul thought of the law as God's and therefore had to ask about its meaning. The question comes to him from the traditional *Heilsgeschichte*.

16. In both sections Paul "proves" by the law that obedience of the law is not necessary.

17. On the way in which Gal. 3:19f. sets the law over against God, see recently Terrance Callan, "Pauline Midrash: The Exegetical Background of Gal. 3:19b," *JBL* 99 (1980): 549–67.

18. E. P. Sanders, *Paul and Palestinian Judaism* (Philadelphia: Fortress Press, 1977) pp. 442–47; esp. pp. 474f. (hereafter cited as *PPJ*).

19. Above, chapter 1 n. 63.

20. "Us" in Gal. 3:13 means everyone, Jew and Gentile alike: Franz Mussner, "Theologische 'Wiedergutmachung.' Am Beispiel der Auslegung des Galaterbriefs," *Freiburger Rundbrief* 26 (1974): ll; Luz, *Geschichtsverständnis*, p. 152 (it includes Gentile Christians); Peter von der Osten-Sacken, "Das paulinische Verständnis des Gesetzes im Spannungsfeld von Eschatologie und Geschichte," *EvTh* 37 (1977): 561.

21. It is not necessary to enter the discussion of what these *stoicheia* were. I take Gal. 4:8f. to show that Paul had pagan deities in mind.

22. E.g., Bo Reicke, "The Law and This World according to Paul," *JBL* 70 (1951): 259–76: there is identity between the angels of 3:19 and the *stoicheia* of chap. 4. He correctly observed, however, that there is essential identity between "we" and "you" in this section. The pronouns do not refer to different groups.

23. Thus J. A. Fitzmyer, "Saint Paul and the Law," *The Jurist* 27 (1967): 27: "tantamount to a return to [the same] slavery"; Eckert, *Verkündigung*, pp. 93, 110, 128, 232. Räisänen (*Paul and the Law*) points out that the angelic law-givers are not precisely paralleled with the *stoicheia*. Paul, Räisänen observes, did not think through the logic of his argument, since the solution is clearer than the problem. He concludes: "Paul's point in Galatians 4 is the polemical one of suggesting that man's plight under the law is identical with his plight under the elements." Cf. also the discussion of the law and the *stoicheia* in George Howard, *Crisis in Galatia* (New York: Cambridge University Press, 1979), pp. 66–78. He points out that it would be incorrect to isolate a supposed characteristic of each, such as legalism or ritualism, as the object of Paul's opposition and as providing a common denominator.

24. Cf. Eckert, *Verkündigung*, pp. 25 f.: Paul's thought is characterized as *Kontrastdenken*; there is seldom a middle position. So also Räisänen, *Paul and the Law*.

25. The different answers in Romans to the question of the function of the law are deftly handled by Ferdinand Hahn, "Das Gesetzesverständnis im Römer- und Galaterbrief," *ZNW* 67 (1976–77): 41–47: the law brings knowledge of sin in 3:20; in 5:12., 20f. the connection between the law and sin is put in terms of *Heilsgeschichte*; the same connection is put existentially in 7:7–24. I shall later propose that this distinction does not adequately account for all of 7:7–24. Cf. Räisänen,

Paul and the Law: "Paul seems to understand the relation between the law and sin in different ways in different passages."

26. J. A. T. Robinson, *Wrestling with Romans* (Philadelphia: Westminster Press, 1979), pp. 37, 66.

27. Cf. C. E. B. Cranfield, *The Epistle to the Romans*, vol. 1 (Edinburgh: T. & T. Clark, 1979), pp. 340f.

28. There are good summaries of various treatments of Romans 7 in Luz, *Geschichtsverständnis*, pp. 158–68; Richard Longenecker, *Paul: Apostle of Liberty* (New York: Harper & Row, 1964), pp. 86–97; 109–16; J. A. T. Robinson, *Wrestling with Romans* (Philadelphia: Westminster Press, 1979), pp. 82–88; James D. G. Dunn, "Rom. 7,14–25 in the Theology of Paul," *TZ* 31 (1975): 257–73. As Dunn especially makes clear, there have been basically three interpretations of Romans 7: (*a*) the anthropological (it depicts the plight of humanity before and apart from Christ); (*b*) Paul's own experience prior to Christ, but seen from his present perspective; (*c*) his continuing autobiographical experience.

29. On the question of whether or not there is in 7:13 a distinction between the original intention behind the giving of the law and the law's factual function, see Hübner, *Gesetz*, p. 64 and the literature cited there. I take it that at least there is a distinction between God's intention and sin's use of the law: the law is no longer simply the instrument of God's will.

30. Rom. 7:14 is often seen as marking a shift in the argument, but usually the emphasis is put on the change to the present tense. Robinson (*Wrestling with Romans*, p. 88) correctly observes that this is the wrong emphasis. The present tense is required by the general proposition that "the law is spiritual," and the emphasis is on the contrast between the spiritual law and human nature, the *ego* which is *sarkinos* (7:14b).

31. *Sarkinos* in 7:14 emphasizes "the state of human nature in its own strength" (Robinson, ibid., p. 90). This is especially clear in 7:18, "in my flesh." Before the argument is complete, however, Paul will relate the weakness of human flesh to the Flesh conceived as a power which opposes God's spirit; see esp. 8:8.

32. Bultmann explained the object of "willing" in Rom. 7:14–25 as "life" rather than the commandments. See "Romans 7 and the Anthropology of Paul," in *Existence and Faith* (Cleveland and New York: World Publishing Co., Meridian Books, 1960), p. 152. But the question is what one *does*. Note *prassō* and *poiō* in 7:15. Bultmann's forced interpretation continues to be influential. Thus Leander Keck ("The Law and 'The Law of Sin and Death' [Rom. 8:1–4]: Reflections on the Spirit and Ethics in Paul," in *The Divine Helmsman*, [New York: KTAV, 1980], p. 53) interprets "the requirement of the law" in Rom. 8:4 as "the right intent of the law — life."

33. Beker, *Paul the Apostle*, pp. 236–43. In this section he criticizes the view which I took in *PPJ* as being purely theological and as ignoring the dimension of Paul's experience (p. 237; 242 n. 22). Beker overlooks the role which I actually assigned to Paul's experience: "What is distinctive about Paul's view of the law . . . [is] that Christ saves Gentiles as well as Jews. This was not only a theological view, but it was bound up with Paul's most profound conviction about himself, a conviction on which he staked his career and his life: he was the apostle to the Gentiles. . . . Further, it was a matter of common Christian experience that the Spirit and faith come by hearing the gospel, not by obeying the law" (*PPJ*, p. 496). Thus Beker

and I do not disagree that there is a connection in Paul's view of the law between theology and experience. The disagreement is over how to state that experience. In *PPJ* I identified the experience as Paul's call to be apostle to the Gentiles and as the common experience of the Spirit. See further below, pp. 151–53.

Robert H. Gundry makes a thoroughgoing attempt to explain Romans 7 as autobiographical, and he notes that this sort of explanation is making a resurgence: Robert H. Gundry, "The Moral Frustration of Paul before His Conversion: Sexual Lust in Romans 7:7–25," *Pauline Studies* (Grand Rapids: Wm. B. Eerdmans, 1980), pp. 228–45. See also Dunn, "Rom. 7,14–25 in the Theology of Paul" (Paul's continuing autobiographical experience).

34. This is the position which Bultmann made famous in "Romans 7 and the Anthropology of Paul." For a recent and extreme statement, see Walther Schmithals, *Die theologische Anthropologie des Paulus. Auslegung von Röm. 7,17 − 8,39* (Stuttgart: Kohlhammer Verlag, 1980), p. 7: "An essential characteristic of this text is its theological direction towards humanity. Paul expounds no teaching about God, but rather describes man, who stands before God as sinner and believer."

35. Paul Meyer, "Romans 10:4 and the End of the Law," in *The Divine Helmsman* (New York: KTAV, 1980), p. 67.

36. Beker's phrase, *Paul the Apostle*, p. 240.

37. See, for example, Meyer, "Romans 10:4 and the End of the Law."

38. Cf. Seyoon Kim, *The Origin of Paul's Gospel* (Tübingen: J. C. B. Mohr [Paul Siebeck], 1981), p. 308: "Since God justifies man apart from works of law, by his grace in Christ and on the basis of his faith, the Gentiles as well as the Jews can be justified through faith alone. This is what Paul argues for whenever he comes to unfold his doctrine of justification."

39. For another example see Byrne, *"Sons of God" − "Seed of Abraham"* (Rome: Biblical Institute Press, 1979), pp. 92f., 231.

40. *PPJ*, p. 474.

41. Hahn, "Gesetzesverständnis," p. 59. It accords with this that Hahn regards Galatians as dealing almost exclusively with Judaism (p. 51).

42. Above, n. 20. See also Howard, *Crisis*, pp. 58f., and Hübner's critique of Hahn, *Gesetz*, pp. 134f.

43. Friedrich-Wilhelm Marquardt, *Die Juden im Römerbrief* (Zürich: Theologischer Verlag, 1971), p. 19 and passim.

44. Markus Barth, "Die Stellung des Paulus zu Gesetz und Ordnung," *EvTh* 33 (1973): esp. 508, 511.

45. Some commentators (e.g. Robinson, *Wrestling with Romans*, p. 36) avoid the difficulty posed by 3:19 by inserting between the proof-texts of 3:11–18 and the conclusion which Paul draws in 3:19 a Jewish objection: "these texts refer to the Gentiles." Paul replies that Scripture *also* condemns Jews (3:19). But this exchange is simply not evident in the text. Paul takes the scriptural quotations to cover all humanity throughout: note 3:9f.: "all people . . . as it is written." Here as elsewhere Paul, with no explanation, puts *all* under the law.

46. The two statements are slightly different. In 2 Corinthians 3 "sin" is not mentioned, and the law ("the written code") is said to kill. In Rom. 7:9–13 Paul attributes death to sin, which makes use of the law.

47. Räisänen, "Paul's Theological Difficulties with the Law," in *Studia Biblica 1978*, vol. 3 (Sheffield: JSOT Press, 1980), p. 306.

48. I am especially indebted here to Räisänen, ibid., pp. 305 f.; *Paul and the Law*.

49. Against the distinction see S. Lyonnet, "St. Paul: Liberty and Law," *The Bridge* (Newark, N.J.: The Institute of Judeo-Christian Studies, Seton Hall University, 1962), p. 232.

50. The latter position is Hübner's interpretation of Romans, which he summarizes thus: "Christ is the end of the fleshly misuse of the law" (*Gesetz*, p. 129). Hübner understands "under the law" in Rom. 6:14 to mean "under the Lordship of the perverted law" (p. 115). The word "perverted" is frequent in this section of Hübner's book. Though he did not have Hübner in mind, Keck's remark is to the point: "Where does Paul ever speak of something bad that has befallen the Torah in such a way as to pervert it?" ("The Law and 'The Law of Sin and Death'," p. 47).

51. We pointed out above, chapter 1, n. 114, that this view cannot be derived from Rom. 10:4. The point here is more general.

52. Bultmann, *Theology*, vol. 1, p. 341.

53. Ernst Käsemann, *Commentary on Romans* (Grand Rapids: Wm. B. Eerdmans, 1980), p. 94. Cf. Paul Wernle, *Der Christ und die Sünde bei Paulus* (Freiburg: J. C. B. Mohr [Paul Siebeck], 1897), pp. 96–99; Wolfgang Schrage, *Die konkreten Einzelgebote in der paulinischen Paränese* (Gütersloh: Gerd Mohn, 1961), pp. 94, 232, 238.

54. Herman Ridderbos, *Paul: An Outline of His Theology* (Grand Rapids: Wm. B. Eerdmans, 1975), p. 179. This general view is very common. Thus Robinson, *Wrestling with Romans*, p. 51: the law is constantly regarded from two viewpoints, as the will of God and as a way to salvation.

55. Note C. K. Barrett's formulation: "the law was open to two kinds of response, a faith-response and a works-response" ("Romans 9:30 – 10:21," in *Essays on Paul* [London: SPCK, 1982], p. 144).

56. N. 1 above.

57. The point of Hübner's distinction between God's intention in giving the law and the angels' (above) is that to attribute the intention to provoke sin to God would be cynical: *Gesetz*, pp. 28f.

58. Räisänen, "Paul's Theological Difficulties," p. 307: "I am unable to harmonize the two sets of statements [i.e., the positive and the negative]. The common explanation that Paul rejects the law as a way of salvation but retains it as an expression of God's will in ethical regard only restates the problem in different words."

3

The Law Should Be Fulfilled

Doing the Law

We have seen, in Rom. 6:14 – 8:8, that Paul holds that Christians are not under the law, which is connected with sin and the flesh; that the law has the function of bringing sin to knowledge or causing it to be exceedingly sinful; that fleshly humans cannot obey what the law requires; and that those in the Spirit do fulfill the law. This general sequence (not the views peculiar to Romans 7) characterizes Galatians as well. After Paul argues at length that righteousness comes not by law, but by faith (Gal. 2:15 – 3:18), he turns to ask why God gave the law (3:19), and explains that it is connected with sin and thus leads up to salvation through faith negatively (3:22–24). Christians are no longer under the law (3:25). Yet they do (or should) fulfill "the law" or "the law of Christ" (5:14; 6:3). The three principal points, especially as they appear in Galatians, provide the structure of our present treatment: (1) No one is righteoused by doing the law. (2) What, then, is the reason for the giving of the law? What is its function? Since the answer connects the law in some way with sin, Paul often follows this point up by saying that Christians are not under the law. (3) Christians do, or should, fulfill the law. The sequence of topics is more complicated in Romans than in Galatians, but it is not basically different. Points one and two appear together, and in that order, in Rom. 3:20. The same sequence can be observed in chapter 4 (4:13, the promise is not through law; 4:15, the law brings wrath) and in chapter 5 (5:1, we are righteoused by faith; 5:20, the law increases the trespass). Rom. 6:14, then, states that Christians are not under sin, since they are not under the law, and this is repeated in 7:4–6. In 7:7–13 Paul returns to the connection of law with sin; in 8:2 he says that Christians are not under "the law of sin and death," and in 8:4 he says that the requirement of the law is fulfilled in Christians. He reaffirms that Christians should fulfill the law in 13:8–10.

Once Paul says that righteousness is not by the law, the rest of the sequence of statements about the law is easily understandable. The law must have been given for some purpose. When its function is described as being connected with sin, it is again understandable that he says that Christians are not "under" it. Yet he also thought that Christians should live in accordance with God's will, and he saw that will as expressed in the Scripture: thus Christians obey the law.

The statements about the law which we considered in chapters 1 and 2 (or similar ones) apparently led some to think that Paul was an antinomian or worse: that the consequence of his message was that evil should be multiplied so that grace would abound (see Rom. 3:8; 6:1). The letters which we have, however, show that he had definite ideas of correct behavior, that he thought that Christians should live holy and blameless lives, and that he was horrified when they did not do so.[1]

The principal summary phrases which Paul employs when describing how Christians should behave are these:[2]

Gal.	5:14:	"the whole law": love your neighbor
	5:22:	fruit of the Spirit: love, joy, etc.; opposite sexual immorality, idolatry, etc. (5:19–21)
	6:2:	"the law of Christ": bear one another's burdens
1 Cor.	7:19:	"the commandments of God": not circumcision
	9:21:	*ennomos Christou*: not *anomos theou*
Rom.	8:4:	*to dikaiōma tou nomou*
	12:2:	the will of God, the good, the pleasing, and the perfect (a list follows)
	13:8–10:	the law: four commandments plus any others: summarized by love your neighbor
Phil.	1:11:	fruits of righteousness
1 Thess. 3:13; 4:3–7; 5:23; 1 Cor. 1:8; 7:34; 2 Cor. 7:1; Phil. 1:9–11; 2:15f.:		
		blameless, guiltless, holy, pure, and the like

A full discussion of Pauline ethics is beyond the scope of the present essay, yet some general view of Pauline ethics and of the role of correct behavior in the Christian life is necessary in order to understand what Paul says about the law. We should also pay attention to the concrete instructions about behavior which he gives. Concrete instructions can help control interpretation of the general or theoretical statements about the relationship between behavior and the law. Rather than begin with a passage-by-passage exegesis of the places in which Paul urges obedience to "the law" or to some aspect of it, I shall offer some general observations about the relationship between behavior and the law as it emerges in his letters, hoping thereby to preserve a focus on the law, while not ignoring relevant passages in which the word *nomos* does not occur.

1. We should note first the remarkable degree to which Paul's admoni-

tions are in accord with the law and with Jewish tradition. As Heikki Räisänen puts it, "Paul obliged his Gentile converts to lead a decent life according to normal Jewish standards."[3] The summary which Paul twice gives, to love the neighbor (Gal. 5:14; Rom. 13:8–10) is, as is well known, a quotation of Lev. 19:18 and is a summary well-known in Judaism.[4] Further, Paul's vice lists generally feature prominently the sins most characteristic of Gentiles as the Jews saw them: idolatry and sexual immorality.[5] In other words, not only the summary "love your neighbor," but also its concrete working out shows Paul's education and point of view. There is nothing self-evident, on the basis of the principle "love your neighbor," about saying that homosexuals would not inherit the kingdom of God (1 Cor. 6:9–11). Similarly the principle does not, abstractly considered, ban fornication. Paul apparently felt the standard Jewish repugnance for Gentile sexual practices.

Paul did not work out a full halakic system,* his rulings seem to be ad hoc, and many of them may have come as a surprise to his converts, since they do not necessarily follow from the admonitions to love the neighbor and walk by the Spirit. Thus we may reasonably infer that his first concern was not to inculcate Jewish behavior in his converts. 1 Corinthians seems to show that he regarded correct (that is, decent Jewish) behavior as the self-evident result of living by the Spirit and did not spend a lot of time teaching it. Thus behavior had to be corrected by letter. It is also true that he does not often appeal to Biblical *commandments* as the ground for his view. Thus he goes to considerable length to show that idolatry is wrong on typological and christological grounds in 1 Corinthians 10, and the argument depends on the use of the Bible as Scripture, but neither here nor in Rom. 13:8–10, where commandments are cited, is the first commandment mentioned.

We should also note that not all the admonitions and prohibitions in the lists of correct and incorrect behavior (e.g. Gal. 5:19–23; 1 Cor. 6:9–11) are peculiarly Biblical or Jewish. Paul's view of divorce goes back to one form of the Jesus tradition (1 Cor. 7:10f.). His complete prohibition of consorting with prostitutes (1 Cor. 6:15–20) goes beyond Jewish law and is based on his interpretation of union with Christ. Phil. 4:8, where the emphasis is "think good things" rather than "act correctly," is not easily traced to Jewish tradition.

Thus he neither developed nor taught a full system of behavior, he did not often explicitly derive his rulings from Biblical commandments (even when he used Scripture to support them), and not all his views of correct

---

*Halakah is detailed and applied law.

behavior were in strict accord with Biblical law and Jewish tradition. Nevertheless, the Jewish content of Paul's ethical views is striking and noteworthy.

2. When Paul uses the word "law" or "commandments" in connection with behavior, he never makes a theoretical distinction with regard to what aspects of the law are binding, nor does he in any way distinguish "the law" which Christians are to obey from the law which does not righteous, which ties all humanity to sin, and to which those in Christ have died. This is a controversial point, and it should first be noted that we shall immediately ask whether or not Paul made de facto distinctions between the law which Christians obey and the Mosaic law. The present point is that he made no generalizing or theoretical distinction.

Hans Hübner has proposed that Paul does make a distinction in Galatians, which is indicated by the change from "the whole law" (5:3) to "all the law" (5:14). The "whole law" of 5:3 is to be viewed as the Mosaic law understood quantitatively: a law consisting of numerous individual commandments that cannot be adequately fulfilled.[6] "All the law" is entirely different, and it has no reference to the Jewish Torah.[7]

Hübner's proposal gets Paul out of a difficulty. Paul is to continue to state the opposition between the Christian life and the law in Gal. 5:17 by saying that those who are led by the Spirit are not under the law. How, then, could he mean the same law in 5:14 as in Galatians 3; 5:3; and 5:17? Thus it is tempting to look for another "law" in 5:14. The difficulty with Hübner's proposal, however, is that it requires us to think that Paul made an intentional shift in the meaning of the word "law" and indicated it by changing the modifying word from "whole" to "all," and that he then defined this different law by quoting the Mosaic law. Hübner's solution, I fear, is overly ingenious, especially since there seems to be a simpler way of understanding the course of the argument.

We should first give two prima facie reasons for understanding "all the law" in Gal. 5:14 as not being theoretically distinguished from the law of Moses. In the first place, Paul was Jewish, and he quotes a passage on which was based a standard Jewish summary of the law.[8] That a person of his antecedents could use this quotation to mean a law that has nothing to do with the law of Moses is hard to believe. Secondly, within a relatively short period of time he will quote the same passage as summarizing four of the ten commandments and "any other commandment" (Rom. 13:8–10). Hübner, to be sure, thinks that Paul changed his mind about the law almost entirely between writing Galatians and Romans. As we noted in chapter 1 above, Hübner thinks that Paul's objection to the law in Romans is that the law leads to boasting. It should be fulfilled by Christians, though not in a boastful manner.[9] I have already argued against Hübner's interpretation of Romans 3 – 4 and 9:30 – 10:13. Here I shall only note that, prima facie, one would expect Paul to mean the same thing when he quotes the same passage in two letters which are so close together chronologically.

But to understand Gal. 5:14 we must understand the way in which Paul argues: paradoxically, and by flinging his opponents' terms back at them. Gal. 5:14, in the context of the argument as a whole, says this: You are urged by "some" to accept circumcision and the law in order to be true descendants of Abraham. You must not. I did not preach the law, but faith, by which you received the spirit (3:1-5). Further, those who are Christ's are the sons of Abraham (3:29). If you start with circumcision you must keep the entire Jewish law (5:3). If you think that you will be righteoused by doing the law, you are cut off from Christ (5:4). *Besides*, I can tell you the *real* way to fulfill the law: love your neighbor as yourself. Doing that *actually* fulfills the entire law (5:14).

This same type of argument appears in 1 Corinthians in connection with wisdom. Paul argues thus: You are tempted to follow someone else, who offers wisdom. I did not preach wisdom, but the cross (1 Cor. 1:18). God destroys wisdom (1:19). But, in fact, I have and can give you *real* wisdom (2:6). In 1 Cor. 2:6 Paul continues to say that his wisdom is not the "wisdom of this age," while in Gal. 5:14 he does not introduce terms which distinguish the entire law from the Mosaic law. The style of argument, however, is the same: wisdom, as is the law, is combatted by recalling what Paul preached (Gal. 3:1-5; 1 Cor. 1:17, 23; 2:4) and by the use of one or more proof-texts (Gal. 3:6-14; 1 Cor. 1:19). Paul then indicates that following him leads to what his converts desire. In the case of wisdom he distinguishes it theoretically from the wisdom of the world but does not reveal the content, appealing, rather, to the Spirit (1 Cor. 2:10). In the case of the law, he makes no theoretical distinction, but does summarize the content: love your neighbor. In both cases he is employing a debating device. No matter what temptations or values others offer his converts, he, Paul, can provide them with what they want.

He does not explain *how* one who does not accept circumcision can fulfill the entire law. He simply asserts it, and the assertion was doubtless made easy by the fact that in Judaism the law was often summarized in a similar way, with no indication of how loving the neighbor would in fact lead to doing all that God commanded.[10]

Gal. 6:2 is probably to be understood along the same lines. The law, now characterized as "the law of Christ" is actually fulfilled when one bears another's burdens. It is futile to try to determine, on the basis of Galatians, how the "law of Christ" would differ from "the entire law" of 5:14 or from the Mosaic law.[11] The connection with 5:14, in fact, is very close. "Bear one another's burdens" is probably not to be distinguished from "love your neighbor as yourself," except that the former is not a quotation from Scripture. The reader of Galatians, if none of Paul's other letters were available, might well be confused by Paul's saying "do not accept the law; you will fulfill the entire law if you love your neighbor as yourself; you are not under the law; you fulfill the law by bearing another's burdens." But the reader would not understand that Paul intends by "law" in 5:14 and 6:2 a law which is entirely distinct from the other one.[12] That is what I mean by saying that Paul makes no theoretical distinction. What is concretely urged in 5:14 and 6:2 falls within the Mosaic law; and just how, if at all, the law which Christians are to obey differs from the Mosaic law is not clarified by any further definition.

We can put the matter one other way. The reader of Galatians can understand Paul as saying "you are not under *the* law, but nevertheless you are under *a* law, the law of Christ, which commands love of the neighbor" *or* "you are not under the law, but nevertheless you should fulfill it, not by being circumcised, but by loving your neighbor: that is real fulfillment." I think that the latter is by far the more likely meaning, especially since the law which is to be fulfilled is Lev. 19:18.

There is also no theoretical distinction in Romans. In Rom. 3:31, as Abraham Malherbe has pointed out, Paul sets up an extreme and erroneous deduction from his theology ("we overthrow the law") and then counters it in a way which has well-known rhetorical parallels. The strong "uphold" is the rhetorical counter to "overthrow." From the context one sees that "the law" which is to be upheld is one which must be conformable to the equality of Jew and Gentile, but the rhetorical question and answer do not permit "the law" in v. 31 itself to be defined and nuanced.[13]

In Rom. 8:3–4 Paul writes that the purpose of God's sending his son was that Christians "would fulfill the requirement of the law." Several scholars have argued recently that the law in Rom. 8:1–4 is the same as the law in Romans 7, but viewed from a different perspective. It is the same law, and the distinction is the situation of the one whom it confronts. It is a law of sin and death for those under sin, but a law of the Spirit of life for those in the Spirit.[14] Although "law of the Spirit of life" in Rom. 8:2a seems clearly a play on the word *nomos*, as we argued before,[15] it is certainly true that there is no explicit distinction drawn between the "requirement of the law" which is fulfilled in Christians according to 8:4 and the law which non-Christians cannot do in 7:14–25 and from which they are liberated according to 8:2b.[16] But not only is there no explicit distinction between the law of Rom. 8:4 and the Mosaic law, the course of the argument requires them to be the same. Non-Christians are in the flesh and cannot fulfill the law — none of it — yet Christians, who are in the Spirit, fulfill it. If "the requirement of the law" in 8:4 is different from "the good" which is commanded by "the law of God" (7:16, 18, 22), the distinction is lost on the reader, and besides, the contrast which Paul is drawing between being in the flesh and being in the Spirit becomes pointless. In the flesh one *cannot* do the good which the law demands (7:18–22; 8:5a, 7–8); those in the Spirit fulfill the law (8:4).

We should also note that the distinction in Rom. 8:1–4 is not that Christians take a different attitude toward the law from that of non-Christians in Rom. 7:14–25; 8:5, 7f. There is nothing about attitude (e.g., to compile enough merit to boast) in either section. The question is about ability.[17] Those in the flesh, despite their best efforts, which Paul does not criticize, cannot do what the law requires; those in the Spirit can and do.

We shall briefly note, since the point is not controversial, that Rom. 13:8–10 makes no obvious distinction between the law that Christians should obey and the Mosaic law. There Paul not only quotes Lev. 19:18, but also itemizes four of the ten commandments and adds "and any other commandment" as being included in Lev. 19:18.

The fact that Paul summarizes the law with a sentence which does not logically include all the law (Gal. 5:14), and that when he does list commandments he gives a selective list (Rom. 13:8–10) does not in and of itself indicate that the content of the law has been changed. When other Jewish teachers, in summarizing the law, cited one law or a few commandments (the commandment to love the neighbor, perform acts of charity, avoid idolatry, and the like)[18] they did not intend to reduce the law, nor did they explain how the commandment stated could include all the commandments. The lack of an explanation is thus in line with Paul's tradition. On the other hand, other Jewish teachers did not cite a commandment as summarizing the whole law after forbidding circumcision and connecting the law with sin. For this reason Paul's summaries constitute a substantial problem. Nevertheless, he provides no explanation.

There is, then, appreciable tension between the view that Christians are not under the law at all — they have died to the law, not just to part of it and not just to the law as perverted by pride, but to the law as such — and the view that those in Christ fulfill the law — not just aspects of it, and not just the law when pursued in the right spirit. Thus it will come as no surprise to discover that both positions cannot be maintained in detail. The pressure to make a distinction, to clarify the situation of those in Christ vis-à-vis the law, is evident in 1 Cor. 9:19–21, where Paul describes his own situation. He is free from all human constraint, but he has made himself a slave for the sake of his mission.

> To the Jews I became as a Jew, in order to win Jews. To those under the law [I became] as [one] under the law — not being myself under the law — in order that I might win those under the law. To the lawless [I became] as lawless — not being lawless with regard to God, but in [the] law of Christ — in order that I might win those who are lawless.

The phrase *ennomos Christou*, which is virtually untranslatable, though here translated "in [the] law of Christ" for the sake of convenience, is parallel to the preceding negative, "*not being lawless* with regard to God" (*mē ōn anomos theou*). But it is also defined by the preceding "*lawless*," which Paul also says he was.[19] Paul is obviously attempting to formulate how he can live *outside* the law when evangelizing Gentiles and living among them, yet remain *within* the law of Christ and thus of God. He is attempting to formulate that possibility, yet the passage does not say how he can manage both.[20] The truth is that he has no clear way of defining his own situation theoretically. When among the Gentiles he does not observe the Jewish law: that is clear in Gal. 2:11–14. Yet he does not regard himself as outside the law of God, since he is *ennomos Christou*. If this is a reference to his obeying the words of Jesus, it is certainly an obscure one. It is better to read it as an assertion, which is based on the conviction that Christians both stand in a right relationship to God and live in accordance with his will, but which is no more thought through in a systematic way than Gal. 5:14 and Rom. 8:4. Christians, of whom Paul is here the example, are not *under* the law, but they are not thereby lawless toward God. Paul here as elsewhere wants to maintain that Christians are "lawless," yet at the same time not really lawless: they are outside the law yet fulfill it.

3. Fortunately, we do not remain forever unable to penetrate what Paul "really thought" about observance of the law, despite the fact that he does not formulate in a clear theoretical way how it is that Christians are not under it but fulfill it. There are enough explicit rulings on concrete aspects of the Jewish law that we can see that he made de facto distinctions about which parts Christians should obey.

a) We begin, again, with Galatians. There Paul rules out, for Gentile converts, circumcision and thus formal commitment of the Jewish law. In and of itself circumcision does not matter (6:15), but accepting it in order to become a descendant of Abraham is excluded. Further, it is wrong for

Jewish Christians to follow the laws which govern eating (whether the laws which prohibit certain foods or the laws of purity is not clear)[21] when in company with Gentile Christians (2:11–14). Third, the observance of the special days and seasons which are required by Jewish law is tantamount to returning to idolatry (4:10).

b) Romans and 1 Corinthians show that Paul was not inconsistent with regard to these three laws or groups of laws. Circumcision is explicitly excluded, as a matter of indifference, from "the commandments of God" (1 Cor. 7:18f.). 1 Corinthians 8 and 10, especially 10:27, show that Paul expected Christians to eat Gentile food, and in Rom. 14:1–4 Paul indicates that what food is eaten is basically a matter of indifference. Different people may follow different convictions. In Rom. 14:5f. a similar comment is made about "days."

These discussions are not precisely the same. Romans, in chapter 14 as elsewhere, is calmer and better balanced toward both Jew and Gentile than is Galatians. In Galatians accepting circumcision and the Sabbath is seen as returning to bondage on the part of the Gentile converts, while observing the dietary code is hypocrisy on the part of Jewish Christians. In Romans 14 and 1 Cor. 7:17f. Paul recognizes that Jews will probably carry on observing the traditional Jewish commandments; 1 Cor. 7:17 *expects* them to do so; Romans 14 *allows* the commandments to be kept. 1 Cor. 7:17–20 expects Jews to remain circumcised; 1 Corinthians 8 recognizes divergent points of view about food; Romans 14 recognizes divergent practices about food and days.

Behind these divergences, we can see that the three items which have been excluded for the Galatian Gentile converts before Paul tells them how to keep "the whole law" received special attention and were never enforced by him on his Gentile converts.

Although Paul offered no theoretical basis for this de facto reduction of the law, can we perceive a principle on the basis of which he excluded (or considered optional) certain laws, while requiring others? Some would propose that Paul kept the law's "ethical" aspects but rejected its "cultic" parts.[22] There is obviously something to that sort of distinction, although it is anachronistic. Further, it is not precise: is the prohibition of idolatry (which Paul kept, though without citing a commandment) ethical or cultic? Paul also does not define Christian behavior as keeping the "spirit" of the law as distinct from observing it literally. He is aware of the inner/outer distinction, as Phil. 3:3 and Rom. 2:29 show.[23] Yet this distinction does not govern his treatment of concrete laws. He does not oppose circumcision in Galatians as mere externalism, nor is his criticism of Peter based on this ground

(Gal. 2:11–14). Phil. 3:3 and Rom. 2:29 are very instructive in this regard: they show that Paul had access to a thoroughly Jewish way of avoiding the literal observance of commandments without renouncing them as such.[24] Yet he did not make use of it in the principal discussions of the law. Circumcision is flatly rejected for his Gentile converts; "days" and food laws are explicitly held to be optional. They are not to be "truly" kept in the spirit, while being disregarded in practice.

We should also note that in no case does Paul give any hint that he has in mind a second dispensation which can be called "the law."[25] The passages which favor fulfilling the law, we have seen, all have in mind the Mosaic law, at least in theory, and when Paul deletes circumcision he does so either without explanation (1 Cor. 7:19) or on the basis of Genesis (Galatians 3, Romans 4), not on the basis of the arrival of the messianic age. Even 2 Corinthians 3 (to be discussed more fully in chapter 4), where the term "new covenant" appears, does not indicate that a second law has been given with Christ. Rather, the veil which covers the law of Moses has been removed (2 Cor. 3:15f.). The law, for Paul, is not only the will of God, it is the will of God as revealed in Jewish Scripture, even though it turns out in concrete application to be distinguished in the ways that we have noted.

Within Jewish literature which is more or less contemporary with Paul there is a distinction between commandments which govern relations between God and humans and commandments which govern relations between human and human (*mitsvot bēn adam le-Maqom; mitsvot bēn adam le-adam*).[26] Can we say that this distinction forms the basis on which Paul chose which commandments need be obeyed? Not precisely, since monotheism again will not fit into the second category.

There is, however, something which is common to circumcision, Sabbath, and food laws, and which sets them off from other laws: they created a social distinction between Jews and other races in the Greco-Roman world. Further, they were the aspects of Judaism which drew criticism and ridicule from pagan authors.[27] Jewish monotheism also set Jews apart from Gentiles, but it seems not to have drawn the ridicule of pagans in the way that Sabbath, food laws, and circumcision did.[28] In any case, belief in one God is a point which Paul could not conceivably have questioned.

I do not wish to propose that Paul consciously deleted from the law which Christians are to keep the elements which were most offensive to pagan society on purely practical grounds, so that pagans would find it relatively easy to convert. We should recall, rather, two of his principal convictions: all are to be saved on the same basis; he was called to be the apostle to the Gentiles. Putting these convictions into practice understandably resulted

102

in deleting circumcision, Sabbath, and food laws from "the whole law" or "the commandments of God." Yet we must also bear in mind that Paul himself offered no theoretical basis for the de facto reduction of the law. We can say that he meant in fact a *reduced* law when he said that the law is fulfilled in the requirement to love the neighbor only because we can observe the ways in which he reduced it, not because he himself admits that he reduced it. He still calls it "the whole law."

We cannot determine to what degree he was conscious of his own reduction of the law.[29] He certainly knew that circumcision, Sabbath observance, and dietary restrictions were commanded in the Scripture; and it was certainly with full intent that he said that they are not binding on those in Christ. These points cannot be disputed. Yet he offered no rationale for his de facto limitations, but insisted that those in the Spirit keep what the law requires (Rom. 8:4). The degree to which he could change the content of the law, while still saying that it should be kept, is strikingly clear in 1 Cor. 7:19, which I regard as one of the most amazing sentences that he ever wrote: "Neither circumcision nor uncircumcision counts for anything, but keeping the commandments of God."[30]

Paul may have been hampered from facing in a theoretical way his reduction of "the law" by the general view in Judaism that the law is one and that all parts were equally ordained by God.[31] Deliberate rejection of any commandment was, in the later rabbinic formulation, tantamount to rejecting the God who gave it.[32] Paul, therefore, in explicitly holding some parts of the law not to be binding, or to be optional, went well beyond the bounds of contemporary Judaism. Yet even so he could not bring himself to say that he thereby rejected the law or Scripture, and certainly not the God who gave it. On the contrary, he maintained that he upheld the law (Rom. 3:31) and that Christians should and did fulfill it (Gal. 5:14; Rom. 8:1–4). He seems to have "held together" his native view that the law is one and given by God and his new conviction that Gentiles and Jews stand on equal footing, which requires the deletion of some of the law, by asserting them both without theoretical explanation.

To this whole line of discussion it may be objected that Paul did not conceive Christian behavior in terms of law: his ethics are grounded on the Spirit and on love of the neighbor.[33] The positive aspect of this objection should not only be admitted, it should be emphasized. I would further emphasize that some aspects of behavior which Paul recommends, or considers mandatory, are derived from his conception of the meaning of union with Christ (e.g., 1 Cor. 6:15). Further, as we noted above, his lists of right and wrong actions are not entirely Jewish. Granting all this, we should nevertheless note that what the Spirit leads Christians to do is "what the law requires" (Rom. 8:4). Further, "what the law requires" turns out not to be what is logically or necessarily entailed by "living in the Spirit" and loving the neighbor. These principles in and of themselves, as we observed above, do not rule out homosexuality or even incest — as 1 Corinthians 5 makes clear. This is not to say that Paul made no effort to connect the behavior which he required with the love commandment. In 1 Corinthians 8, for example, he tries to bring even the prohibition of idolatry under the rubric "love thy neighbor."[34] This was not entirely satisfactory, as his further argument in 1 Corinthians 10 shows. His handling of sexual practices and idolatry (including here "food offered to idols") indicates both his deeply held Jewish convictions and his struggle to reformulate Jewish prohibitions in terms of Christian principles.

Our present concern, however, is not to offer a full account of what Paul meant by "life in the Spirit," but to understand his treatment (or rather treatments) of the law. Before pressing on to another difficult aspect of Pauline exegesis, we should summarize the results of our study thus far of Paul's positive statements about the law: (1) Paul held the normal expectation that membership in the "in-group" involved correct behavior. One of the ways in which he stated that expectation was that Christians should fulfill the "the law" or keep "the commandments." (2) In the passages in which he requires fulfillment of the law, he offers no theoretical distinction between the law which governs Christians and the law of Moses; put another way, he does not distinguish between the law to which those in Christ die and the law which they fulfill. (3) In concrete application, however, the behavior required of Christians differs from the law of Moses in two ways: (a) Not all of Paul's admonitions have a counterpart in Scripture; (b) Paul deliberately and explicitly excluded from "the law," or held to be optional, three of its requirements: circumcision, days and seasons, and dietary restrictions.

It is obviously difficult to hold together the second and third points. Several recent interpreters, as we have noted, have argued that the law which Christians are to fulfill (e.g., Rom. 8:4) and the law which sin uses to bring death (Rom. 7:10f.) are the same. They hold the two points together by arguing that, while the law is the same, the status of the individual is changed.[35] The strength of this view is that Paul makes no theoretical distinction between "the law" which Christians fulfill and the Mosaic law. Further, the view that it is not the law which changes, but the person, corresponds to the way in which Paul states the matter in Romans 7 — 8: The difference is whether one is in the flesh or in the Spirit. The view breaks

104

down, however, when one asks about concrete application. Even in Romans the law varies in content. It is in Romans 14 that Paul states, in effect, that two groups of laws — those governing days and those governing food — are optional. We cannot get around the fact that Paul, while offering no theoretical basis for distinguishing among the commandments, did make de facto distinctions.

The Law and the Consequences of
Transgression and Obedience

We earlier noted that some would object to our treatment by arguing that Paul did not conceive of Christian behavior as being in accord with law, but as springing from life in the Spirit. Our reply was that, while the second part of that formulation is correct, living in the Spirit and living according to the law are not to be considered as opposites in Paul's view. Living in the Spirit results in obeying the law. We should now take up a second aspect of this potential objection: Paul's injunctions are not to be considered binding *as law*; the law does not function as law in the standard Jewish way.[36] I believe that the best way to pursue the relationship between Paul's admonitions and traditional Jewish thinking about the law is to ask whether or not he maintained the standard connection between deeds on the one hand and reward and punishment on the other. Did he hold, in the way well known in Judaism, that obedience was rewarded, that disobedience was punished, that transgressions within the "in-group" could be atoned for, and that heinous and uncorrected transgression could lead to exclusion? As far as I can tell from the somewhat slight evidence, he did.

Before presenting the evidence for the view that in some ways the law still functioned as law, we should dispose of a standard difficulty and then register a limitation and a reservation. The standard difficulty is how to reconcile Paul's statements about reward and punishment with justification by faith and salvation by grace. The problem is basically a theological one: how to separate Paul from the supposed Jewish doctrine of justification by works. There is now general recognition that Paul's statements about reward and punishment are not just a Jewish "remnant" which can be eliminated from Paul's "own" view,[37] but there does not seem to be a clear view of how to relate them to the rest of Paul's thought.[38] I must confess that I do not see a problem. Paul's statement "not by works of law" has to do with entry into the body of Christ. It is not at all inconsistent that he expects correct behavior on the part of those who are in Christ, nor that he thinks that transgressions on the part of Christians will be punished. This is in accord with the general Jewish view that election and salvation are by God's grace, while reward and punishment correspond to deeds. There is no conflict between God's mercy and his justice, and in fact on this point Paul is a perfect example of the view which is characteristic of first-century Judaism: God judges according to their deeds those whom he saves by his mercy. This distinction contains a degree of oversimplification, since a common Jewish view would be that God tempers even his judgment with mercy by delaying punishment to allow time for repentance, or shows mercy to sinners in forgiving them when they repent. Nevertheless, the basic distinction holds: getting in is purely a result of God's grace; he must judge the deeds of those whom he has chosen, since to do otherwise would be capricious. Paul seems to share this view entirely.

Thus there is, or should be, no theological difficulty in holding together grace and the requirement to obey the law. There are, however, real difficulties in maintaining that Paul regarded the law as functioning as law. A limit to this whole line of inquiry is implicit in Paul's view of the setting of his work. The situation, as he saw it, was this: God had sent his son to save humanity; the time was short; it was Paul's responsibility to spread the message of salvation to those who had no other way of hearing it.[39] Those who responded to the message, though they had been sinners (1 Cor. 6:9–11) and under sin (Rom 3:9), were, through the death of Christ, cleansed of former transgressions and liberated from bondage to sin. Henceforth they were to remain pure and blameless while awaiting the Lord's coming.[40] In this context, in which the coming of the Lord was near and Christians were to remain blameless, it is understandable that the formulation or explication of law as law would have a limited role. Paul developed neither a precise halakah to govern behavior nor a system for the atonement of post-conversion transgressions.[41] As the introductory discussion made clear, Paul most characteristically thought that one who transferred from sin and the flesh to freedom and the Spirit should live accordingly,[42] and much of his paraenesis simply urges his readers to do so. Thus many of his admonitions are so general that they could not function as concrete commandments. An example is 1 Thess. 4:3. Paul, we learn, is opposed to *porneia*, sexual immorality. This means, he says, not taking a wife "in the passion of lust" (4:5), but one cannot from this passage determine the precise definition of what would count as *porneia*. There is a lack of halakic precision.[43] The statements that "God is an avenger" and that disregarding Paul's admonition is an offense against God (4:6–8) show that Paul at one level thought of his instruction on this point as "law." Transgression of the law is actually transgression against the God who gave it,[44] and there is requital. Nevertheless, Paul's instruction still could not actually function as law, since he

does not, at least here, define *porneia* in a way that would allow Christians to know whether or not they had committed it, and he provides no
means of atonement in the case of transgression.[45] That his instructions in
these regards were vague is confirmed by 1 Corinthians, where we see that
he and his converts could draw different conclusions about what counted
as *porneia* (1 Cor. 5:1).

Thus, to reiterate, there is virtually no systematic halakah in his letters,[46]
and we also earlier noted that it is probable that his missionary preaching
did not include much detailed instruction regarding behavior.[47] These observations set a definite limit to the importance of the question of whether
or not the law still functioned as law.

The principal reservation which must stand over this entire discussion
is that Paul as a rule does not cite commandments — either those in the law,
those "from the Lord," or those of his own making — and *then* say that they
should be obeyed. There are only a few instances in which the motive or
rationale behind an instruction is said to be that God commanded it. He
prohibits divorce on the basis of the Lord's word (1 Cor. 7:10). He regards
Deut. 25:24 as the Lord's command that "those who proclaim the gospel
should get their living by the gospel" (1 Cor. 9:8f., 14). More typically,
however, Paul, in dealing with concrete problems, offers an assortment of
arguments (some, to be sure, based on Scripture) without citing a commandment qua commandment to settle the issue. I regard the discussions of pros-
titution and idolatry (eating at an idol's table; 1 Cor. 6:15–18; 10:1–22)
as best typifying the way in which Paul argued on the basis of union with
Christ. 1 Corinthians 10 also shows how he could use Scripture to determine behavior without citing commandments. One may suspect, as I have
proposed more than once, that the real source of many of Paul's views was
Jewish Scripture and tradition; nevertheless, he seldom brings forward a
commandment as deciding a concrete issue.

These and similar considerations understandably have led some scholars
to the view that Paul did not retain traditional Jewish thinking about the
law.[48] In the following discussion I wish to share the effort of some to redress
the balance. It is and will remain difficult to do precise justice to the degree
to which the law still functioned as law for Paul. I wish not to ignore it;
I hope not to exaggerate it.

It was Paul's difficulty with the church at Corinth which pushed him
beyond his tendency to give general admonitions and threats. Here we see
that, when he had to deal in detail with transgression within the Christian
community, reward and punishment, and the possibility of postconversion
atonement, he did so in a thoroughly Jewish way. For our present purposes

it will be sufficient to list the appropriate passages by categories and offer brief comments. The footnotes will indicate where more detailed discussions are to be found.[49]

1. We note, in the first place, Paul's view that transgressions bring suffering and death.[50] In 1 Cor. 11:27–34 he connects illness and death with "eating the bread and drinking the cup of the Lord in an unworthy manner." In 1 Cor. 5:1–5 he indicates his expectation that the man guilty of incest[51] will die as a result of his transgression.[52] The converse of this is that good deeds are rewarded in this life, and it appears in the discussion of sowing and reaping in 2 Cor. 9:6-15 that Paul could hold out the hope of this-worldly reward for charity.[53]

2. Atonement is possible for those in Christ who transgress. In the first two passages mentioned in the preceding paragraph punishment and death result in atonement.[54] One passage (2 Cor. 12:21) implies that repentance is efficacious for restoring a sinning member of the church: in threatening those who do not repent of sexual transgressions with punishment (possibly exclusion or condemnation; the force of "mourn over" cannot be specified),[55] Paul implies that repentance brings restoration.

3. Punishment may be meted out by the community. The man guilty of incest is to be excluded (this is apparently the meaning of 1 Cor. 5:5),[56] and in fact all those guilty of *porneia* and other sins are to be "driven out" (1 Cor. 5:9–13).[57]

4. There is one extended passage in which Paul refers to reward and punishment at the judgment. In 1 Cor. 3:5 — 4:6 Paul compares his work as an apostle with that of Apollos. Each will receive a reward (*misthos*) according to his labor (3:8). With regard to Apollos, who is building on Paul's foundation, Paul cautions — or warns (3:10) — that there are varying degrees of success and failure (3:12),[58] and each one's work will be revealed on the day and tested with fire (3:13). If Apollos's work as builder on the foundation laid by Paul survives, he will be rewarded, but if it is burned up, "he will suffer loss, though he himself will be saved" (3:14f.).[59] There are two underlying views evident in the last two verses: faults unpunished in this world will be punished at the judgment. Further, punishment at the judgment brings atonement, just as do punishment and death in this world.[60]

Paul even entertains the possibility that he himself may have done something which will bring punishment from the Lord on the Day (1 Cor. 4:4f.). He apparently does not consider that his own sufferings (e.g. 2 Cor. 11:23–27) are punishment for unperceived faults; he probably takes them as indicating that he shares the sufferings of Christ (e.g. Rom. 8:17). His self-examination in the light of suffering had thus far revealed no faults for which he deserved punishment, but he was open to the possibility that such faults would emerge at the judgment.

We should also note, for the sake of completeness, that Paul refers to the judgment of Christians in 2 Cor. 5:10[61] and Rom. 14:10. The former passage, like 1 Cor. 3:8, 12, seems to point toward the view that Paul thought of varying but unspecified rewards and punishments at the judgment.[62] Both passages indicate that Paul applies to Christians in general what he says with regard to himself and Apollos in 1 Cor. 3:5 — 4:6.

5. There are some passages in which Paul threatens that Christians can lose their status. The matter is by no means easy to determine.[63] For convenience we divide the passages into various categories.

a) The vice lists may be read as indicating that Christians are condemned if they sin.[64] In Gal. 5:19–21 and 1 Cor. 6:9–10 Paul gives a list of sins which prevent those who commit them from inheriting the kingdom of heaven. The lists, in which idolatry and sexual immorality figure prominently, describe the behavior of non-Christians — those who live according to the flesh (Gal. 5:16–21) or the unrighteous (1 Cor. 6:9). Yet in Galatians Paul warns his readers not to commit such sins, while 1 Cor. 6:9–11 follows the discussion of sexual immorality in chapter 5. Is the implication that Christians will be condemned if they commit the sins which (in Paul's view) typify non-Christian behavior? Probably not. We should recall that, in the one concrete case of sexual immorality with which he deals (1 Cor. 5:1–5), Paul indicates that the person eventually will be saved. The vice lists, with the phrase "not inherit the kingdom of God," are probably traditional, and Paul simply repeats the standard line. George Foot Moore commented about the rabbis that they were "very liberal with homiletical damnation."[65] The same seems to be true of Paul and others who repeated this sort of material.

The power of the traditional vice list is evident in 1 Cor. 5:9–13, where Paul begins by discussing sexual immorality. Having so begun, he continues by including the greedy, the robbers, and the idolaters, and then includes those and others in a list of *Christians* (those who bear the name brother) with whom the Corinthians are not to associate. Could an idolater be a Christian? We return to the problem below. Just now we note that one vice tended to draw in a string of others. It is somewhat dubious that Paul would actually consign to damnation everyone who fits into one of the groups named.

b) Equally uncertain are some of the instances in which Paul fears that he might have labored in vain or that Christians may have believed in vain. Paul fears that his labor will have been in vain if suffering makes the

Thessalonians weaken in faith (1 Thess. 3:5), and he urges the Corinthians not to accept the grace of God in vain (2 Cor. 6:1). Such passages sound ominous, but they are too uncertain to yield sure results. The same comment applies to the "mourn over" statement of 2 Cor. 12:21 and the warning "unless you fail to meet the test" in 2 Cor. 13:5. Perhaps we should classify here Paul's expression of concern for himself in 1 Cor. 9:27, "lest after preaching to others I myself should be disqualified."

c) There are three passages which are more forceful and which indicate that Paul could envisage permanent exclusion from Christianity and, presumably, salvation; but none of these has to do with a wicked deed. Gal. 5:1–4 indicates that those who accept circumcision are cut off from Christ and revert to slavery, the pre-Christian state (cf. also 4:11: "in vain"). The wording of 1 Cor. 15:2 — "unless you believed in vain" — seems to indicate that those who reject Paul's gospel will not be saved. In Rom. 11:22 Paul indicates that Gentile Christians can be "cut off" if they do not continue in God's kindness. The threat here is clearer than the offense.

The false apostles of 2 Cor. 11:13–15 will, according to Paul, meet a bad end, and in Gal. 1:7–9 Paul calls down a curse on those who preach a gospel contrary to his. Whether Paul in a calm frame of mind would have held that other Christian preachers would be condemned is hard to determine.

These passages move us beyond anything which can reasonably be called "the law," but they seem to indicate that reversion to the non-Christian state was, in Paul's view, possible.[66]

6. We are still in quest of an instance in which a sinful *deed* is unmistakably said by Paul to lead to permanent exclusion or condemnation. 1 Cor. 8:11 (apparently echoed in Rom. 14:15; note "on behalf of whom Christ died," "on account of whom Christ died") is intriguing. The point is that there is no harm done if the one who eats food offered to an idol knows that idols have no real existence. If, however, a weak brother sees such behavior and eats food offered to an idol "as really offered to an idol" (8:7), that is, believing in the existence of the pagan deity, the consequence is that he is destroyed. Here idolatry is really committed only if the one who eats also believes that he is worshiping.[67]

In light of the distinction in 1 Corinthians 8, we probably should not read 1 Corinthians 10 as implying that the act of eating at an idol's table leads to damnation. The force of the typological argument is that those who commit idolatry will be killed. Paul continues his typological midrash by including those who commit sexual immorality (10:8), those who put the Lord to the test (10:9), and those who grumble (10:10). Vv. 10:20f. seems to push this discussion beyond 8:11: anyone who eats food offered to an idol participates in a demon, even if not actually in another god, and is excluded from the Lord's table. But 10:27–29 again indicates that idolatry is still partly in the eye of the participant.

It thus appears that, while Christians can revert to the non-Christian state and share the fate of unbelievers, there is no deed which necessarily leads to the condemnation of a believer, although Paul appears to waver with regard to food offered to idols.

Before considering the implication of this discussion of deeds for understanding Paul's view of the law, we should first note how thoroughly at home all of Paul's positions are in Judaism. The passages which we have considered are in and of themselves not detailed or precise enough to allow us to make firm statements about Paul's views of transgression, obedience, reward, punishment, atonement, exclusion, and condemnation. Yet they make such good sense when seen against more or less contemporary Jewish views that some conclusions may be drawn. As did his contemporaries in Judaism, Paul thought that salvation basically depends on membership in the in-group, but that within that context deeds still count. Transgressions must be repented of or they will deserve God's punishment.[68] Punishment itself, however, provides atonement. Both punishment and reward take place within the in-group, whether here or hereafter. Loss and commendation (1 Cor. 3:15; 4:5) are both earned in the sense of "deserved," but salvation itself is not earned by enumerating deeds or balancing them against one another.[69] While there is a firm belief in rewards and punishments which are appropriate to deeds, there is understandable reluctance to say precisely what the reward or punishment will be, especially when recompense is reserved for the final judgment.[70]

The difficulty in determining precisely what, if anything, will permanently exclude and condemn a member of the group does not make Paul's letters atypical. In 1QS certain heinous transgressions lead to expulsion with no hope of return.[71] In rabbinic literature, however, there is no transgression which *in and of* itself condemns. There are statements in rabbinic literature to the effect that those who do a variety of misdeeds will be condemned[72] — as there are in Paul's letters. In this sense we can say that, in both rabbinic literature and Paul's letters, remaining in the in-group is conditional on behavior.[73] In neither case, however, does an act of disobedience bring automatic expulsion. Thus when the rabbis discuss atonement it turns out that every sin can be atoned for.[74] Only willful and unrepentant transgression brings condemnation, since that indicates rejection of God.[75] In the end, it comes down to intention: those who intend to deny the God who gave the commandments have no share in his promises. It is not significantly otherwise with Paul: one who eats at an idol's table and understands himself thereby to be worshiping a real deity is destroyed. The formulations are different, the rabbinic emphasizing the intention of the transgressor and the efficacy of repentance and other means of atonement, and Paul the understanding of the action; but the result is substantially the same. Those who sin and do not repent, in the rabbinic view, show that they intend to deny God. In Paul's view, those who deny their faith lose the salvation which faith brings.

But what has all this to do with the law? The word *nomos* does not appear in any of the passages presently under discussion, and Paul nowhere has a sentence to the effect that those who transgress "the law of Christ" will be punished (or possibly finally condemned) unless there is atonement. Are we correct, then, in introducing the passages which deal with punishment, reward, judgment, exclusion, and atonement into the discussion of the law? I believe that we are.

In the first place, there are some fairly explicit links between passages which mention the law and those which describe correct behavior and its reward or incorrect behavior and its consequences. Thus in Gal. 5:22 "the fruit of the Spirit," which is headed by "love," is to be related positively to "the whole law," which is to love the neighbor (5:14). Those who produce the works of the flesh do not inherit the kingdom of God; thus there is condemnation for not being led by the Spirit and consequently not fulfilling the law of love. There is another link between passages which use the word "law" in a positive sense and those which imply reward and punishment on the basis of deeds in Romans 13 – 14. The general context is the so-called paraenetic section of Romans, and it is here that Paul offers as a summary of "the law" explicit commandments as well as the principle to love the neighbor (13:8–10). It is, then, not surprising that after more instructions, including the word not to judge the brother (14:4), Paul appeals to the idea of God's judgment, which will fall equally on all Christians (14:10). The judgment seems to be positively related to the law which is summarized earlier: Christians are judged according to how well they fulfill the law. Within this passage we are reminded of a point made earlier: the content of the law changes. In Rom. 13:8–10 there is no clue that the law is anything other than the scriptural law; but before saying that Christians will be judged (14:10), Paul indicates that the observance of days and restrictions on food are not essential (14:1–6).

General considerations, however, are more important for seeing the connection between the law and judgment than the slight links between appearances of the word *nomos* and references to judgment and reward or punishment. Paul considers that Christians should behave correctly, and one of the words which he uses to indicate that behavior is "law": they should fulfill the law. He further thinks that they are to be judged according to deeds. The deeds include some things explicitly condemned by scriptural law, such as incest, and other, more general offences which are not dealt with in Scripture and which Paul does not formulate in a halakic way, such as the *porneia* which is mentioned in 1 Thess. 4:1–8 or building on Paul's foundation with faulty material (1 Cor. 3:12–15). These misdeeds bring retribution from God. They are not summed up and said to be condemned by "the law," but the requirements of correct behavior still function *as law*.[76] There is punishment for transgression and reward for obedience.

To put the matter another way, there is no distinction between the manner in which Christians are to fulfill Paul's requirements — whether Paul calls those requirements "the law" or not — and the manner in which Jews traditionally observe the Mosaic law.

It is common to distinguish between the supposed Jewish legalistic view that one is righteoused and judged on the basis of the sum of individual deeds and Paul's view that behavior is conceived as a whole. Thus one finds that the singular form *ergon*, "work," in 1 Cor. 3:13–15 is underlined and emphasized with an exclamation point.[77] This is a false distinction, and it skews exegesis. In the first place, the terms "righteous" and "wicked" in Judaism refer to basic status and orientation, not to the result of enumerating individual deeds.[78] Thus the supposed contrast does not exist. In the second place, Paul's use of the singular and the plural does not lead to the desired conclusion. Paul is perfectly capable of calling the behavior required of Christians "keeping the commandments (*entolai*) of God" (1 Cor. 7:19). "Every good work" in 2 Cor. 9:8 implies a plural conception, and the phrase "any other commandment" in Rom. 13:9 implies that the one law of love includes a multiplicity of commandments. Even where Paul does not use the term "commandment," "work," or "law," he requires individual acts of correct behavior.[79]

Summary

In both Romans and Galatians, after sharp statements which deny that one can be righteoused by works of law, and after connecting the law with sin, Paul nevertheless summarizes correct behavior by saying that those in Christ either do or should fulfill the law. The law which Christians fulfill is not a second law, and in his summary statements Paul does not distinguish it from the Jewish Scripture. When he discusses concrete points, however, we see that he regarded as either wrong or optional three laws or groups of laws: the requirement of circumcision, special days, and special food. The most obvious common denominator to these laws is the fact that they distinguish Jews from Gentiles. The contents of what Paul required differ from the Mosaic law in a second way: many of the aspects of behavior which he regarded as obligatory are not specifically governed by Scripture.

Paul's letters are not halakic, even when they deal with specific points of behavior. He tends not to cite a law and then derive from it rules of behavior. Despite this, however, there is an important sense in which his views of behavior function as law: there is punishment for disobedience and reward for obedience.

We have earlier seen that, when Paul opposed "faith" to "law," the question was what is required to be a member of the group that would be saved. We now see that, when the topic was how people in that group should behave, he saw no opposition between faith and law. Our emphasis on faith *versus* law as an entry requirement should not be taken to mean that, in Paul's view, faith stopped functioning after entry. The life he lives, he lives by faith (Gal. 2:20), and faith should be expressed in love (Gal. 5:6). He urges the Corinthians to stand firm in faith (1 Cor. 16:13). Our point is that, in discussing the behavior appropriate to being Christian, Paul saw no incongruity between "living by faith" and "fulfilling the law." Doing the commandments (1 Cor. 7:19) is integral to living by faith. I am not arguing for the case that, when discussing behavior, Paul became a "legalist," thinking that continuation in the body of Christ must be earned. Rather, when discussing behavior, he emphasized that faith resulted in fulfilling the law; and to some degree the law still functioned as law. The flat opposition between faith and law comes only when he is discussing the requirement essential for membership in the people of God. The important point to observe is that what Paul said about the law depends on the problem which he was addressing.

His answers to questions of behavior have a logic of their own. There is no systematic explanation of how those who have died to the law obey it. Yet he regarded Scripture as expressing the will of God. We should recall that even the statements that righteousness is not by law are supported in part by Scripture. Thus it was natural that, when questions of behavior arose, he would answer by saying, among other things, that Christians should fulfill the law. It is equally understandable that "the law" had to correspond to his view of God's plan: he had sent his son to save all who believe, without distinction. Thus concretely the law was modified by the revelation of the universal lordship of Christ and consequently by the requirements of the Gentile mission.

NOTES

1. The question of the place of ethics, once righteousness is said not to be by law, is one of the standard questions of Pauline exegesis. It is sharply posed, for example, by Ulrich Wilckens, "Was heisst bei Paulus: 'Aus Werken des Gesetzes wird kein Mensch gerecht?'" in *Rechtfertigung als Freiheit: Paulusstudien* (Neukirchen-Vluyn: Neukirchener Verlag, 1974), pp. 110–70.

2. See the list above, p. 9. Note also Paul's description of his own behavior in 1 Thess. 2:10: holy, righteous, and blameless; 2 Cor. 1:12: holiness and sincerity. He regards his own behavior as exemplary (or paradigmatic) for Christians: Phil. 4:9; 1 Cor. 4:16; 11:1.

The list of words which indicate correct behavior could be expanded by including things which should be avoided: "cleansed from every defilement" (2 Cor. 7:1); separate from *porneia* (1 Thess. 4:3; cf. 2 Cor. 12:21); and the like.

3. Heikki Räisänen, "Paul's Theological Difficulties with the Law," in *Studia Biblica 1978*, vol. 3 (Sheffield: JSOT Press, 1980), p. 312. Cf. E. P. Sanders, *Paul and Palestinian Judaism* (Philadelphia: Fortress Press, 1977), p. 513 (hereafter cited as *PPJ*) and the references to Bultmann and Bammel.

4. Despite the suggestion that Paul is influenced by the Stoic idea of "one law" and plays it off against the Jewish idea of "many commandments" (see the discussion in Hans Hübner, "Das ganze und das eine Gesetz," *KuD* 21 [1975]:248–56), I (with many others) regard Paul's summary as Jewish. See H. D. Betz, *Galatians*, (Philadelphia: Fortress Press, 1979), p. 274 and n. 26; *PPJ*, pp. 112–14. We shall return to other questions concerning Gal. 5:14 and Rom. 13:8–10 below.

5. So Gal. 5:19–22; 1 Cor. 5:10f.; 6:9; cf. Rom. 1:18–32. 2 Cor. 12:21 (only sexual sins) is not a full vice list, but refers to sins committed by some (or one) of the Corinthian Christians. It is generally recognized that these lists are derived from Diaspora Judaism. See, e.g., Ernst Käsemann, *Commentary on Romans* (Grand Rapids: Wm. B. Eerdmans, 1980), pp. 49f.

6. Hans Hübner, *Das Gesetz bei Paulus* (Göttingen: Vandenhoeck & Ruprecht, 1980), pp. 38–42. For the last point he refers to his interpretation of Gal. 3:10: the law curses because one cannot do *all* of it.

7. Ibid., p. 116.

8. Shabbath 31a; Tob. 4:15 ("what you hate, do not do to anyone"). For other instances of summarizing the law by citing one or a few commandments, and for secondary literature, see *PPJ*, pp. 112–14 and notes.

9. Ibid., p. 116. Hübner also regards Paul as requiring of Christians a reduced law (*Gesetz*, p. 78), a point to which we shall soon turn.

10. See above, n. 8.

11. The proposal that "the law of Christ" in Gal. 6:2 means the Jesus tradition (W. D. Davies, *Paul and Rabbinic Judaism*, 4th ed. [Philadelphia: Fortress Press, 1980], p. 144; James D. G. Dunn, *Unity and Diversity in the New Testament* [Philadelphia: Westminster Press, 1977], pp. 68f.) cannot be based on Galatians, but depends on noting parallels between Paul's exhortations in other letters and sayings attributed to Jesus. See the lists in Davies, pp. 138–40.

12. In favor of understanding 5:14 as meaning a law other than the Mosaic law, see also Jost Eckert, *Die urchristliche Verkündigung im Streit zwischen Paulus und*

Seinen Gegnern nach dem Galaterbrief (Regensburg: F. Pustet, 1971), pp. 160f., 233. Eckert argues that up to 6:2 the law and Christ were irreconcilable entities. 6:2 is a "paradoxical formulation," but it is equally clear that Paul has in mind an entirely different law from the law of Moses. The content of the law itself has undergone change (p. 161). But the content of 5:14 and 6:2 seems the same, and we may also note that the first fruit of the Spirit (5:22) is love.

Peter Stuhlmacher has offered another distinction. He proposes that the law of Christ is the "Zion-Torah," the prophetically predicted eschatological correspondent to the "Moses-Torah." It is not simply identical with the law of Moses, but rather "brings its spiritual intention to fulfillment" ("Das Gesetz als Thema biblischer Theologie," *ZTK* 75 [1978]:273–75, against Ulrich Wilckens, *Rechtfertigung als Freiheit: Paulusstudien* [Neukirchen-Vluyn: Neukirchener Verlag, 1974], p. 109, who maintains that the law is the same throughout, but that the status of the individual changes). I can only repeat that neither sort of distinction is apparent in Galatians.

13. Abraham J. Malherbe, "ΜΗ ΓΕΝΟΙΤΟ in the Diatribe and Paul," *HTR* 73 (1980): 231–40.

14. Eduard Lohse, "ὁ νόμος τοῦ πνεύματος τῆς ζωῆς, Exegetische Anmerkungen zu Röm 8, 2," in *Neues Testament und christliche Existenz* (Tübingen: J. C. B. Mohr [Paul Siebeck], 1973), pp. 279–87; cf. Ferdinand Hahn, "Das Gesetzesverständnis im Römer- und Galaterbrief," *ZNW* 67 (1976–77): 49, 60; Peter von der Osten-Sacken, "Das paulinische Verständnis des Gesetzes im Spannungsfeld von Eschatologie und Geschichte," *EvTh* 37 (1977): 568. Hübner's formulation (*Gesetz*, p. 125) typifies this view: "The one *for whom* the nomos is the law of the Spirit . . . is freed from the perverted law. . . ." In Hübner's view, this interpretation applies only to Romans. Hübner also notes that in Romans Paul makes a de facto reduction of the law (p. 78). See also Paul Meyer, "Romans 10:4 and the End of the Law," in *The Divine Helmsman* (New York: KTAV, 1980), p. 73. This discussion is related to the discussion of Rom. 3:27, "the *nomos* of faith"; see above, Introduction, n. 26. See also the discussion of dying to the law, above, p. 83.

15. Introduction, n. 26.

16. I am here especially indebted to an exchange of correspondence with Prof. Heikki Räisänen about the meaning of *to dikaiōma* in Rom. 8:4. Räisänen's own view (*Paul and the Law* [forthcoming publication]) is that in Rom. 8:4 *nomos* shifts to mean "the law as interpreted by Paul the Christian," but "Paul does not show any awareness of that shift." We turn to de facto distinctions below. Leander Keck ("The Law and 'The Law of Sin and Death'," in *The Divine Helmsman* [New York: KTAV, 1980], p. 51) opposes reading 8:4 as saying that the Spirit gives the power to fulfill the Mosaic law. He argues that *to dikaiōma tou nomou* means "the right intent of the law — life" (p. 53). This builds on Bultmann's reading of "the good" in Rom. 7:18f. (above, chapter 1, n. 136). But just as "the good" in Romans 7 means the good which the law commands to be *done*, so the "requirement of the law" in Rom. 8:4 is "what the law requires to be done."

17. So Meyer, "Romans 10:4 and the End of the Law," p. 73.

18. *PPJ*, pp. 112–14.

19. Markus Barth ("Die Stellung des Paulus zu Gesetz und Ordnung," *EvTh* 33 [1976]: 516) argues that *ennomos Christou* is not another law than the Torah, but the only holy and good law of God. One can agree in part: Paul had no other law

in mind. Yet he does not precisely observe the Mosaic law; in that respect he is "lawless."

20. We consider below the question of whether or not 1 Cor. 9:17–21 describes Paul's own missionary practice. See chapter 6, pp. 179–90.

21. We do not know whether or not Jews in the Diaspora at this time accepted the extension of the priestly laws of purity to the laity. I presume that they did not, and that the problem in Antioch was about food, not handwashing. For the present purpose the question is of little importance. For secondary literature on the date of the extension of the requirement of ritual purity to the laity, see *PPJ*, p. 154 n. 40.

22. See, for example, Eckert, *Verkündigung*, p. 159: Paul holds at least the "ceremonial" law to be invalid. There is a very astute discussion in Wolfgang Schrage, *Die konkreten Einzelgebote in der paulinischen Paränese* (Gütersloh: Gerd Mohn, 1961), esp. pp. 231–33: Paul never explicitly distinguishes between the ritual and the moral law, yet one can observe that he never cites a ritual law which is valid for Christians, while he does so cite moral laws. Further, Paul factually requires observance of the ethical part of the Bible, even when he does not explicitly cite a law.

23. On the relationship between these two passages, see below, p. 127.

24. We do not know in detail how the allegorists whom Philo criticizes formulated their view of the law. I am here assuming that they did not renounce the law, but argued that it was really kept when one took it in an allegorical-ethical sense. (See Philo, *Migr.* 89–93.) In any case, the position which is evident in Rom. 2:25–29 is that "true" circumcision consists in keeping the rest of the law, not in the outward act of circumcision. There is here no renunciation of circumcision, nor any indication that "true" circumcision is optional. We consider the peculiar character of Romans 2 in this and other respects in the appendix to this chapter.

25. Contrast Davies, *Paul and Rabbinic Judaism*, p. 144: the words of Jesus were for Paul a new Torah. Davies's second point, that for Paul Christ was the wisdom of God, and that in Judaism the Torah was identified with wisdom (pp. 147–76) is not in dispute. I would urge, however, that when Paul used the word *nomos* he meant the Jewish Scripture, or the will of God as revealed in it, not a second code.

26. See *PPJ*, pp. 179, 341, 364. On de facto reduction to the "moral law" or, as he notes, more precisely commandments which govern relations among humans, see Hübner, *Gesetz*, p. 78.

27. Other races in the Greco-Roman world practiced circumcision, but nevertheless it was considered one of the peculiar (and objectionable) marks of the Jew. For the point that circumcision, Sabbath, and food laws were the subject of pagan criticism see M. Stern, "The Jews in Greek and Latin Literature," in *The Jewish People in the First Century* I, 2 (Philadelphia: Fortress Press, 1976), pp. 1101–59, here 1150–59; cf. Jerry L. Daniel, "Anti-Semitism in the Hellenistic-Roman Period," *JBL* 98 (1979): 45–65. A brief summary is this: Seneca: against Sabbath observance; Persius: ridiculed Sabbath; Petronius: circumcision is the main mark of Jews; Martial: attacked circumcision and Sabbath; Tacitus: criticized misanthropy and separatism; Juvenal: ridiculed Sabbath, circumcision, and the exclusion of pork.

28. Jewish worship was ridiculed, but this had more to do with its secret character than with monotheism itself. Thus Petronius proposed that Jews worshipped a pig. See Stern, "The Jews in Greek and Latin Literature," p. 1151.

29. On Paul's consciousness of changing the meaning of "law" and reducing it, see esp. Räisänen, *Paul and the Law*.

30. Circumcision is directly commanded in Lev. 12:3; cf. Gen. 17:9-14.

31. *PPJ*, pp. 112; Moore, *Judaism in the First Centuries of the Common Era*, vol. 1, (Cambridge, Mass.: Harvard University Press, 1927), p. 235.

32. I know of no exception to this view in Jewish literature during the period 200 B.C.E.–200 C.E. Everyone took the view that every law must be *accepted* and that none could be *rejected*. See *PPJ*, pp. 92–96; 134f.; 138 n. 61 (against Hübner's view that the Hillelites required only 51% obedience). Atonement was appointed to deal with conscious or unintentional transgression within the framework of accepting God's right to give the law, but there is a difference between "conscious transgression" and "rejection." Interpretive techniques allowed different groups to define what acceptance of the law actually entailed, and in this way actual and literal obedience or even agreement could be avoided. Thus, for example, no known rabbi accepted the law's own statement that there is no atonement for transgressing the commandment "thou shalt not take the name of the Lord in vain," and different exegetical techniques provided for atonement (*PPJ*, pp. 159f.). Literal observance of some of the Sabbath laws, as is well known, was circumvented in various ways (see Erubin in the Mishnah and the Talmuds). But in all such cases the law was accepted and agreed to, and there was no explicit declaration that it was not binding. As I indicated above (n. 24), I think it overwhelmingly likely that even the allegorists are to be understood along this line. They did not observe the literal law, but they observed its "real" intent.

33. Cf. J. Murphy-O'Connor, "Corpus paulinien," *RB* 82 (1975): 142: the Pauline imperatives are never "laws" in the Old Testament sense. This sort of objection is deftly handled by Schrage, *Einzelgebote*. He gives a summary of the way in which Paul grounds behavior by appealing to the Spirit (pp. 71–75), but also notes that there is no contradiction between living by the Spirit and internal freedom on the one hand and external authority and explicit commandments on the other (p. 76). A good example is 1 Cor. 6:18f., where appeal to the Spirit grounds the explicit injunction against sexual immorality.

34. Osten-Sacken ("Das paulinische Verständnis des Gesetzes," p. 569) correctly observes that the love commandment informs Paul's thought even when it is not cited. We should also observe, however, that 1 Corinthians 8 shows that the connection between what Paul held to be correct and the love commandment is sometimes tenuous, and that Paul must struggle to hold them together.

35. N. 14 above.

36. N. 33 above. This sort of criticism is implicit in Murphy-O'Connor's statement that "it is a fact that Paul never recommends obedience to a particular precept or to a generic law. Obedience is the response to a call of God in Christ" ("Corpus paulinien," p. 140). In Rom. 13:8–10 Paul does, of course, recommend obedience to particular precepts. One may still ask if precepts qua precepts are to be obeyed.

37. G. P. Wetter (*Der Vergeltungsgedanke bei Paulus* [Göttingen: Vandenhoeck & Ruprecht, 1912], p. 155) went so far as to deny that Paul truly thought of reward and punishment. Floyd V. Filson (*St. Paul's Conception of Recompense* [Leipzig: J. C. Henrichs, 1931], pp. 1f.) urged that Wetter and others minimized the role of recompense in Paul's thought, and further that it could not be considered an unassimilated remnant (p 117). This is now generally accepted. See, for example, Georges Didier, *Désintéressement du Chrétien. La rétribution dans la morale de saint Paul*, 1955), esp. pp. 13 n. 25, 17, 219; L. Mattern, *Das Verständnis des*

Gerichts bei Paulus (Zürich and Stuttgart: Zwingli Verlag, 1966); Ernst Synofzik, *Die Gerichts- und Vergeltungsaussagen bei Paulus* (Göttingen: Vandenhoeck & Ruprecht, 1972), esp. p. 9 (characterizing reward and punishment as "Jewish" once meant eliminating it from a legitimate place in Paul's own thought, but this should not be the case); Calvin J. Roetzel, *Judgment in the Community* (Leiden: E. J. Brill, 1972); Karl P. Donfried, "Justification and Last Judgment in Paul," *ZNW* 67 (1976): 90–110.

38. The studies listed in the preceding note generally deal with reward and punishment in connection with justification by faith or salvation by grace. Thus Filson stated the problem as how to deal with recompense, given Paul's emphasis on God's grace (*Recompense*, p. 14). A typical way of reconciling grace and works is presented by Herman Ridderbos, *Paul: An Outline of his Theology* (Grand Rapids: Wm. B. Erdmans, 1975), p. 179: works are good "where meritoriousness is not in question." There is a summary of positions in Roetzel, *Judgment*, pp. 1–13. Roetzel himself is of the view that justification by faith and judgment by works do not stand in a "dialectical relationship" in Paul. "Any attempt to reconcile these motifs may be more of a concern of the western theologian for consistency than a concern of Paul's" (p. 178). My own view is different: there is no difficulty in reconciling the two: justification by faith has to do with entry; judgment by works with behavior after entry.

39. Rom. 13:11–14; 15:17–24.

40. E.g., 1 Thess. 5:23; Phil. 2:15f. See the passages listed above, pp. 9, 94.

41. Cf. Paul Wernle, *Der Christ und die Sünde bei Paulus* (Freiburg: J. C. B. Mohr [Paul Siebeck], 1897), p. 69: it appears that Paul never asked himself by what means a Christian who sinned could attain forgiveness; Floyd Filson, *Recompense*, pp. 16f.; 84: Paul emphasized perfect behavior and did not provide for Christian repentance.

42. Above, pp. 6f., 94.

43. I give some examples of the kinds of questions which must be decided in order to convert general laws into halakah in *PPJ*, pp. 76–78.

44. Cf. above, at n. 32.

45. Paul also does not specify what the punishment for transgression is; but, since he leaves the punishment to God, the failure to be specific is characteristic of Jewish thought. The rabbis, for example, give detail with regard to punishment only when the offense is to be handled by a human court.

46. Paul's discussion of marriage (1 Cor. 7:1–16, 25–40), even though he qualifies part of it as only his opinion (7:25, 40), is close to halakah, since various possibilities and contingencies are considered and evaluated, though not in every case ruled on.

47. The emphasis here is on "systematic" and "detailed." Paul had a clear idea of correct behavior; but he apparently did not formulate his views in a halakically precise way. One further example: Rom. 13:13f. indicates that behavior appropriate to Christians would not include a list of things, including "reveling and drunkenness." For this to be halakah, Paul would have to say how much cheerful mirth and enthusiasm constitutes "reveling" and how much imbibing is required for "drunkenness."

48. See, for example, Murphy-O'Connor, n. 33 above. Rudolf Bultmann's formula was that Christians are free from the demand of the law (that is, from the law *as* law), but nevertheless obligated to it. He cited, quite correctly, 1 Cor. 6:12

119

and 10:23 ("all things are lawful"). See *Theology of the New Testament*, vol. 1 (New York: Charles Scribner's Sons, 1951–1955), p. 341. The present point is that, when Paul stated the "nevertheless" (nevertheless still obligated), the law functioned as law.

49. Filson's work on recompense (1931) remains a very valuable and comprehensive survey of the passages in which Paul may be considered to provide for the punishment of Christians in this world (including death), punishment at the judgment (including condemnation), and the rewards to be expected by Christians (see the outline, p. 85). Naturally one may disagree with his interpretation of individual passages, but he is correct in allowing for the presence of all these views in Paul's letters. In the present brief survey I intend only to lead up to the question of the bearing of these themes on Paul's view of the law.

It may be worthwhile to distinguish the difference in overall viewpoint between this work and Filson's. He saw the problem as being how Paul's acceptance of recompense squares with his belief in God's grace and mercy. He argued that, as a Pharisee, Paul put the emphasis on recompense, while allowing some room for mercy (p. 13); as a Christian he put grace at the center, while not surrendering the notion of recompense (pp. 13f., 127). In this discussion Filson frankly indicated his acceptance of Schürer's and Bousset's view of Pharisaism in contrast to Moore's (p. 7). I have already indicated that the supposed conflict between grace and works dissolves, both in Paul and in other forms of Judaism, once one realizes that grace applies primarily to election and salvation, recompense to deeds within the in-group: God judges according to their deeds those whom he saves by his mercy (above, pp. 105f.).

The more recent works by Didier, Mattern, Synofzik, Roetzel, and Donfried (n. 37) take up different aspects of reward, punishment, and judgment. None offers as complete a canvass of the whole field as Filson's.

50. Filson (*Recompense*, p. 85) correctly noted that suffering, in Paul's view, is often not the result of sin, but part of sharing Christ's sufferings.

51. Lev. 18:8 forbids a man to "uncover the nakedness" of "his father's wife," and this passage provides Paul's wording. We thus cannot tell whether the woman was the man's mother or stepmother.

52. The uncharacteristic use of *pneuma* and *sarx* in 1 Cor. 5:5 opens the possibility of other interpretations. Thus Mattern has proposed that the judgment of the community keeps the sinner a Christian and leads to his redemption at the final judgment. *Sarx*, she argues, indicates the whole person, who "dies" to sin, not literally. *Pneuma*, then, also is the whole person, who is saved (Mattern, *Gericht*, pp. 105–8). It is certainly true that Paul does not usually use *sarx* for the human body, but he does so in Phil. 1:22–24, and that seems to yield the best sense here.

Donfried has also proposed a revised translation of 1 Cor. 5:1–5, arguing that *pneuma* means the Spirit (of God) ("Justification and Last Judgment," pp. 107–9), but his suggestion is adequately answered by Synofzik (*Vergeltungsaussagen*, p. 154). Various possibilities for understanding "that the spirit be saved" are also discussed by Göran Forkman, *The Limits of the Religious Community* (Lund: CWK Gleerup, 1972), pp. 144–47.

53. Cf. Mattern, *Gericht*, pp. 151–93, esp. 162–68. Mattern's entire discussion of reward for deeds in Paul is based on a faulty comparison with reward and punishment in rabbinism, where, she holds, the view is that deeds are balanced and

weighed, the reward for a majority of good deeds is salvation, and so forth (pp. 176, 192f.). She must then try to distinguish Paul's view of reward and punishment from that of the rabbis. She argues that in Paul's view judgment is not according to deeds as such: "Das Gericht geht nach Paulus vielmehr über die unterschiedliche Partizipation des Christen am Werk Gottes" (p. 192). Hairsplitting distinctions of this sort do not seem helpful. In 2 Cor. 9:6–15 Paul vaguely, but nevertheless unmistakably, holds out the promise of reward for good *deeds*, specifically charity. Mattern is correct, as we shall see in discussing 1 Cor. 3: 5 – 4:6, that Paul could think of varying degrees of reward.

54. Moule points out that, in 1 Cor. 11:29–32, "it depends upon the person's response . . . whether [the punishment] proves to be remedial, and to be a judgment which will prepare him for salvation at last, or whether it plunges him further into a condition of fatal self-concern" (C. F. D. Moule, "The Judgment Theme in the Sacraments," in *The Background of the New Testament and its Eschatology* [New York: Cambridge University Press, 1954], pp. 464–81, here 481). I do not see a reference to self-concern, but otherwise the point is well made. Paul here is in full accord with the general Jewish view that suffering should be accepted as God's chastisement in order for it to atone.

As elsewhere, Mattern tries too hard to distinguish Paul's view from the rabbinic. She argues that the judgment of the Lord preserves the community as community and thus it escapes the condemnation of the world (*Gericht*, pp. 101–3, 108). But *en humin polloi* ("many among you") in 11:30 cannot mean the community; it refers rather to some individuals in the community.

55. Cf. "not spare" in 2 Cor. 13:2.

56. So, for example, Forkman, *Limits*, p. 172.

57. Wernle regarded the exclusion of 1 Cor. 5:11, 13 as less far-reaching than the total ban of 5:3–5. He connected 5:11, 13 with 2 Cor. 12:21 and concluded that 1 Cor. 5:11 does not refer to a "definitive exclusion," but to a temporary punishment which is retracted when the sinner repents (*Der Christ und die Sünde*, p. 47). Forkman (*Limits*, pp. 149–51) takes 1 Cor. 5:9–13 to refer to partial expulsion.

58. Filson correctly, in my judgment, found the idea of varying but unspecified rewards here (*Recompense*, p. 109; cf. 115, 126).

59. It is difficult to determine the relationship between "receive a reward" in v. 14 and "be saved" in v. 15. Wetter argued that Paul started to say that there are gradations within salvation but could not describe them, and so took refuge in the rabbinic idea of punishment as atoning, though he did not really believe in it. There is no distinction between "receive a reward" and "be saved" (*Vergeltungsgedanke*, pp. 114f.). I think that it is likely that Paul held both views – that there is reward for work at the judgment (though it is unspecified) (v. 14) and that punishment at the judgment atones and thus saves (v. 15). He simply does not lay them out clearly.

60. Donfried ("Justification and Last Judgment," pp. 105f.) argues that the passage does not refer to the sins of individual Christians nor to salvation at the final judgment. I agree with much of what he says about the context, but the last judgment seems clearly in view, and there is no reason to distinguish the treatment of the apostles from that accorded to other Christians. Cf. Synofzik, *Vergeltungsaussagen*, pp. 39–41 and 153 (in reply to Donfried).

61. In 2 Cor. 5:10 the "we" refers to Christians: so Mattern, *Gericht*, p. 155 (all Christians, living and dead); Filson, *Recompense*, p. 88; Donfried, "Justification and Last Judgment," p. 105.

62. Above, n. 58.

63. See Donfried, "Justification and Last Judgment," pp. 106–10, with references to earlier literature. The most complete list of passages is in Filson, *Recompense*, pp. 89–97.

64. Donfried, "Justification and Last Judgment," p. 107.

65. G. F. Moore, *Judaism in the First Centuries of the Christian Era* vol. 2, p. 388 n. 4.

66. So also Mattern (*Gericht*, pp. 118, 213), although she bases her conclusion on other passages. Thus she thinks that Phil. 3:18 refers to former Christians (pp. 112–15).

67. Cf. Mattern, *Gericht*, p. 117: it depends on faith, not the action as such.

68. One may note the prominence of punishment in the DSS, especially in 1QS, and the relative lack of emphasis on repentance, as well as the overwhelming rabbinic stress on repentance. Paul mentions repentance to God only once and punishment or chastisement more often. The view of punishment as atoning is widely attested in rabbinic and other sources (Ps. Sol.), however, and Paul's view is in any case too undeveloped to allow one to say that it is especially connected to any one movement in Judaism.

69. *PPJ*, e.g., p. 126.

70. *PPJ*, pp. 125–28.

71. 1QS 7.1f., 16f.

72. The lists tend to get longer: compare Sanhedrin 10.1–3 with ARNA 36. In the early literature the sins which exclude are those which require deliberate denial of God, such as idolatry. See *PPJ*, pp. 134f.

73. See *PPJ*, pp. 92–97, 146f., 236f. (rabbinic lit.); 295f. (DSS); 362, 371, 397 (Apocrypha and Pseudepigrapha); 451f.; 503; 518 n. 6 (degree to which membership is conditional on behavior in Paul). G. B. Caird (in his review of *PPJ*, *JTS* 29 [1978]: 542), expressed surprise that I said that for Paul, as for Judaism generally, good deeds were the condition of remaining "in." I hope here to clarify the issue.

74. *PPJ*, p. 162.

75. *PPJ*, pp. 177, 182.

76. See Schrage, *Einzelgebote*, pp. 96–102: "The obligatory character of the apostolic demands is not narrower than that of the law," and Paul's concrete requirements can be called "law."

77. Synofzik, *Vergeltungsaussagen*, p. 41; cf. Hübner, "Das ganze und das eine Gesetz," pp. 244f.; Hahn, "Gesetzesverständnis," p. 61 (the justified person does not fulfill the law of works, *erga*; Paul does not use the plural); Mattern, *Gericht*, pp. 141–51; J. Christiaan Beker, *Paul the Apostle* (Philadelphia: Fortress Press, 1980), pp. 247f.

78. *PPJ*, index, *s.v.* "The Righteous."

79. Correctly Marcus Barth, "Die Stellung des Paulus zu Gesetz und Ordnung," p. 506; Schrage, *Einzelgebote*, pp. 95–98; Hoheisel, *Das antike Judentum in christlicher Sicht* (Wiesbaden: O. Harrassowitz, 1978), p. 200 ("impliziert der neue Weg des Glaubens seinerseits das Prinzip der Werke").

Appendix: Romans 2

I have thus far studiously avoided mentioning Rom. 1:18 — 2:29, which must be considered in discussing the requirement to do the law. I have not yet mentioned it because I think that its peculiar point of view requires separate treatment. The word *nomos* occurs eleven times in Romans 2, and discussion will focus on that chapter.[1]

There is general agreement on the purpose of the section. It is intended to demonstrate (or illustrate) the universal sinfulness of all (3:9, 20), so as to lay the ground for Paul's solution: righteousness by faith in Christ.[2] The basic theme of the first four chapters of Romans is that all can be saved equally on the basis of faith. The word "equally" emphasizes the equal opportunity of access on the part of the Gentiles. Thus the sustained negative argument: not by works of the Mosaic law, which would favor the Jews. Special attention, however, is paid to the Jews in the argument that they are also culpable, the argument which dominates chapter 2.

The section which begins with 1:18 fits Paul's main purpose because different parts of it condemn both Jew and Gentile. It also depicts both as being judged on the same basis, since "God shows no partiality" (2:11). Yet there are difficulties. There are internal inconsistencies within the section, not all the material actually lends itself to the desired conclusion, and there are substantial ways in which parts of it conflict with positions which Paul elsewhere adopts.

Before going into the difficulties in detail, and considering how scholars have dealt with them, it will be useful to indicate the view of the section to which I have been led. I think that in Rom. 1:18 — 2:29 Paul takes over to an unusual degree homiletical material from Diaspora Judaism, that he alters it in only insubstantial ways, and that consequently the treatment of the law in chapter 2 cannot be harmonized with any of the diverse things which Paul says about the law elsewhere.

The principal incongruity within the section is easily spotted and well known: the Gentiles are condemned universally and in sweeping terms in 1:18–32, while in 2:12–15, 26 Paul entertains the possibility that some will be saved by works. The rhetorical point, to be sure, is to lend force to the condemnation of the Jews (2:14: even Gentiles are better than you Jews!); nevertheless 2:12–15 and 2:26 do not square well with the conclusion that all are under the power of sin (3:9, 20). The manner in which Paul can roundly condemn the Jews for flagrant disobedience (2:17–24) also causes some surprise, since in Rom. 10:2 he characterizes his kin as zealous for the law, and in Gal. 2:15 he contrasts Jews with "Gentile sinners." The exaggerated description of Gentile sexual immorality in 1:18–32 is not too surprising in light of such passages as 1 Cor. 6:9–11, but the description of Jewish behavior in 2:17–24 is unparalleled.

We should pay special attention to the exaggerated character of the section.[3] Numerous scholars have regarded Paul's "description" of Gentile and Jewish behavior in Romans 1 – 2 as a telling condemnation. Thus Floyd Filson wrote that "the bulk of 1:18–32 is a report of contemporary conditions" on the "basis of personal observation."[4] Franz Mussner cites Romans 1 – 2 as showing that Paul was convinced "by experience" that no one fulfills the law.[5] Herman Ridderbos describes 2:1 – 3:20 as "the great indictment of Judaism" and 2:1–12 as a "telling accusation."[6] J. Christiaan Beker states that 2:23f. shows that the Jew, by his immorality, "empirically" contradicts the boast in the law.[7] He regards Romans 1 – 5, especially chapter 2, as a "factual" account of Jewish transgressions which "was meant to be intelligible to his Jewish audience."[8] Rom. 1:18 – 2:29, in other words, is read as an objective description of human inability to fulfill the law, inductively arrived at, which is the counterpart to the existential description of the same human condition in Rom. 7:14–25. But Rom. 7:14–25 is itself an exaggeration, being part of a statement that those in the flesh are entirely unable to observe the law, while those in the Spirit keep it. Paul's passion there lends seriousness to the passage, and we may all perhaps be forgiven for thinking that it is a profound statement of the human condition.[9] It is best seen, as we argued above, and as Heikki Räisänen has pointed out, as an exaggerated view of the non-Christian life which depends on Paul's view of life in the Spirit.[10] It is tortured (and therefore it appears profound) because Paul is wrestling with the problem of exonerating God from intending the law to bring sin and also with the effort to separate the law from sin altogether.

The acceptance of Rom. 1:18 – 2:29 as an objective, inductive statement of the human condition, however, shows that we have become too accustomed to thinking of Paul as stating not only the truth of the gospel, but also the gospel truth. That is too flat, even too credulous a reading. Beker, for example, takes it that here Paul states what is really wrong with the law: the Jews did not obey it.[11] Did they all rob temples? One must press behind Paul's exaggerated rhetoric if one is to grasp the origin of Paul's thought about the law. One also must not conflate Rom. 1:18 – 2:29 with Romans 7. The former passage does not argue that no one *can* obey the law (that is the argument in 7:14–25), but that everyone has been guilty of gross and heinous sins. Or rather, part of the section makes this accusation. In several verses, as we shall note in detail below, the possibility is entertained that some obey the law perfectly well. Let me put the matter clearly. Paul's case for universal sinfulness, as it is stated in Rom. 1:18 – 2:29, is not convincing: it is internally inconsistent and it rests on gross exaggeration. In Paul's own time this sort of exaggerated statement may have had rhetorical force;[12] but nevertheless we should recognize that Rom. 1:18 – 2:29 was not written to give an objective, or even a consistent, description of Jews and Gentiles. Paul knows what conclusion he wants to draw, and it is the conclusion which is important to him, since universal sinfulness is necessary if Christ is to be the universal savior.[13] This only points out, to be sure, what can be discovered in other ways: Paul did not come to his view of sin and salvation by beginning with an analysis of the human plight.

There are more substantial ways, however, in which the section raises questions. There is, first, the famous statement that those who do the law will be righteoused (2:13). Further, Paul's statement about repentance (2:4) has no true parallel and is at best atypical. The "hearing and doing" theme (2:13) has numerous parallels in Jewish literature, but none in Paul's letters. The phrase *dikaios para tōi theōi* ("righteous before God," also in 2:13) is also without a Pauline parallel and appears to rest on a Semitic Jewish formulation.[14] The statement in 2:27 that Gentiles who keep the law will judge Jews who do not is at variance with Paul's view that Christians ("the saints") will judge the world (1 Cor. 6:2). Even when we realize that Paul was fully in favor of good works, we must nevertheless admit that the emphasis on actually doing the law is remarkable (the passages are listed below).

There have been several ways of responding to the problems which these points raise. Four of them can be dealt with expeditiously, while two require somewhat more detailed consideration. The first three have been fully discussed by Günther Bornkamm: (1) The Gentiles of 2:14 are Gentile Christians, not Gentiles who obey the Jewish law.[15] (2) Paul is speaking hypothetically: if anyone could obey the law he would be righteoused; but no one can. This explanation depends in part on supposing that Paul's objection to the law is that it could not be satisfactorily fulfilled.[16] (3) The doers of the law in 2:13 are those who do the law in the right way, not according to the mode of a supposed Jewish legalism, but on the basis of faith.[17] Bornkamm correctly objected to these harmonizing proposals,[18] but he put forward a fourth, which I at one time accepted.[19] (4) Rom. 2:13 only means that Christians will be judged in the future, which is in accord with such passages as 2 Cor. 5:10 and Rom. 14:10. As I put it, only the use of the future passive form of *dikaioun* to mean "judged" is unusual.

None of these proposals is satisfactory. (1) The entire passage is about Jews and Gentiles — all humanity — and the law. The Gentiles are not Gentile Christians. (2) There is nothing hypothetical about the statement that some Gentiles will satisfactorily obey the law. It is simply impossible to take 2:14 and 2:27 to mean that *if* even Gentiles were to obey the law they would be justified, but they cannot. Paul says that those who do keep the law *will condemn* those who do not (2:27). The point of the chapter (as will be explained more fully below) is not that no one *can* keep the law: several verses mention those who do keep it. (3) The condemnation of the Jews is that they do not keep the law, or do not keep it well enough, not that they keep it in the wrong spirit.

Having been given time to repent of my own former explanation of 2:13, I should say what is wrong with it. Rom. 2:13 is entirely unlike Rom. 14:10, 2 Cor. 5:10, and other passages in which Paul mentions judgment according to deeds, for the other passages refer to Christians; Rom. 2:13 refers to *all humanity*: all, whether Jew or Greek, are judged by one standard, the law. Those who have done the law will be considered righteous.

Ernst Käsemann has fully realized how difficult it is to fit Romans 2 into the rest of Paul's thought, and in his comments on most of the chapter he resists attempts to harmonize. Thus he argues forcefully that the Gentiles in 2:13–16 are not Gentile Christians,[20] and he also maintains that in 2:14 Paul does not speak hypothetically.[21] He further sees that in 2:26 the question remains whether or not one keeps the law:

> The expression τὰ δικαιώματα τοῦ νόμου in v. 26 characterizes unequivocally the attitude of strict adherence to the law which demonstrates membership in the saved community. . . . The reference of δικαιώματα, as in Deut. 30:16, is to the whole Torah . . . , defined by legal statements.2[22]

Despite this, the Gentiles who are mentioned in 2:27 are, according to Käsemann, hypothetical. They must be: it would be wrongheaded of Paul consistently to fashion "a constantly more favorable picture of the Gentile and then [to measure] against him the ideal Jew."[23] What, then, is the way out, to keep Paul from being wrongheaded? The key is v. 29. There we see, urges Käsemann, that Paul does have Gentile Christians in mind. "Only thus does the context make sense and achieve a theological climax."[24] The change is proved by noting the words *gramma* and *pneuma* (letter and spirit). They show that Paul is writing in the Christian sense.[25] Those who have the spirit keep the law.

In Käsemann's view, then, there are three distinct moments in the chapter. Up to v. 26 Paul writes from the Jewish perspective and requires obedience to the Jewish law as the ground of salvation. In v. 27, however, Paul suddenly speaks hypothetically and means that if Gentiles (not Gentile Christians) could obey the law they would be able to judge Jews who break it. In v. 29 the perspective changes again, and the reader sees that those who live by the Spirit are true Jews.[26] This requires a rereading of the chapter in light of the final verse,[27] where the Christian perspective is expressed.

The greatest value of Käsemann's treatment is that it shows how tortured exegesis must be if one holds that the chapter must reach a Christian theological climax but nevertheless takes most of the chapter (down to v. 26) at face value. The double shift of perspective seems intrinsically unlikely. More important, it is not justified by the text. The statement about the Gentiles in 2:27 is no more hypothetical in wording or tone than 2:14. Käsemann thinks that it must be hypothetical because otherwise Paul would be wrongheaded, but this is not truly an argument. Further, the use of *pneuma* in 2:29 is not distinctively Pauline. The obvious reading of the verse is that the "spirit" of v. 29 is opposite "flesh" in v. 28 and parallel to "heart" in v. 29. The distinction is not the one most usual in Paul, according to which the Flesh and the Spirit are conceived as powers which oppose each other (e.g. Rom. 8:9), but the one more in accord with normal Greek and Jewish usage (and known also from Paul: 2 Cor. 7:1), according to which "flesh" is the physical body and "spirit" is the inner self ("heart").[28] That is, the spirit is not the Spirit of God, but the spirit of the human who obeys the law. The true Jew is one who keeps the law, who does not make an external show, who may not be physically circumcised ("in the flesh"), but who is circumcised internally, in secret; it is a spiritual, not a literal, circumcision of the heart (*en tōi kryptōi . . . kai peritomē kardias en pneumati ou grammati*). The true Jews of 2:26–29 are not the same as the true Jews of Philippians 3, who are those who "glory in Christ Jesus." Nor are they the same as the true descendants of Abraham in Galatians 3 and Romans 4, who are those who have faith in Christ. Thus far we have seen no evidence that at any point in Romans 2 does Paul step outside the Jewish perspective.

It is not novel to find in Romans 2 material from Diaspora Judaism. It is generally recognized that much of the material in 1:18 — 2:29 is derived from pre-Pauline Jewish tradition. Käsemann, for example, thinks that 2:4 may be based on the language of Jewish prayer and that 2:17–24 contains formulations of the Diaspora synagogue.[29] The relationship between Rom. 2:17–18. and Wisd. of Sol. 15:1–3, on knowing the law, is also often pointed out. The author of the Wisdom of Solomon holds that "to know thee is complete righteousness," and this view, or one similar to it, is under attack in Romans 2. Käsemann and others see here a Pauline (Christian) attack on the Jewish view, which takes Jewish guilt lightly,[30] but it is better to see the matter as an inner-Jewish debate on whether or not knowledge necessarily leads to right action, a debate which would be easily understandable in the Greek-speaking Diaspora. There are several other aspects of the chapter which also point to a context in inner-Jewish debate and exhortation: criticism for reliance on descent,[31] the exhortation to do as well as hear the law,[32] the reminder that conscience is the true judge,[33] the question of how much of the law Gentiles need to obey in order to be righteous,[34] and the question of what constitutes true circumcision.[35]

Perhaps the most thoroughgoing way of dealing with the Jewish perspective which governs 1:18 — 2:29, while still holding that Paul has substantially shaped the material, is that of Claus Bussmann.[36] He argues that we should regard the section as containing selections from Paul's own missionary preaching.[37] According to this view, Paul drew on synagogue material[38] but nevertheless stamped it with his own point of view.[39] Yet when one compares the section with other passages which Bussmann regards as reflecting Paul's missionary preaching, the difference is blatant: the other passages, such as 1 Thess. 1:9f., are christocentric. 1 Cor. 1:21–24, which Bussmann cites as the inner-Pauline parallel to Rom. 1:18 — 3:20,[40] in fact helps us see more clearly how distinctive Rom. 1:18 — 2:29 is. In 1 Cor. 1:21–24, Paul says of his own preaching that "we preach Christ crucified." In fact all the clues which point toward Paul's own missionary message have the gospel of the crucifixion and resurrection as their main theme.[41]

Bussmann passes over this distinction and maintains that in another way Paul put his own stamp on Romans 2. The distinctive Pauline motif is that all are under the power of sin.[42] Now, that this is Paul's conclusion (3:9, 20) is beyond doubt. Further, the passage on the Gentiles, 1:18–32, fits the conclusion. We may not be convinced that the passage is an accurate description of Gentile behavior, but the sweeping character of the denunciation does square with the argument that all are in sin. Chapter 2, however, does not really argue that all are condemned. All are judged on the same basis, but the results are by no means in accord with the universal character of the conclusions in chapter 3. The offer of salvation on the basis of fulfillment of the law is held out repeatedly, and not in terms which make one think that the offer is hypothetical or that the goal is impossible to achieve:[43]

> 2:7: "To those who by patience in well-doing seek for glory and honor and immortality, he will give eternal life."
>
> 2:10: ". . . glory and honor and peace for every one who does good."
>
> 2:13: "The doers of the law will be righteoused."
>
> 2:14f.: Gentiles who do what the law requires will be held innocent.
>
> 2:25–28: Those who keep the law will condemn those who do not.

All this is much further from the conclusion in 3:9, 20 than is generally realized. It is often said that Paul, having condemned all Gentiles in 1:18–32, makes an exception of some in 2:14 in order to drive home the case against the Jews. It is certainly correct that 2:14 and 2:27 are intended to emphasize the condemnation of those Jews who do not keep the law ("but break the law," 2:27), but the chapter as a whole does not naturally lead up to the conclusion that no one keeps the law — much less that the law cannot be kept. The chapter lacks the distinctive Pauline motif which Bussmann attributes to it, the emphasis on the condemnation of all.

Paul's conclusion, in fact, comes as something of a surprise after reading chapter 2. The conclusion which would naturally follow from chapter 2 is "repent and obey the law from the bottom of your heart, so that you will be a true Jew." If God's forbearance is intended to lead to repentance (2:4), and if even some Gentiles are better observers of the law than you Jews (2:14, 27), and if all will be judged on the same basis, heartfelt observance of the Mosaic law (2:13, 28), surely what one should do is to examine one's motives to make sure they are pure, to be sure that observance of the law is not merely external, and to act in such a way as not to bring disgrace on the synagogue (2:24; not the church: contrast 1 Cor. 14:23); in short to repent and to mend one's ways.

I think that the best way to read 1:18 — 2:29 is as a synagogue sermon. It is slashing and exaggerated, as many sermons are, but its own natural point is to have its hearers become better Jews on strictly non-Christian Jewish terms, not to lead them to becoming true descendants of Abraham by faith in Christ.[44]

I find, in short, no distinctively Pauline imprint in 1:18 — 2:29, apart from the tag in 2:16. Christians are not in mind, the Christian viewpoint plays no role, and the entire chapter is written from a Jewish perspective. The question throughout chapter 2 is whether or not one does the Jewish law, not as the result of being in Christ, but as the sole determinant of salvation.

"Doing" is emphasized as nowhere else in Paul's letters. We have seen that it is not un-Pauline to require good works, but the concentration on doing the law is nevertheless striking. In Romans 2 Paul mentions doing and not doing (*prassō*, 2:1, 2, 3, 25; *poieō*, *poiētēs*, 2:3, 13f.), works (*erga*, *ergon*, 2:6, 7, 15), obeying and disobeying (*peithō*, *apeitheō*, 2:8), doing good and evil deeds (*ergazomai to agathon*, *katergazomai to kakon*, 2:9f.), transgressing (*parabasis*, *parabatēs*, 2:23, 25, 27), keeping (*phylassō*, 2:26), and fulfilling (*teleō*, 2:27). That it is the Jewish law as such which is to be done is indisputable in 2:12, 13, 17, 18, 23, 25. The meaning of *nomos* in v. 14 is more difficult, but Bornkamm has convincingly argued that the difference is the mode of revelation, not the contents.[45]

The thrust of the whole is summed up in 2:25–29 (once the characteristically Pauline interpretation of "spirit" is seen not to be present in 2:29). What is at stake is whether or not one is a good Jew, a good Jew as judged not on the basis of sharing Abraham's faith, but of obedience to the law.

There are, however, two points which seem not to be entirely in accord with reading the chapter as a non-Christian, inner-Jewish discussion of how to be a true Jew. One is stated by Käsemann as he leads up to the position that, by 2:29, Paul's perspective has changed. He argues that "there were no uncircumcised Jews," and thus that 2:28, which states that a real Jew need not be circumcised, is not written from the perspective of Judaism. Räisänen points out that the expectation that, to be righteous, Gentiles must fulfill the entire law (the implication of 2:13 and 2:27) is not a standard Jewish view. It is well known that, in the rabbinic discussions of "righteous Gentiles," it is envisaged that they will keep part of the law (e.g., the "Noachian commandments"), not the same law as is required of Jews.[46]

These two points are, indeed, unexpected in Jewish synagogue material, especially if we use the standard of rabbinic literature to establish the characteristics of that material. Does that lead to the conclusion that Paul is responsible for them? I think not, for neither point is any more Pauline than it is rabbinic. The general proposition that judgment is according to the law is not the difficult point. What is atypical is the view that all humanity will be judged and either justified or condemned according to the same law. If we take the position that Paul did not compose 2:12–15 *de novo*, but used traditional material, we must admit that we do not know the contents of "the law" in the original setting of the passage. One might speculate that in a homiletical presentation the question might be left vague.[47] The law which Gentiles are to obey, and which is ascertainable by nature, cannot be the same as the Torah *if* one thinks concretely and in detail. People do not always think that way, however, and we may also assume that not every Jewish sermon would maintain the careful rabbinic distinction between laws which Gentiles might reasonably be expected to follow and those which require revelation and special instruction. We do not have a corpus of Diaspora synagogue sermons with which to compare Romans 2, and thus we can adduce no proof that 2:12–15 is a non-Christian Jewish theme. Nevertheless, I regard that as more likely than the view that Paul composed it.

The situation is a little better with regard to Rom. 2:25–29. The argument that circumcision is truly accomplished when the (rest of) the law is fulfilled is not entirely without parallel in Jewish literature. As Peder Borgen has pointed out, the discussions of circumcision in Philo reveal that some Jews thought that "true" circumcision had been accomplished when the ethical aspects of the law had been fulfilled.[48] That is very close to the position on circumcision taken in Rom. 2:25–29: circumcision consists in doing what (the rest of) the law requires. This position is not rabbinic,[49] but it does seem to be Jewish.[50] It is at least not Pauline. If we may judge by Philippians 3, Paul would say that those who glory in Christ Jesus are truly circumcised.

Thus at no point do we find a convincing argument that Paul has shaped the material to his "own" point of view.

In that case, why is the chapter in Romans at all? The first answer has already been given. In one respect the chapter fits into Paul's argument: it puts Jew and Gentile on the same footing — not, to repeat, as Paul does in Romans 3 and 4 (all have equal opportunity to be righteoused by faith in Christ), but nevertheless on equal footing. Different parts of it, though not in a consistent or objective way, lead up to 3:9. Perhaps the special circumstances in which Romans was written are also a factor. In writing to a church which he did not know, Paul may have used traditional material to an unusual degree.

I may anticipate the objection that I have separated 1:18 — 2:29, and in particular Romans 2, too sharply from the rest of Paul's thought. I can only reply that I think that emphasizing the difference in viewpoint is essential. Let me, however, offer one or two final remarks to clarify the position which is taken here.

I do not mean to imply that the section is an interpolation, or that the material should be dismissed from the Pauline corpus because it is internally inconsistent and it reflects a point of view different from Paul's "own." It is routinely observed, when pre-Pauline Christian material in one of Paul's letters is being discussed, that even if Paul did not compose the passage under consideration, he did incorporate it, and he could not have done so if it went completely against the grain.[51] The same observation can be made with regard to Romans 2. Yet there is a difference: the hymn in Phil. 2:6–11 is a christological hymn, and the formula in Rom. 1:3f. is also christological; in Romans 2 we are dealing with a point of view which at no point reflects

131

specifically Christian thinking. That in itself is not unique when sins are being listed. Paul's virtue and vice lists do not reflect a particularly Christian point of view. His more detailed discussions of behavior sometimes do (as in 1 Cor. 6:15–18), but in general Paul's view of right and wrong behavior reflects standard Hellenistic Jewish thinking. Nevertheless, even when one considers that Paul is not always consistent, that he not infrequently incorporates and makes use of material which he did not coin, and that he often draws on Diaspora synagogue traditions in discussing behavior, Romans 2 still stands out. It stands out because it deals directly with salvation and makes salvation dependent on obedience to the law. What is said about the law in Romans 2 cannot be fitted into a category otherwise known from Paul's letters, and for that reason it has been dealt with in an appendix.

NOTES

1. It is not necessary for the present purpose to decide whether the Jews are exclusively in mind from 2:1 on. There has been considerable discussion about just where the change of emphasis from Gentile to Jew takes place. See, e.g., F. Flückiger, "Zur Unterscheidung von Heiden und Juden in Röm. 1, 18–2,3," *TZ* 10 (1954): 154–58. For a summary of positions, see Dieter Zeller, *Juden und Heiden in der Mission bei Paulus*, 2d. ed. (Stuttgart: Verlag Katholisches Bibelwerk, 1976), p. 149 and n. 36.

2. J. Cambier, "Le jugement de tous les hommes," *ZNW* 67 (1976–77): 187; L. Ramarosan, "Un 'nouveau plan' de *Rm 1*, 16 – 11, 36," *Nouvelle Revue Théologique* 94 (1972): 951; Günther Bornkamm, "Gesetz und Natur (Rom. 2, 14–15)," *Studien zu Antike und Urchristentum* (Munich: Chr. Kaiser, 1963), pp. 93f.

3. See Heikki Räisänen, "Paul's Theological Difficulties with the Law," in *Studia Biblica 1978*, vol. 3 (Sheffield: JSOT Press, 1980), pp. 308f.

4. Floyd V. Filson, *St. Paul's Conception of Recompense* (Leipzig: J. C. Hinrichs, 1931), p. 29.

5. Franz Mussner, *Der Galaterbrief* (Freiburg: Herder, 1974), pp. 191f.

6. Herman Ridderbos, *Paul An Outline of His Theology* (Grand Rapids: Wm. B. Eerdmans, 1975), p. 135.

7. J. Christiaan Beker, *Paul the Apostle* (Philadelphia: Fortress Press, 1980), p. 82.

8. Ibid., p. 242.

9. I accept with thanks Räisänen's rebuke: "Paul's Theological Difficulties with the Law," pp. 310f., referring to *PPJ*, p. 509. The view that Romans 7 is "a profound analysis" was, as Räisänen points out, inconsistent with my other comments on the chapter (*PPJ*, p. 475). Cf. above, p. 75.

10. Räisänen, "Paul's Theological Difficulties," pp. 310f.

11. Beker, *Paul the Apostle*, pp. 246f., 242. He combines Romans 2 and 7 in this argument.

12. Cf. Ezek. 33:25f.: "You eat flesh with the blood, and lift up your eyes to your

idols, and shed blood. . . . You resort to the sword, you commit abominations, and each of you defiles his neighbor's wife. . . ." Closer to Paul's time, note Ps. Sol. 8:9f.: "They wrought confusion, son with mother and father with daughter; they committed adultery, every man with his neighbor's wife." Perhaps not all the priests really did all these things. From the other point of view, it may be surprising that in Romans 2 there are no charges of sexual misconduct on the part of the Jews, so common are such charges in polemic.

13. We recall here the point made earlier (p. 4), that not every argument on behalf of a position shows what Paul "really thought."

14. For discussion and passages, see L. Mattern, *Das Verständis des Gerichts bei Paulus* (Zurich and Stuttgart: Zwingli Verlag, 1966), pp. 123–40. On "righteous before God" see Otto Michel, *Der Brief an die Römer*, 12th ed. (Göttingen: Vandenhoeck & Ruprecht, 1963), p. 77 n. 1. Mattern's discussion is very instructive. She sees how atypical Rom. 1:18 – 2:29 is and resorts to an unconvincing distinction in order to fit it into Paul's thought. Paul, she acknowledges, is not actually (*wirklich*) discussing Christians in 2:5ff., but he really (*faktisch*) has them in mind (p. 137 n. 37). She continues, "Das Gericht, von dem Rö 2 spricht, hat nur die Aufgabe, die endgultige Scheidung zwischen Glauben und Unglauben zu treffen. . . ." (p. 138). Are we to conclude that although faith is not actually mentioned it really is meant?

15. E.g. C.E.B. Cranfield, *The Epistle to the Romans*, vol. 1 (Edinburgh: T. & T. Clark, 1979), p. 152; A. König, "Gentiles or Gentile Christians? On the Meaning of Rom. 2:12–16," *Journal of Theology for South Africa* 15 (1976): 53–60; F. Flückiger, "die Werke des Gesetzes bei den Heiden," *TZ* 8 (1952): 17–42, esp. p. 17 n. 3.

16. See Andrea van Dülmen, *Theologie des Gesetzes bei Paulus* (Stuttgart: Verlag Katholisches Bibelwerk, 1968), pp. 76f.; 253 n. 69; Karl Hoheisel, *Das antike Judentum in christlicher Sicht* (Weisbaden: O. Harrassowitz, 1978), p. 200 (cf. p. 187).

17. A thoroughgoing recent example is that of J. Cambier, "Le jugement de tous," note p. 210: those who "anticipativement . . . acceptaient le Christ."

18. Bornkamm, "Gesetz und Natur," pp. 107–11.

19. *PPJ*, pp. 515f. So earlier Bornkamm, "Gesetz und Natur," p. 110. Cf. Ernst Käsemann, *Commentary on Romans* (Grand Rapids: Wm. B. Eerdmans, 1980), pp. 57f., on Rom. 2:6.

20. Käsemann, *Romans*, p. 73.

21. Ibid.

22. Ibid.

23. Ibid.

24. Ibid., p. 75.

25. Ibid., pp. 76f.

26. Many scholars understand the true Jew and true circumcision of 2:28f. in the Christian sense, pointing to Phil. 3:3. See, for example, Peter Richardson, *Israel in the Apostolic Church* (New York: Cambridge University Press, 1969), pp. 138f. Räisänen argues that the word *pneuma* indicates that in 2:29 Paul has "glided" into discussing Christians: *Paul and the Law*.

27. Käsemann, *Romans*, p. 76: The last sentence of chap. 2 "alone brings out the point and reveals the intention of the whole."

28. The Greek contrast would be "body" or "flesh" and "soul" (*psychē*) oftener than "spirit." For references, see *TDNT* 6: 390, n. 335; *TDNT* 7: 103.

29. Käsemann, *Romans*, pp. 70f. Cf. Zeller, *Juden und Heiden*, p. 149; Leander Keck, *Paul and His Letters* (Philadelphia: Fortress Press, 1979), p. 10. Bornkamm's treatment deserves special consideration. He notes that "Paulus heir ganz von den Voraussetzungen des Juden aus denkt und redet" ("Gesetz und Natur," p. 110). He also fully sees the dependence on Diaspora Jewish modes of speech and thought (as well as on popular philosophy, which could have been already adapted by the synagogue), but argues that Paul uses his sources to make a different point from that of the Jewish apologetic tradition on which he drew. See especially Günther Bornkamm, "The Revelation of God's Wrath," *Early Christian Experience* (New York: Harper & Row, 1969), pp. 47–70. There are several points in Romans 2, however, which seem to me to reflect inner-Jewish debates rather than Paul's use of Jewish material from a Christian viewpoint: (1) The question of whether or not there are righteous Gentiles (Rom. 2:14f., 27f.); (2) The question of whether or not knowing the law necessarily leads to righteousness (Rom. 2:13; Wisd. of Sol. 15:2f.); (3) The question of true obedience—whether outward or inward (Rom. 2:28f.; Deut. 30:2, 6; Jer. 31:33; 1QS 5:5; and often in other Jewish literature).

30. Käsemann, *Romans*, p. 54.

31. Rom. 2:17, 28; cf. Philo, *De Virtutibus* [*On the Virtues*] 206: All humanity should remember that "those who have no true excellence of character should not pride themselves on the greatness of their race." Cf. *De Praemiis et Poenis* [*On Rewards and Punishments*] 152.

32. Rom. 2:13; cf. Philo, *De Praemiis* 79, 82: "If, he says, you keep the divine commandment in obedience to his ordinances . . . , not merely to hear them but to carry them out by your life and conduct. . . ." "Now while the commandments of the laws are only on our lips our acceptance of them is little or none, but when we add thereto deeds which follow in their company. . . ."

33. Rom. 2:15; cf. Philo, *De Praemiis* 206, end: the only true judge is conscience.

34. This is a frequent topic in rabbinic literature. The answer given in Romans is unusual. See below.

35. See below.

36. Claus Bussmann, *Themen der paulinischen Missionspredigt auf dem Hintergrund der spätjudisch-hellenistischen Missionsliteratur* (Frankfurt and Bern: H. Lang, 1971), pp. 108–11, with references to earlier literature.

37. On this, see also Käsemann, *Romans*, p. 34.

38. Bussmann, *Missionspredigt*, pp. 111–22.

39. Ibid., pp. 121f.

40. Ibid., p. 109.

41. Cf. *PPJ*, pp. 444–46.

42. Bussmann, *Missionspredigt*, p. 122.

43. Ferdinand Hahn ("Das Gesetzesverständnis im Römer- und Galaterbrief," *ZNW* 67 [1976–77]: 36f.) sees that the possibility of complete fulfillment of the law is entertained in Romans 2. That possibility is excluded only later, in Hahn's view.

44. O'Neill has put the difference between chap. 2 and the rest of Romans precisely: "Paul is trying to show [the Christians in Rome] that even though they might seem to be keeping the requirements of the Law pretty successfully the Law itself

says that this way of being righteous . . . is wrong (see chapter 3). But the section in front of us is unaware of that problem, and assumes that the only question is whether or not a man keeps the Law." He adds: "The present argument leads to the same conclusion, that Gentiles as much as Jews can be rewarded with eternal life by God, but it gets there by ignoring Paul's main problem. Of course God will reward righteousness, but, on the basis of the present passage, the best way to help Gentiles to be righteous would be to preach to them the law." J. C. O'Neill, *Paul's Letter to the Romans* (Baltimore: Penguin Books, 1975), p. 48.

45. The law in 2:14 is the same law of God, which the Jews knew through Moses and the Gentiles through nature: Bornkamm, "Gesetz und Natur," p. 101. Käsemann (*Romans*, p. 64) argues against Bornkamm on the ground that Paul does not restrict the Torah to the moral law. The logic is that the Gentiles could have known only the moral aspect of the law "by nature," and thus the content of the law which Jews know must be different from that which Gentiles know. It is clear in The Wisdom of Solomon 14 — 15, as in Rom. 1:18–32 and several of the vice lists, that the two typical Gentile sins, as Jews saw them, were idolatry and sexual immorality, and that monotheism — as well as moral points such as sexual behavior, murder, lying, and perjury — should be perceived "by nature." It seems likely that, in the homiletical material which lies behind Rom. 1:18 — 2:29, these things were considered to constitute "the law." It seems to me that, while a Jewish author — whether Paul or anyone else — would know that the law contains things other than the requirement of monotheism and moral rectitude, for homiletical purposes discussions of obeying and being judged by the law might very well be limited to those points. One may note also the rabbinic point that acceptance of the prohibition of idolatry is acceptance of the whole law (Sifre Deuteronomy 54; see *PPJ*, p. 135). That is not true in detail, but it could be regarded as true for homiletical purposes. Quoting part of the law as the whole law, or referring to only aspects of the law as "the law," raises a problem, as we shall immediately note, if we think systematically, concretely, and in detail. Homileticians and others looking for a succinct statement of the law do not necessarily think that way. Cf. above, p. 99 and n. 18.

46. See *PPJ*, pp. 210f. and nn. 28, 30.

47. N. 45 above.

48. Peder Borgen, "Observations on the Theme 'Paul and Philo'," in *Die Paulinische Literatur und Theologie* (Aarhus: Forlaget Aros, 1980), esp. pp. 86–9, 91f. The principal passages in Philo are *Migr.* 92 and *Quest. Ex.* II.2. The important point is that the "allegorists" interpret circumcision ethically, not primarily noetically.

49. Borgen, ibid, p. 88, notes that according to bShabbath 31a Hillel gave the status of "proselyte" to one who obeyed the Golden Rule. Subsequent physical circumcision was, however, expected.

50. Cf. Neil J. McEleney, "Conversion, Circumcision and the Law," *NTS* 20 (1974): 332: "while circumcision was normally the approved way of a man's becoming a Jew, there were those who did not believe it was necessary in every case."

51. In this connection it is often said that, by adding a word or phrase, he "corrected" the view of quoted material. See Käsemann, *Romans*, p. 13.

4

The Old Dispensation
and the New

Our fourth category is in some ways a subcategory of the second, since it has to do with the role of the law in *Heilsgeschichte*. Yet it is different, since the angle of vision is different. In two passages Paul directly compares, in an evaluative way, the old dispensation and the new. These passages are 2 Cor. 3:4–18 and Phil. 3:3–11.

The distinctiveness of these two passages is seen in part by noting the question which they do not address. They do not ask about God's will or intention in giving the law. We saw above that in Galatians 3 and Rom. 4:15; 5:20; 7:7–13, when Paul discusses the function of the law, or God's purpose in giving it, in light of the sending of Christ, he connects it in some way or other to sin, so that the law served negatively to lead up to what God had intended all along—salvation for all on the basis of faith. In Rom. 7:10; 7:14 — 8:4 he says that God gave the law, which is good, to lead to life, but that sin or the flesh foiled that aim, with the result that God had to redeem the situation by sending his son (Rom. 7:25; 8:3). The passages presently being considered compare and contrast the law with life in Christ, but they leave aside the question of what God had intended in giving the law.

They are different from other passages in another way. When Paul says that righteousness is not by law, there is no evaluation of life under the law, and thus no evaluation of Judaism as (what we would call) a religion. Those passages have to do with how one enters the body of Christ, and they especially stem from the argument about Gentiles, although Paul applies the principle "not by works of law" to Jews as well as Gentiles. But they do not assess life under the law; they simply say that it does not lead to "righteousness" or to being in Christ.

Something like assessment does appear, however, in the two passages now in view. In 2 Corinthians 3 Paul compares the covenant (*diathēkē*, 3:14) or dispensation (*diakonia*, 3:7) which came through Moses with the new *diathēkē* (3:6) or *diakonia* (3:8) of which he is *diakonos* (3:6). It is in part a comparison of Paul and Moses, in part a comparison of the covenants of

137

which they are ministers. What Paul has to say by way of evaluative comparison is this: "What was glorious has no glory in comparison with the surpassing glory" (3:10). It is only the new dispensation that devalues the old. This is equally clear in 3:14: the Jews who read Scripture do not see because of a veil which is taken away only through Christ.

Although the basic comparison in 2 Cor. 3:10f. is straightforward, these verses in their own way reveal the dilemma about the law which constantly plagues Paul's discussions of it. We note in the first place that the law kills (2 Cor. 3:6) and that the Mosaic dispensation is called the dispensation of death (3:7) and condemnation (3:9). The dispensation of the Spirit (3:8) or of righteousness (3:9) gives life (3:6). This black and white contrast between the law and death on the one hand and the Spirit and life on the other is familiar from such passages as Rom. 8:2. In Romans 7, we recall, Paul had been struggling to hold together his native conviction that the law was given by God and is good with his new conviction that life comes only through Christ and that therefore the law cannot save. This same problem seems to be reflected in 2 Corinthians 3. This dispensation of *death* was *glorious!* (3:9). Paul does not explain how it is that something which condemns and kills can be glorious. He is caught here as elsewhere between two convictions, but here there is no struggle to resolve them; he states them both as facts.

If he had started with the conviction that the law condemns and kills, and if he had, before his conversion, been in quest of a way out, we would expect a more consistent expression of the view that what is wrong with the law is that it kills. He says that often enough, to be sure. Yet when he actually formulates a direct sentence which says how it comes to be that the law which God gave has become the law of sin and death, he says only that its glory has been surpassed and that it now has no glory at all (3:10f.). The black-and-white contrast between the dispensation of death and the dispensation of life is also formulated as a contrast between degrees of whiteness: what was glorious and what is more glorious. The simplest explanation of this dual form of contrast seems to be that he came to relegate the Mosaic dispensation to a less glorious place *because* he found something more glorious and that he *then*, thinking in black-and-white terms, developed the death/life contrast. I cannot see how the development could have run the other way, from an initial conviction that the law only condemns and kills, to a search for something which gives life, to the conviction that life comes by faith in Christ, to the statement that the law lost its glory because a new dispensation surpasses it in glory.

There is a second point in this chapter at which we see Paul's difficulty in dealing with the law. In 3:7 he attaches the descriptive participle "passing away" or "being abolished" to the "glory" with which the law was given (*tēn doxan . . . tēn katargoumenēn*). One would think from this that the law itself abides, but that it has lost (or is losing) its glory. This line of thought, or a related one, is seen to be continued in 3:14–16: the old covenant is still read; when non-Christian Jews read it, it is veiled; when Christians read it, it is not. In 3:11, however, it is the law itself which is passing away. The neuter participle *to katargoumenon* (what is passing away) refers not to the glory with which the law was given, as does the feminine participle in 3:7, but to *what* was given (v. 10: *to dedoxasmenon*), that is, the law. Morna D. Hooker, however, has argued that what is being abolished in 3:11 is not the law itself. It could hardly be, since "scripture provides [Paul] with his primary witness to Christ." What is becoming obsolete is rather the ministry of Moses — a relationship with God based on "obedience to the letter of [the] law." The two phrases in 3:11 (*to katargoumenon*, "passing away" or "being abolished"; *to menon*, "remaining") both refer to the law, but to different aspects of it. It is passing away as a system which offers life to those who obey it; it abides "in so far as it is seen as a witness to Christ."[1] I do not agree with Hooker's explanation of the two participles in 3:11. It seems much more natural to take "what is passing away" to refer to "what was [given] in glory" (3:10), that is, the Mosaic dispensation as such, and "what remains" to refer to "the surpassing glory" (3:10), that is, the new dispensation. Hooker's explanation highlights, rather, a true ambiguity in Paul's position. On the one hand the law is a law of condemnation and death, and it (not just an aspect of it) is passing away; on the other hand only its splendor has passed away while it still remains and testifies to Christ. I do not find here a conscious distinction between two aspects of the law. We see, rather, the two sides of a dilemma: the law was glorious, its only "fault" is that it has been surpassed in glory, and it can still be correctly read by Christians. What is wrong with non-Christian Jews is only that they have not turned to the Lord (3:15f.). On the other hand, since the law does not save, Paul says that it only condemns and kills and that it itself is passing away in favor of the new dispensation, which remains.

Paul also compares the two dispensations in an evaluative way in Phil. 3:4–11. Here he speaks in the first person; and, as Georg Eichholz has noted, he sees his own experience as paradigmatic.[2] The comparative statement is this: "Whatever gain I had, I counted as loss for the sake of Christ" (3:7). This reflects precisely the same view as that of 2 Cor. 3:9–11, where the law lost its glory only because of the surpassing glory of the new dispensation. In Philippians we also get an insight into the "black or white" thinking which we have often noticed: once a greater good appears, what was formerly good is regarded not just as second best, but as "loss." In Philippians, however, Paul does not draw out the negative conclusion about the law by saying that it is a law which brings only death. He continues, rather, by contrasting two righteousnesses. If he gains Christ, and is found in him, he will have not his own righteousness, which was based on law, but another righteousness, one which comes from God on the basis of faith in Christ and which consists in being found in Christ and sharing his sufferings (3:8–10). The only thing that is wrong with the old righteousness seems to be that it is not the new one; it has no fault which is described in other terms. Paul has confidence in the old righteousness, but, as we said above,[3] his "fault" as a zealous Pharisee was not his attitude, but boasting in a "gain" which he later saw as "loss."

We should here recall that we have seen this same attitude in Rom. 9:30 – 10:13. The Jews will not be saved because they seek the righteousness based on the law, zealously to be sure, but blindly, because real righteousness is based on faith in Christ.

Numerous scholars emphasize the words translated "own" in Phil. 3:9 (*mē echōn emēn dikaiosynēn*) and Rom. 10:3 (*tēn idian zētountes*), taking the emphasis to be against supposed Jewish self-righteousness and in favor of accepting righteousness as a gift.[4] I do not for a moment doubt that, had the problem been posed to Paul, he would have come out strongly against merit-seeking self-righteousness, but I do not think that that is the force of these two phrases. In Romans he draws a contrast between two righteousnesses, one based on law and sought by the Jews in ignorance of the other one, "the righteousness of God," which is based on Christ apart from the law (Rom. 10:3f.). In Philippians he contrasts the righteousness which he once had by virtue of being Torah-observant, which was "gain," with the righteousness based on faith in Christ, called "the righteousness from God." He thus knows about two righteousnesses.[5] The difference between them is not the distinction between merit and grace, but between two dispensations. There is a righteousness which comes by law, but it is now worth nothing because of a different dispensation. *Real* righteousness (the righteousness of or from God) is through Christ.[6] It is this concrete fact of *Heilsgeschichte* which makes the other righteousness wrong, not the abstract superiority of grace to merit.

Thus we see that when Paul speaks in a direct way about the two dispensations (2 Corinthians 3), or about the relative good of life under the law and life in Christ (Philippians 3), his thought is dominated by the surpassing value of life in Christ. What is surpassingly valuable becomes, in Paul's mind, what is exclusively valuable. In light of Christ the law loses its glory entirely (2 Cor. 3:10), and righteousness under the law changes from "gain" to "loss" (Phil. 3:7). It seems to be this way of thinking that leads him to give the law a purely negative role: it kills (2 Cor. 3:6).

NOTES

1. Morna D. Hooker, "Beyond the things that are written? St. Paul's use of Scripture," *NTS* 27 (1981): 303f. Cf. W. D. Davies, "Paul and the People of Israel," *NTS* 24 (1977): 11f.: the participles "passing away" in 2 Cor. 3:11, 13 refer not to the law, but to the ministry of Moses and the glory on Moses' face.

2. Georg Eichholz, *Die Theologie des Paulus im Umriss* (Neukirchen-Vluyn: Neukirchener Verlag, 1972), pp. 224f.

3. P. 44.

4. Rudolf Bultmann, *Theology of the New Testament*, vol. 1 (New York: Charles Scribner's Sons, 1951–1955), I, p. 267; Ernst Käsemann, *An die Römer* (Tübingen: J. C. B. Mohr [Paul Siebeck], 1974), p. 271 ["die Werke der Leistungsfrömmigkeit"] [ET: *Commentary on Romans* (Grand Rapids: Wm. B. Eerdmans, 1980], p. 281).

5. Herman Ridderbos (*Paul: An Outline of His Theology* [Grand Rapids: Wm. B. Eerdmans, 1975], p. 170) correctly sees that "in Paul this righteousness acquires a content altogether its own and entirely divergent from Judaism," although I cannot follow him in finding that the difference is expressed "above all in the word 'to impute'." On two righteousnesses, cf. also J. A. Sanders, "Torah and Christ," *Interpretation* 29 (1975):380; E. P. Sanders, *Paul and Palestinian Judaism* (Philadelphia: Fortress Press, 1977), pp. 505f.

6. Räisänen, "Legalism and Salvation by the Law," in *Die paulinische Literatur und Theologie* (Aarhus: Forlaget Aros, 1980), p. 71: "The Jews' establishment of their own righteousness . . . is . . . identical with their rejection of Christ"; "the root of the evil lies in a christological failure, not in an anthropological one."

5

Conclusion: Paul and the Law

Summary of Results

The main burden of the argument of Part One is stated in the phrase "Different Questions, Different Answers." We have repeatedly seen that Paul's various statements about the law are not the result of theoretical thought about the law as such, but spring from and serve other convictions. The main lines of his discussions of the law are determined by christology, soteriology (especially their universal aspects), and what we may call Christian behavior. On these subjects he had definite ideas, despite appreciable variety in expression, and when the law came up in connection with them they determined what he said about it.

In discussing how one can be saved (more precisely, be put in the proper state preparatory to final salvation), Paul always said "through Christ" and "not by law." The meaning is that neither agreement to observe the law nor actual observance of it can be set as the condition for entering the community of those who faith in Christ. Faith in Christ itself — sometimes clarified by the phrases "dying with Christ" or "sharing his suffering" — is the only means of entry.

The limitation of the argument that righteousness is not by law to the question of how one *enters* the body of those who will be saved is seen better when we observe that otherwise Paul can treat as matters of indifference, or of one's personal conscience, the aspects of the law about which he waxes so vociferous in most of Galatians. Circumcision does not matter (1 Cor. 7:19; Gal. 6:15), and days and food can be decided by each individual (Rom. 14:1–6). When the topic changes, what he says about the law also changes.

Since Paul retained his native conviction that God gave the law, but had also come to the conviction that Christ saves and that therefore the law does not, he naturally had to give some account of God's purpose in giving the law and of the law's function in God's overall plan. This problem plagued him and led to some of the most difficult and tortured passages in the surviving correspondence. He was still struggling with it in what is

143

probably his last letter, Romans, and no single statement encompasses neatly all of his attempts to deal with it. One can say in general terms that, in dealing with this question, he connected the law with sin. Most often he did so by subordinating both the law and sin to God's purpose. God intended that the law enslave everybody (!) under sin, *so that* he could have mercy equally on all (Gal. 3:22–24; cf. Rom. 5:20f.). In Romans 7, however, the relationship among God's will, sin, and the law changes. In 7:7–13 Paul depicts sin as using the law against the purpose of God. The law still *produces* transgression (by prohibiting it), but this is not in accord with God's intention. In 7:14–25 it is the flesh, or "another law," which prevents the individual from obeying the law and which leads to transgression. God's will is that the law be obeyed, but those "in the flesh" are unable to do so. In every case the solution is found in God's sending of his son.

When it came to concrete acts, Paul, as a good Jew, thought that his converts should act in accord with the will of God as revealed in Scripture, not in accord with the customs of the Greeks — much less in accord with any new enthusiasm which would permit such things as incest. Here, we have noted, Paul made only three exceptions of which we have knowledge. He handed down no halakah, and thus we have only ad hoc decisions. Whether more cases would have produced more exceptions we cannot say; but it is clear that his ethical views were basically Jewish.

Finally, we have seen that, when it came to evaluating the Mosaic dispensation vis-à-vis the dispensation in Christ, Paul found the former, glorious as it had been, to be worthless.

Central Concerns and Lack of System

The lack of systematic thinking about the law is principally apparent at two places. One is the conflicting connections which Paul makes between the law and sin (our category 2). He can say that God intended that the law enslave or produce transgressions, that sin used the law against the will of God, but still that it produced transgression, and that because of the weakness of the flesh humans are unable to do the good which God both wills and commanded. All these statements are understandable as springing from the dilemma which we have characterized as resulting from two deeply held convictions — that God gave the law and that salvation is by faith in Christ for all. Paul's first formulation of which we have knowledge, that of Galatians, made a positive connection between the law and sin and attributed sin directly to the will of God. One can well understand that this formulation was not satisfactory. At any rate, we see it partially continued in Romans (5:20), but other formulations emerge. According to one,

144

God's will was that the law would lead to life, but Sin used the law to provoke transgression. According to the other, the weakness of the flesh keeps people from doing the good which God wills and which is expressed in the commandments.

These formulations also raise problems. One places Sin outside the control of God and elevates it to the status of an autonomous power. The other breaks the positive connection between the law and sin (a connection which was obviously troublesome) and places the flesh outside God's control. It leads Paul to speak of the law as an attempt to produce good which failed, and finally, since he could not attribute failure directly to God, to distinguish between God and the law: *God* does what the *law* could not do (Rom. 8:3). One does not know what further combinations among sin, the law, and God's will Paul might have attempted, but it seems justifiable not to regard any one of these as Paul's true, final, and unalterable view. We do see, however, some views which can be so described: God gave the law; God wills the good; God's intention to save will ultimately prevail; God has provided for salvation by sending his Son.

The unsystematic character of Paul's thought about the law also comes distinctly to the fore when he discusses correct behavior. He makes no distinction between the law which does not righteous and to which Christians have died and the law which those in the Spirit fulfill.[1] This situation presents a standard exegetical problem, and it need not be elaborated again. Our "solution," it will be recalled, was that each statement (righteousness is not by the law; Christians fulfill the law) springs from one of Paul's central convictions. One has to do with how people enter the body of those who will be saved, one with how they behave once in. He did not abstract his statements about the law from the context in which they were made, nor did he consider them in their relationship to one another apart from the questions which they were intended to answer.

We have seen in the course of discussion several attempts to make unified sense of Paul's various treatments of the law. The most notable ones of recent years have been (1) that Paul's thought developed between Galatians and Romans[2] and (2) that the law is the same in all Paul's comments, but seen from a different perspective.[3] I have disagreed on numerous points with the proponents of these views, but it should also be noted that there are some agreements. The statements about the law in Galatians and Romans, especially those which deal with its function and its relation to God's will and to sin, are not identical. They seem to me to be varying attempts to solve the same problem, however, rather than reflections of a fundamental development in Paul's thought.

145

There are several variations of the basic position that Paul's statements about the law result from seeing it from different perspectives:[4] the law is seen either in connection with sin or in connection with promise;[5] it is seen as a way of salvation or as a norm of life;[6] as it encounters those in the flesh or those in the Spirit;[7] as a means to the achievement of self-righteousness or as an expression of the will of God to be obeyed in faith.[8] Of these, the last has, in my judgment, no support. I find no instance in Paul of a distinction with regard to the interior attitude with which one obeys the law. When Paul objects to "works of law," he never objects to the intention to achieve merit by them,[9] and when he recommends obedience to the law he never mentions attitude one way or the other. The third position which is mentioned above — that the law is the same, but seen as it encounters either one in the flesh or one in the Spirit — can be subdivided. We have dealt fairly extensively with the argument that the difference between those in the flesh and those in the Spirit (Rom. 7:14 – 8:8) is one of attitude; the recent arguments of Eduard Lohse, Hans Hübner, and others, as they apply to Romans, are only a variant of Rudolf Bultmann's position. They suffer from the additional burden of arguing that "the *nomos* of faith" in Rom. 3:27 means "the Mosaic law when observed in faith," while "*nomos* of the Spirit of life in Christ Jesus" in Rom. 8:2a means "the Mosaic law when observed in the right spirit."[10]

Rom. 7:14 – 8:8, however, is subject to a different interpretation and one which has, in my view, more merit: the real fault with the law is that it does not enable those in the flesh to fulfill it. Paul Meyer, for example, connects the theme of inability in Rom. 7:14-25 — which is unquestionably there — with Rom. 1:18 – 2:29, which he also reads as an argument based on inability, and Rom. 9:30 – 10:4, which he takes as saying that Jews did not succeed in obeying the law.[11] I have argued against this interpretation of Rom. 1:18 – 2:29 and 9:30f. above. It remains here to offer some general considerations against making the inability/ability distinction of Rom. 7:14-25 central to Paul's thought about the law.

This distinction fails as an explanation of Paul's divergent statements about the law because it does not cover important aspects of what Paul said about the law. It can explain why Paul said that the law kills, but it really offers no explanation of the various statements about the law in Galatians. If one takes fleshly inability as a starting point, the debate about whether or not there is righteousness according to law is hard to explain, and the statements that God *intended* the law to enslave everyone to sin (Gal. 3:22-24) become incomprehensible. In fact the distinction between inability in the flesh and ability in the Spirit does not explain how Paul came to formulate "Christ" and "law" as mutually exclusive alternatives (Philippians 3). The distinction between "law in the Spirit" and "law in the flesh," were it basic to Paul's view, should have been reflected elsewhere than Rom. 7:14 – 8:8. Why would he then need the formula "faith in Christ apart from law" versus "works of law" as a flat alternative? It is understandable that Paul moved from the debate about entry requirements (one is not righteoused by the law) *to* the various explanations of the function of the law (the law enslaves, the law brings knowledge of sin, the law kills); but it is very difficult to posit as the basic distinction that the law kills those in the flesh but is life to those in the Spirit, and then to move to *diverse* explanations of the function of the law and finally to the statement that the law does not righteous. Further, the flesh/Spirit distinction does not explain Paul's de facto changes in the content of the law. It is noteworthy that those who argue in greatest detail that the law in Paul's thought is always the same, but is seen from different perspectives, do not consider concrete cases. If the basic thing "wrong" with the law is that humans are unable to fulfill it, there is no reason to have those in the Spirit, who have been given the ability, fulfill only part of it. In the Spirit one should certainly be able to obey the laws governing circumcision, food, and days. If, however, what is basically wrong with the law is that it does not provide entry to the people of God for Gentile as well as Jew (which has been provided by faith in Christ), it is easily understandable why Paul ruled out, or held to be optional, those three parts of the law.

I do not think that it is wrong to seek an inner unity which holds together everything which Paul says about the law. The search is even encouraged by the fact that Paul makes no theoretical distinction between different aspects or parts of the law. Nevertheless, I have come to the conclusion that there is no single unity which adequately accounts for every statement about the law. Against those who argue in favor of mere inconsistency, however, I would urge that Paul held a limited number of basic convictions which, when applied to different problems, led him to say different things about the law.[12] Even at the point at which Paul may most obviously be charged with true incoherence, the statements in Romans 2 that the sole basis of salvation is fulfillment of the law, we can see that he has been led to make use of material which is contrary to one of his central convictions (salvation by faith in Jesus Christ) by the desire to assert another one (the equality of Jew and Gentile). Nevertheless Romans 2 remains the instance in which Paul goes beyond inconsistency or variety of argument and explanation to true self-contradiction.

In terms which I used earlier, I still see Paul as on the whole a "coherent," though not a "systematic" thinker.[13] Heikki Räisänen has objected, arguing that "Paul the theologian is a less coherent and less convincing thinker than is commonly assumed."[14] As far as I can tell, we disagree only about terminology. If each divergent statement comes from an identifiable "central conviction," I would call Paul a "coherent" thinker. If he does not relate his various conclusions to one another, he is "unsystematic." Whether he is "convincing" is another problem. Few moderns will be convinced that he "proves" his case against circumcision by quoting Gen. 15:6 and ignoring Gen. 17:9–14, just as few will find his conclusion in Rom. 3:9 to be proved by Rom. 1:18 – 2:29 (even though many commentators, with a deep commitment to believing Paul, write as if his arguments were still convincing). The obvious fallback position is that Paul's basic views are true, even if the arguments in favor of them are not always convincing to moderns. I must leave this, however, to theologians in the strict sense of the word.

Galatians and Romans

Appreciable attention has lately been given to the differences between Galatians and Romans, attention which is based on the quite correct observation that Paul's statements on similar subjects should not be conflated without regard to their particular settings. Hübner and John W. Drane have offered theories of development in which the law plays a substantial part.[15] Thus it is necessary to give separate attention to the relationship between the two letters. This will by no means be a full account, but points will be presented in a summary fashion.

1. Differences in tone and address are to be recognized. Both are written to Christian communities, but Galatians is written in a polemical setting against the views of Christian missionaries who are undermining Paul's work. Romans, on the view of it taken here, is written with other views in mind. but not directly against Paul's opponents within the Christian movement.[16]

2. In both Paul takes the unvarying position that the only way to become a true descendant of Abraham is by faith. Thus the position that righteousness is not by law does not alter. Further, in both he regards faith as the only means of entry for Jew and Gentile, although this view is applied to Jews much more elaborately in Romans than in Galatians, where it appears only in 2:15f. In both letters the status of Jew and Gentile prior to faith is the same, and in both there is an equation between being under the law and "in the flesh,"[17] although again the argument that Jews are "under sin" is much fuller in Romans than in Galatians. Gen. 15:6 (Abraham

was righteoused by faith) is used typologically in both letters, although some of the details of the argument are different.[18] Thus Hübner correctly notes that the reference to 430 years in Gal. 3:17 does not reappear in Romans. In Rom. 4:10 the priority of faith to law is reduced to the interval between Genesis 15 and Genesis 17.[19]

3. In both letters Paul, after asserting that righteousness is not by law, deals with the problem of the purpose and function of the law. It is in his answer to this question that the greatest shifts take place, although the positive connection between the law and sin is continued, at least through Rom. 7:13.

4. When Paul discusses correct behavior, he quotes Lev. 19:18 in both letters (Gal. 5:14; Rom. 13:8–10). In the latter passage Paul also cites four of the ten commandments. It is difficult to assign a reason for the greater explicitness of Romans. It is possible that he had become aware of the fact that some of his statements were subject to being interpreted as leading to antinomianism (Rom. 3:8; 6:1f., 15). This explanation would also account for the explicitly favorable statements about the law in Romans (3:31; 7:7, 12), but it nevertheless remains speculative.[20]

5. Hübner has argued that in Galatians observance of the law is *completely* excluded, while in Romans it is not. On his reading of Galatians, he has to consider it remarkable that Paul did not view the Jerusalem Jewish Christians who followed the law as necessarily lacking faith.[21] Similarly, he thinks that Paul's attribution of some positive value to circumcision in Romans reflects a development in his thought.[22] It should be noted, however, that important aspects of the law are regarded as optional in both letters: Gal. 6:15 (which Hübner does not cite) states that in and of itself circumcision is indifferent, and this is the position taken on Sabbath and food laws in Rom. 14:1–6.

In general, then, Hübner's contrast between the two letters seems too sweeping.[23] As Räisänen puts it, "several of the contradictions in Paul's thought are already seen in *Galatians*, and most are still there in *Romans*."[24]

The Origin of Paul's Thought
About the Law

In discussing the adequacy of the view that the law is always the same in Paul, but that the status of the person whom it encounters changes, I argued in part from what I consider to be the sequence of Paul's thought: If Paul's thought is anchored in the distinction of Rom. 8:3–4, I cannot understand how he could have come to say the things about the law which he says in Galatians, particularly in the section which deals with the function of the law in God's plan (Gal. 3:22, 24: the law was given in order to enslave so that salvation would be by faith in Christ). I can, however, understand the reverse development.

Although comments have been made about them along the way, it will be useful to give separate consideration to two difficult and interrelated problems: the sequence of Paul's thought and its source or sources. These are areas to which we obviously have no direct access, and attempts to penetrate them are hindered by a factor to which we referred in the introduction, the possible distinction between the reasons for which Paul held a view and the arguments which he adduced in its favor.

In seeking the source of Paul's thought about the law principal interest has always attached to his negative statements, particularly that obeying it does not lead to righteousness and that Christians are freed from it, since the law, along with sin and the flesh, is part of the old order to which Christians die. How did Paul come to this negative judgment? Two principal explanations have fixed on the law itself. Either it is impossible to fulfill or obeying it leads to boasting, or both.

There are two arguments against these explanations. One is simply exegetical. There is no clear instance in which Paul says that the law does not righteous *because* it is impossible to obey, nor in which he finds fault with it because obeying it leads to self-righteousness. Thus I argued above that the focus of the argument in Gal. 3:8–14 is not on the word "all" in 3:10, that Gal. 5:3 does not say that all the law *cannot* be obeyed, and that Rom. 1:18 – 2:29 does not rest on the view that it is impossible to obey the law. Similarly we saw that the discussion of boasting in Rom. 3:27 – 4:5 does not lead to the conclusion that the fault of the law is that it leads to self-righteousness. An argument against legalistic self-righteousness has been found in numerous passages in Romans and elsewhere. It is said that faith excludes the law because it excludes boasting *in one's own merit* (Rom. 3:27); that the Jews erred because they pursued righteousness by *meritorious achievement* (9:32); that "their own righteousness" is the righteousness of *legalistic achievement* (10:3); that when Paul renounced his own righteousness by the law he renounced *achievement which leads to merit* (Phil. 3:9).[25] But the italicized phrases must be added by the commentator. It is more natural to read each passage in a different way.

There is, however, another argument which is even more convincing than the exegetical analysis of individual passages. I have argued elsewhere, and also at numerous points in the present work, that Paul thought from solution to plight rather than from plight to solution.[26] If this be true, it rules out all the positions which find the source of Paul's negative statements about the law within the system of law itself. If the source of Paul's thought about the law was that the law cannot be fulfilled, or that fulfilling it leads to boasting,[27] or that it is weak and unable to produce real righteousness (Rom. 8:3), we would have to assume that his thought sprang from an analysis of the human condition and of the place of the law in the human condition prior to faith. This, however, seems very unlikely.

It is unlikely in part because of the variety of ways in which he states the human plight and the role of the law in that plight. We have seen, for example, that he puts all humanity equally under the law.[28] He can hardly have come to this position by analyzing the human condition, and few parts of his letters are more illogical than those in which he equates the status of Jew and Gentile prior to faith. Thus we observed that in Galatians 3 – 4 he says both that "we" were under the law (3:23) and that "we" were slaves of the *stoicheia* (4:3). This sort of simple equation is explicable as coming from his conviction that everyone equally needs to be saved by faith in Christ, but it is hardly descriptive of the actual condition of Jews and Gentiles prior to faith, as his own distinction between "Gentile sinners" and "Jews" (Gal. 2:15) shows. Similarly the labored attempt to make Jews and Gentiles equally guilty in Rom. 1:18 – 2:29 is best seen as springing from the need to lead up to the conclusion in Rom. 3:9, rather than as the process of thinking which actually produced that conclusion. The conclusion "all are under sin" is not accounted for by his arguments in favor of it, but by the prior conviction that all must have been under sin, since God sent his son to save all equally.

We have also noted time and again that he has diverse accounts of the role of the law in God's plan (our category 2). The very diversity and lack of agreement indicates that no one of these statements can stand as the source of his thought. We see, rather, a struggle to explain why God gave the law, a struggle which is necessitated by his twin convictions that the law does not save and that it must have been part and parcel of God's overall plan.

We move, I think, to the center of Paul's thought and the source of his negative statements about the law when we consider the point at which Christ and the law are antithetical. The clearest and, I think, most revealing passage is Phil. 3:4–11. In commenting on this passage Georg Eichholz has perceptively stated that "the encounter with Christ has for Paul the consequence that Christ becomes *the middle of his theology*, just as previously the Torah must have been the middle of his theology."[29] In Philippians 3 two righteousnesses, one by the law and the other by faith in Jesus Christ,

151

are posed as mutually exclusive alternatives. This sharp either/or is expressed in similar terms in Rom. 10:3, although the more frequent formulation is that righteousness is not by law, but by faith in Christ.

Philippians 3 also directs our attention to Paul's conversion/call as the source of the flat opposition between righteousness by law and righteousness by faith.[30] Paul had one righteousness and gave it up in favor of a better, with the consequence that he viewed the former as not just second best, but as "loss." We should also recall that Paul regarded the revelation of Christ to him to entail his apostleship to the Gentiles (Gal. 1:16). The revelation was not just that Jesus was the Jewish messiah (though Paul doubtless thought that), but that he was appointed to be savior and Lord of the whole universe.[31]

Thus we come to the following train of experience and thought: God revealed his son to Paul and called him to be apostle to the Gentiles. Christ is not only the Jewish messiah, he is savior and Lord of the universe. If salvation is by Christ and is intended for Gentile as well as Jew, it is not by the Jewish law *in any case*, no matter how well it is done, and without regard to one's interior attitude. Salvation is by faith in Christ, and the law does not rest on faith.

It seems fairly simple, with this as the beginning point, to understand how Paul came to hold the various positions which we see in his letters. If righteousness were by the law, Christ's death would not have been necessary. But God sent Christ to save; therefore righteousness is not by law (Gal. 2:21; 3:21). After this absolute rejection of righteousness by the law, and after making an absolute dichotomy between the law and Christ, however, Paul still had to "justify the ways of God to men." He had to explain why God gave the law, and those explanations connect it with sin and lead to his most negative statements about it. But then he also had to offer guidance for behavior.

I think, in other words, that the sequence of themes in Galatians (the law does not lead to righteousness *since* righteousness is by faith; God gave the law in order to lead up to salvation by faith in a negative way; Christians fulfill the law, summarized by Lev. 19:18) shows the way in which Paul actually thought.

We can never exclude with certainty the possibility that Paul was secretly dissatisfied with the law before his conversion/call. If one is to look for secret dissatisfaction, however, it might be better to look to his stance toward the Gentiles than to his possible frustration with his own situation under the law, or to his analysis of the situation of Jews under the law. It is by no means inconceivable that he had native sympathy for the Gentiles and chafed at the Jewish exclusivism which either ignored them or which relegated them to second place in God's plan. We have seen it to be a main theme that Jew and Gentile are on equal footing, both in their situation prior to faith and with regard to the means of entry to the people of God. It may be that this reflects a conscious or unconscious concern with the situation of the Gentiles which antedates his conviction that his mission was to bring them into the eschatological people of God. This, like other attempts to penetrate Paul's precall thought, is entirely speculative. It seems to me, however, a more likely speculation than the one that holds that his analysis of the law as it related to his own people already led him to see that the way of the law was unsatisfactory, either because they were incapable of living up to the demands of the law or because they boasted in their ability to do so.

We have thus far posited as the reason for Paul's virtual equation of the law with the flesh, sin, and death his "black-and-white thinking": since the law does not save, it becomes not just second best, but is ranged on the side of the forces of evil. Yet we should also be open to the possibility that this extreme reversal was at least partially conditioned by Hellenistic pessimism, by the *Zeitgeist* which saw humans as enslaved by powers over which they had little or no control.[32]

There is, however, one point at which his native precall convictions do unmistakably come to the fore. It is often asked how Paul could have said that he upholds the law, or that the whole law should be fulfilled, after he said that no one is righteoused by works of law. There seems to be a good reason for this in Paul's own biography. As a Jew, he regarded the law as embodying the will of God and its precepts as self-evidently true except when he had cause to renounce them. It is thus natural that when he dealt with behavior he had recourse to the law. This may have led to logical inconsistencies, but humanly it is quite understandable.

There is a final question in considering the source of Paul's thought: why did he draw conclusions which others in his situation, or in a similar situation, did not? He was by no means the only Jew who thought that Jesus was the messiah, or that his death and resurrection had saving significance,[33] or that God had vindicated Jesus although he was cursed by the law; nor was he the only one who thought that, in the last days, Gentiles would join God's people. He was certainly not the only one to read Gen. 15:6. His opponents in Galatia doubtless did not deny that those in "the Israel of God" should have faith in Christ; they simply did not grant that faith in Christ excluded acceptance of the law. Gentiles, in their view, should accept Jesus and also be circumcised and accept the law. This will, as far as I see, always remain a question; there are only speculative answers. Perhaps Paul saw the unfairness involved in asking Gentiles to accept the law: they would remain second-class citizens. Or perhaps he thought more radically than, for example, Peter: if Gentiles are to be brought in it means that *all* distinctions must be obliterated. This sort of radicalness would agree with his tendency toward extremes. In any case, we must recognize the peculiarity of Paul's thought.

This means that the positions which he takes on the law are not *simply* the logical consequence of his new convictions. In arguing that his statements about the law spring from one or more of his central convictions, not from analytical thought about the law itself, I do not mean to argue that his conclusions were necessitated by his convictions in a purely logical way.[34] It is very likely that other Jewish Christians shared his principal convictions — that one should have faith in Christ, that the end was near, and that it was time for Gentiles to join the people of God — without drawing the conclusions about the law which Paul drew.[35] Paul's position remains unique, as far as we know, to him.

Paul's Critique of Judaism and of Legalism in General

I argued above that Paul's criticism of Judaism, which is traditionally and correctly sought, at least in part, in his statements about the law, hinges on two points: christology and election.[36] Non-Christian Jews are faulted in such passages as Rom. 9:30 — 10:13 for failure to have faith in Christ. In other passages, such as Rom. 3:27, it is the view that Jews have favored status which is under attack, and the argument about who is a true descendant of Abraham (Galatians 3; Romans 4; cf. 9:6, "For not all who are descended from Israel belong to Israel") implies a rejection of the Jewish view of election. These are the same points of criticism which I attributed to Paul in *Paul and Palestinian Judaism*, pp. 550–52. They are repeated here in part because so many readers seem to have misunderstood the argument. In particular, Professor W. D. Davies has taken the statement that Paul faulted Judaism for not being Christianity to mean that I wish to make a complete chasm between Judaism and Christianity,[37] and others have taken me to mean that Paul had no substantial critique of his native faith.[38]

What must be noted in Paul's critique of Judaism is that it is a critique of his native religion as such, and it is a critique which covers what is Judaism by definition. He does not say that the law was unable to be fulfilled by some and is therefore inadequate as a means to righteousness; nor does he say that fulfilling it leads to self-righteousness on the part of a few. As far as I can determine, inability and self-righteousness do not figure at all in his statements about the law (except for the extreme statement of fleshly inability in Rom. 7:14–25). When he criticizes Judaism, he does so in a sweeping manner, and the criticism has two focuses: the lack of faith in Christ and the lack of equality for the Gentiles. Both of these points figure in Rom. 9:30 – 10:13, both are related to his call to be apostle to the Gentiles, and both strike at Judaism as such.

I wish to do more, however, than merely reiterate points previously made. Other scholars have seen that Paul's arguments against the law are largely christological — that point is hardly novel — but have nevertheless maintained that the christological criticism goes hand in hand with a criticism of Jewish legalism. "Legalism" then becomes generalized as the human tendency to self-achievement which true theology must counter. I think that neither of these further steps is justified by strict exegesis of Paul's letters.

We may take Ernst Käsemann's *Commentary on Romans* as offering a good example of both tendencies. In commenting on Rom. 9:30f. Käsemann offers this interpretation: "The point is that the will of God which calls for righteousness cannot be reached in the law, this being misunderstood and made a summons to achievement" (p. 277). The phrase *tēn idian* [*dikaiosynēn*] ("their own righteousness") in Rom. 10:3 means this: "one's own righteousness" which is "oriented to works of pious achievement" (p. 281). He continues by saying that this is "the typically Jewish offense which is grounded in ζῆλος" (zeal) (p. 281).[39] Having said this he proceeds to the correct insight that Paul does not generalize about legalism but "asserts the change in lordship and for this reason argues primarily in terms of christology" (p. 282). But he then proceeds to his own generalization:

> Israel, which regarded even faith as a work of the law, could not reach the goal because only Christ enables us to recognize the true will of God and only the Spirit enables us to fulfill it. The Mosaic Torah comes to an end with Christ because man (*der Mensch*) now renounces his own right in order to grant God his right (p. 283).

The connection between Israel, legalism, and generalized theology continues. Two further examples: on Rom. 10:14–21: "According to vv. 18ff. the guilt [scilicet, of Judaism] consists precisely in refusal of grace" (p. 293); on Rom. 11:6: "Not sins, but pious works prevent Judaism from obtaining the salvation held out to it, and keep it in bondage" (p. 302).

I regard most of the quoted material to be more or less blatant eisegesis,[40] even if eisegesis which rests on long and venerated (perhaps too venerated) tradition. The finding that Paul criticized his kinsmen for zeal for good works

155

is simply bewildering. In Paul's principal discussions of the fault of the Jews he charges that they did not do the law well enough (Rom. 2:17) and that doing the law does not lead to real righteousness because that comes by faith in Christ (Rom. 10:3f.), but not that their fault consisted in their zeal for pious works.

The point of this section of the conclusion, however, is to focus on two aspects of Käsemann's position; for they, I think, reveal why this position has endured so long and is still found persuasive by many.

One aspect is the direct connection between christology and the renunciation of self-striving. This is seen in the long quotation above from p. 283. "Only Christ enables us to recognize the true will of God. . . ." That is fair enough as a statement of Paul's view, but it is immediately interpreted by saying that "man" (*der Mensch*, humanity as such) "renounces his own right." The prime point of accepting Christ becomes the renunciation of achievement, and those who deny Christ are necessarily guilty of self-assertion. Once this interpretation is made, it is easy enough to read Paul's *christological objections* to Judaism as if they were directed against Jewish *self-righteousness*. Thus the correct exegetical perception that Paul *opposed Judaism* and that he *argued christologically* becomes — without argument or exegetical demonstration, but on the ground of basic theological assumptions — an assertion that he opposed *the self-righteousness which is typical of Judaism*. This step has doubtless been facilitated by more than a century of reading Jewish literature as evidencing self-righteousness. But the supposed objection to Jewish self-righteousness is as absent from Paul's letters as self-righteousness itself is from Jewish literature.

It will be helpful to consider what a discussion of attitude would have looked like if Paul had offered one. Rabbinic literature is replete with discussions of "directing the heart" when one does what the law requires (see *PPJ*, pp. 107-9). The concern that, in doing the law, one do so with the right attitude of devotion to God was doubtless present in the synagogues of the first century, and it is reflected in Rom. 2.28f. The teachers of the law were doubtless aware that obedience could become external only, and they warned against that danger. We may reasonably think that some Jews performed the law with the wrong attitude. But it is the rabbis who are concerned with this problem, not Paul. Paul, then, had ready at hand a criticism of externality and thus of legalism on the part of *some*. What is remarkable is that it is not employed, except in his use of traditional material in Romans 2. He provides no analysis of the defects from which individual Jews might suffer. His criticism of his native religion has nothing to do with whether or not some within it are inclined towards self-righteousness, much less does he charge Judaism as such with that fault.

The second aspect of Käsemann's treatment on which I wish to comment is the way in which the supposed criticism of Judaism is individualized and generalized. Thus one notes that Paul's complaint that most Jews reject the preaching of Christ (Rom. 10:18–21) is generalized to mean that they reject *grace* (Käsemann, p. 293, quoted above). But surely non-Christian Jews saw themselves as remaining in the grace of God by remaining loyal to the covenant. Only if one simply equates "the word of Christ" (10:17) with grace can one say that they rejected grace. Paul himself very likely made such a connection, and thus *he* can accuse his compatriots of rejecting the Christian gospel (Rom. 10:14–21) and of rejecting grace (11:6; cf. 6:14f.). But for Paul the burden of the criticism falls on the rejection of Christ; it is that which proves that Jews seek their own righteousness. There is no charge that Judaism historically inculcates what we now call self-righteousness; nor is there a charge that individual Jews harbored that attitude. For a modern theologian to say that *in fact* the fault of the Jews was that they were self-righteous he must not only share Paul's assumption that rejection of Christ *is* rejection of grace, he must then add the assumption that Jews rejected grace *because* they preferred righteousness by merit. This not only individualizes and generalizes the discussion of the failure of the Jews in Romans 9 – 11, it makes a historicizing leap: individual Jews rejected grace as such and were thus in fact guilty of zeal for self-righteousness (see the quotation above from Käsemann, p. 281). This pulls Paul's discussion out of its setting in several ways. Romans 9 – 11 is anchored in the problem of Jewish rejection of the Christian gospel in light of God's intention to save them, but to do so on the basis of faith in Christ; Jewish fault is seen by Paul as a *collective* one which consists in the rejection of the Christian message (see especially 10:18–21), not in individual self-righteousness.

Generalization is also seen in the way in which Käsemann can shift to the first person ("us") and can speak of "der Mensch."[41] This mode of generalizing is typical of the school to which Käsemann belongs, but it is by no means limited to it. One of the frankest instances of generalizing, which in more disguised fashion pervades many of the more technical discussions of the law in Paul, is seen in Leander Keck's popular book on Paul:[42]

Nomos means a way of life, a way of relating to God by meeting obligation. Although in the first instance "law" refers to the Scripture, particularly the Pentateuch, Paul's reference to the *stoicheia* shows that *nomos* is not restricted to the law of Moses. What interests Paul is the "lawness of law," whatever

157

the particular law or obligation might be. Paul thinks phenomenologically about law. This is why he shows no concern to salvage law by distinguishing one law from another, the cultic from the moral law (e.g. the Decalogue). If one lives by law, by meeting requirements, it does not matter which law is being obeyed. To live by law, to meet obligations in order to relate rightly to God (to do "the works of the law"), is not to live by sheer trust in God's grace (p. 86).

I disagree with all this: I cannot see that Paul used *nomos* to refer to the *stoicheia;* we have repeatedly seen that Paul did not think phenomenologically about law,[43] and even the relatively minor point that the Decalogue is an example of moral law is incorrect. But what is principally to be countered here is the view that Paul's objection to the law is an objection to "a way of life, a way of relating to God." This interpretation leads Keck to an extraordinary interpretation of Paul's position in the controversy with the Galatians: "meeting requirements and sheer trust in God do not mix" (p. 87). The generalizing equation, in which "the requirement to be circumcised and accept the Mosaic law in order to enter the people of God" (my interpretation of the issue at stake in Galatia) becomes "meeting requirements" (Keck's interpretation), leads Keck to a statement which he must immediately retract. After saying that "meeting requirements" and "trust" do not mix, he has to write, "trust/faith does not abrogate obligation categorically" (p. 89).

We must be clear about where the fault of the generalization lies. Keck argues that the question of circumcision in Galatians is paradigmatic; whatever one would offer as a supplementary requirement to faith would be equally wrong (p. 88). That is a fair enough generalization if one limits the topic to the basic membership requirement. Paul would doubtless have opposed any other form of initiation as vigorously as he did circumcision. Keck's statement may, however, easily lead to a false conception of the position taken by the missionaries who opposed Paul: it may sound as if the other Jewish Christians opposed faith in Christ or even the general view that one should trust God. They almost certainly did not see their position as meaning that. Nor did Paul accuse them of holding such a position. Generalizing more clearly goes astray when Keck—along with many others—says that what was at stake was a way of relating to God, a way of life. Both Paul and Judaism (and, I presume, the opposing missionaries in Galatia) thought that "doing" was *integral* to life in the in-group and *required* of members. That is why Keck must correct his statement that meeting requirements and faith do not mix: all the parties to the debate were in favor of "doing" and of requirements, Paul no less than anyone else.

They all thought that "faith" and "requirements" mix perfectly well. The question was what requirements would be demanded and *what significance* was attached to them. The specific requirement in view was circumcision — a practice that in and of itself, Paul held, did not matter (Gal. 6:15; 1 Cor. 7:19). The significance attached to it, however, was that accepting it meant accepting the Mosaic law as essential for membership in the people of God. Paul's objection was not that the Mosaic law requires "doing," but that if acceptance of the Mosaic law were the crucial point for membership in God's people, the descendants of Abraham, Christ would have died in vain (Gal. 2:21).

The dispute in Galatians is not about "doing" as such. Neither of the opposing factions saw the requirement of "doing" to be a denial of faith. When Paul makes requirements of his converts, he does not think that he has denied faith, and there is no reason to think that Jewish Christians who specified different requirements denied faith. The supposed conflict between "doing" as such and "faith" as such is simply not present in Galatians. What was at stake was not a way of life summarized by the word "trust" versus a mode of life summarized by "requirements," but whether or not the requirement for membership in the Israel of God would result in there being "neither Jew nor Greek."

In saying that the debate between "faith" and "law" is a debate about an entry requirement, I do not mean to imply that, for Paul, faith was required only at the point of entry to the body of Christ. On the contrary: faith in Christ would always be part of life in him, and trust in God should never waver. His opponents would doubtless have said the same. There was no dispute over the necessity to trust God and have faith in Christ. The dispute was about whether or not one had to be Jewish.

Once the flat opposition in Paul's letters between "faith" and "law" is seen to have to do with the central membership requirement, rather than with a whole way of life, there will be less embarrassment about giving full weight to the positive statements which Paul makes about the law, about being blameless, and about punishment for transgression and reward for obedience. Perhaps, too, when faith is seen as not being the opposite of "good works" in and of themselves, there will be less pressure to think that Paul accused Judaism *of* good works — of legalism and reliance on self-achievement.

One last clarification is necessary. The debate about the law in Galatians 3 and Romans 3 — 4 is primarily (in Galatians exclusively) an inner-Christian one. Paul's criticism of Judaism is implied in Galatians 3, in the argument about who are the true descendants of Abraham, and becomes clearer in Romans 3 — 4, where Jewish privilege in claiming that status is repeatedly denied. Paul focuses on Judaism as such in Romans 9 — 11; 2 Corinthians 3 and Philippians 3. When he does so, his criticism is not that Jews were guilty of zeal for good works — to which, we have repeatedly observed, Paul had no objection. The criticism is twofold: that Jews who pursued righteousness by the law did not have faith in Christ and that they relied on the election of Israel "according to the flesh." We have said enough about christology and should now note that, in denying the efficacy of the election, Paul strikes at something which is crucial to Judaism. One need not be or become Jewish to be a descendant of Abraham; God is God of Jew and Gentile alike (Rom. 3:29), which means not especially of Israel;[44] he shows no partiality (Rom. 2:11); despite native privileges (Rom. 3:2; 9:4f.), Israel has no true advantage before God (Rom. 3:9); there is no distinction between Jew and Greek (Rom. 3:22; 10:12). Before we wax too smug about this denial of Jewish exclusivism and privilege, it must be recalled, as Nils A. Dahl has pointed out, that Paul is no less particularistic.[45] He excludes from the "descendants of Abraham" Jews who do not have faith in Christ (as I shall argue in the next chapter). He opposes Jewish particularism, but introduces another kind. His Christian opponents, as well as non-Christian Jews, would doubtless have agreed that God intended to be God of all humanity, but they would have seen that intention as being limited by human willingness to consent to *their* membership requirements: circumcision and acceptance of the law.[46] That may be narrower in its effect than Paul's requirement of faith in Christ, but the difference is not a black-and-white one between universalism and particularism.[47]

Law and Scripture

Having written this many pages about the law, I do not wish to leave entirely out of account one of the more interesting — if also more frustrating — potential subtopics, the relationship of "the law" to "the Scripture" and to the will of God. The basic observation in dealing with law and Scripture in Paul has always been that Paul can cite the law against itself.[48] Most obviously, he cites the Bible to prove that circumcision is not required in order to be a descendant of Abraham. In this case he does not quote the passage which definitely connects circumcision with membership in the family of Abraham (Gen. 17:9–14), nor the actual commandment ("on the eighth day the flesh of his foreskin shall be circumcised," Lev. 12:3), but he can hardly have been ignorant of them. He can also find two different righteousnesses in Scripture and say that one of them (by implication, not

160

the other) saves (Rom. 10:5–10). He also manages to have the law condemn those who are under it (Gal. 3:10, quoting Deut. 27:26).

This has naturally led to a search for a distinction in Paul's own mind between the law (or the aspect or part of it) with which he agrees and the law (or aspect or part) with which he disagrees. There have been numerous proposals. A. T. Hanson, for example, sought a distinction between the covenant on Sinai, which was outdated in Paul's view, and the rest. The stone tablets (2 Cor. 3:3) are part of the outdated Sinai covenant.[49] One objection to this division leaps to the eye: Rom. 13:8–10 commends obedience to four of the ten commandments. A few minutes with the concordance will also reveal that Paul makes no terminological distinction between what he favors and what he rejects: he uses both *nomos* (law) and *graphē* (Scripture), but not in a way which leads to a clear distinction. Thus *nomos* sometimes means "Scripture" (Rom. 3:19; 7:1; 1 Cor. 14:21).[50] I shall here cut short a potentially long and detailed discussion: there is no explicit distinction which indicates that he had sorted out in a systematic way the true from the untrue parts or aspects, or the fulfilled parts (Rom. 8:4) from the parts or aspects which are surpassed or being rendered inoperative (2 Cor. 3:10f.).[51]

It is not unheard of in the history of Jewish exegesis to cite one scriptural passage against another, or even to subvert without acknowledgement the clear meaning of the text. The device developed in rabbinism of bringing a third passage to decide between or clarify two others is well known, as is the quotation (in the Covenant of Damascus) of Gen. 1:27 against Deut. 24:1 (CD 4:20f.). Rabbi Eleazar got around the obvious meaning of Exod. 20:7 (the Lord will not hold guiltless the one who takes his name in vain) by appealing to Exod. 34:7 as justification for revising the reading of 20:7, so that it says, in effect, that God will hold guiltless the one who repents. In the four means of atonement attributed to Rabbi Ishmael the same commandment is circumvented without acknowledgement. The rabbi simply says that, taken together, repentance, the Day of Atonement, suffering, and death will atone for transgression of a commandment for which the Bible itself says there is no atonement.[52]

Paul's treatment of the Bible differs partly in degree, partly in kind. This would be clear if all we had were Rom. 14:1–6. Two large categories of law — those governing food and days — are dismissed as optional. The matter of degree is sufficiently obvious, and equally obvious is the offense to the normal Jewish view of the Bible. I think that the type of dismissal might stick in the normal Jewish throat — assuming that there was such a thing —

even more. "Say anything!" my hypothetical Jew would cry, "Say that Ezekiel corrected Deuteronomy, say that true obedience is inward and not external, say that in the Diaspora many laws are irrelevant; but *don't* say that when God gave the law he didn't *care* whether or not it would be obeyed!"

Years ago George Foot Moore posed the problem of how a Jew of Paul's antecedents could by implication deny the central Jewish doctrine of repentance and forgiveness as the way to salvation.[53] The question has proved hard to answer, although I think that there is an answer.[54] But what about the present problem? How could a Jew of Paul's antecedents, while still viewing Scripture as Scripture, and quoting it to show God's plan and intention, say that some of its commandments are optional?

Though I wince at the possible anachronism of the phrase, I think that Paul had found a canon within the canon. He did not formulate it, and I doubt that he consciously reflected on it. We perceive it in operation. It is this: those parts of the Scripture which mention faith, righteousness, Gentiles, and love are in, as are those which accuse Israel of disobedience; parts which disagree with this interior canon, particularly the point about the Gentiles, whether explicitly or by implication, do not count.

Behind this reading of the Scripture we see the great convictions which determined Paul's career: God has appointed Christ for the salvation of the world, for the salvation of all without distinction. God always intended this — he proclaimed it in advance to Abraham — and his will is uniform and stated in Holy Writ. That salvation is being accomplished now, in the last days, with himself, Paul, unworthy though he is, as the apostle whose task is to bring in the Gentiles.

NOTES

1. We may note in this connection that the law can be limited to the past (e.g. Gal. 3:24f.) and can also be considered as continuing, though surpassed (2 Cor. 3:14f.). Note Heikki Räisänen's comment: "Thus we find two conflicting lines of thought in Paul's theology of the law. Paul asserts both the abolishment of the law and also its permanently normative character. Throughout he refrains from making any distinctions within the law." "Paul thus wants to have his cake and eat it. Depending on the situation, he asserts, as it were, now the *katalysai*, now the *plērosai* of Matt. 5:17" (*Paul and the Law* [forthcoming publication]).

2. So especially Hans Hübner, *Das Gesetz bei Paulus* (Göttingen: Vandenhoeck & Ruprecht, 1980).

3. This is the way in which Hübner explains the various statements *within* Romans. See *Gesetz*, pp. 118–29. See above, chapter 3 n. 14.

CONCLUSION

4. See Heikki Räisänen's critical analysis of the ways of dealing with Paul's diverse statements, "Paul's Theological Difficulties with the Law," in *Studia Biblica 1978*, vol. 3 (Sheffield: JSOT Press, 1980), pp. 302–4.

5. Ferdinand Hahn, "Das Gesetzesverständnis im Römer- und Galaterbrief," *ZNW* 67 (1976–77): 41, 49, 57, 60f.

6. Wolfgang Schrage, *Die konkreten Einzelgebote in der paulinischen Paränese* (Gütersloh: Gerd Mohn, 1961), p. 232.

7. Peter von der Osten-Sacken, "Das paulinische Verständnis des Gesetzes im Spannungsfeld von Eschatologie und Geschichte," *EvTh* 37 (1977): 568.

8. Schrage, *Einzelgebote*, pp. 76f.; Hübner, *Gesetz*, pp. 118f.; cf. Ernst Käsemann, *Commentary on Romans* (Grand Rapids: Wm. B. Eerdmans, 1980), p. 94.

9. See above, pp. 32–35, on Rom. 3:27 – 4:4, where the question of merit is often found.

10. Above, Introduction n. 26; pp. 32–43; pp. 98f., esp. n. 14.

11. Paul Meyer, "Romans 10:4 and the End of the Law," in *The Divine Helmsman* (New York: KTAV, 1980), pp. 59–78. We should especially note, against Meyer, that Rom. 10:3 says that Jews were ignorant of and did not submit to *another* righteousness than that which comes by law, not that they failed to obey the law (Meyer, pp. 69–71). The latter is the argument of 7:14–25, but not of 10:3f.

12. This is basically in agreement with the way J. Christiaan Beker (*Paul the Apostle* [Philadelphia; Fortress Press, 1980]) views Paul's thought, but he seems not to employ his own hermeneutical key in discussing the law. In different parts of his book he offers different interpretations of Paul's rejection of the law, but there is little explanation of how they are to be related. See, for example, pp. 186f.; 237; 240; 246. His statement of "coherence" (p. 243) does not take into account one of his explanations of Paul's motive in Galatians 3, the Lordship of Christ for the Gentiles (p. 240).

13. E. P. Sanders, *Paul and Palestinian Judaism* (Philadelphia: Fortress Press, 1980), p. 518 (hereafter cited as *PPJ*).

14. Räisänen, "Paul's Theological Difficulties," p. 314.

15. Hübner, *Gesetz*; John W. Drane, *Paul, Libertine or Legalist?* (London: SPCK, 1975). The position taken here is much closer to that of Beker, *Paul the Apostle*, pp. 94–108.

16. Cf. Wilhelm Wuellner, "Toposforschung und Torahinterpretation bei Paulus und Jesus," *NTS* 24 (1978): 463–83; Paul Wernle, *Der Christ und die Sünde bei Paulus* (Freiburg: J. C. B. Mohr [Paul Siebeck], 1897), pp. 91f.

17. See Gal. 5:16–18, 4:21–31; Rom. 7:1–4. George Howard (*Crisis in Galatia* [New York: Cambridge University Press, 1979], p. 13; cf. p. 86 n. 47) misses the degree to which law and flesh are equated in Galatians.

18. Ulrich Luz (*Das Geschichtsverständnis des Paulus* [Munich: Chr. Kaiser, 1968], p. 184) argues that Romans 4 has a "phenomenological" orientation, Galatians 3 a "historical" one. In any case, Abraham is a typological proof that righteousness is by faith.

19. Hübner, *Gesetz*, p. 45.

20. An even more speculative possibility is that Paul became aware of the need to cite specific laws because of the Corinthian difficulties. The relative dating of

Galatians and the Corinthian correspondence is uncertain and doubtless will remain so. Hübner, however, argues that Galatians precedes the Corinthian correspondence (*Gesetz*, p. 91 and p. 157 n. 47). For the difficulty, see Udo Borse, *Der Standort des Galaterbriefes* (Bonn: Hanstein, 1972); Gerd Lüdemann, *Paulus, der Heidenapostel*, vol. 1 (Göttingen: Vandenhoeck & Ruprecht, 1980), pp. 122–36.

21. Hübner, *Gesetz*, p. 25.

22. Hübner, *Gesetz*, pp. 46f.

23. Cf. Jack Suggs, "'The Word is Near You': Romans 10:6–10 within the Purpose of the Letter," in *Christian History and Interpretation* (New York: Cambridge University Press, 1967), p. 298: In Romans Paul makes his position, which has not altered, "as palatable as possible."

24. Räisänen, "Theological Difficulties," p. 302.

25. Käsemann's commentary on Romans constitutes a thorough reading of that letter, and by implication of Paul's theology, in terms of an attack on "achievement" (*Leistung*). Thus, for example, he holds that the Jews misunderstood the law as a summons to achievement (*Romans*, p. 93). Rom. 3:27 is a criticism of "self-boasting" (*Selbstruhm*) (ibid., p. 102); Rom. 9:30–33 is an attack on the Jewish misunderstanding of the law as a summons to achievement (ibid., p. 277); in Rom. 10:5 Paul says that Moses "demands action understood as achievement" (ibid., p. 284); and so it goes for verse after verse. See the next subsection, on Paul's supposed criticism of legalism.

26. *PPJ*, pp. 442–47; as above, pp. 35f.; 125.

27. Thus Käsemann (*Romans*, pp. 88f.) reasons as follows: *since* authentic obedience is not realized by doing the law, "the service of the law and that of Christ are mutually exclusive."

28. Above, pp. 68f.; 81–83.

29. Georg Eichholz, *Die Theologie des Paulus im Umriss* (Neukirchen-Vluyn: Neukirchener Verlag, 1972), pp. 224f.

30. See Eichholz, ibid., and the next note.

31. Cf. Luz, *Geschichtsverständnis*, pp. 218–20: The Damascus experience must have led Paul to evaluate his former life, especially if from the beginning he was called to preach to Gentiles. There is an excellent discussion in Peter Stuhlmacher's article, "Das Ende des Gesetzes, *ZTK* 67 (1970): 14–39: starting with Paul's conversion he shows that the two dominating forces in Paul's life were "the Jewish law in its Pharisaic interpretation" and "the gospel of Christ" (p. 24). The gospel is primarily christological and this confirms the either/or of Christ or the law (p. 29). From an earlier period we should cite the discussion of Otto Pfleiderer, *Paulinism*, vol. 1, (London: Williams and Norgate, 1887), p. 3. There is a recent account of the relation between Paul's conversion and his insistence that righteousness is not by law by J. G. Gager, "Some Notes on Paul's Conversion," *NTS* 27 (1981): 697–704. Gager's model, however, leads him to say that Paul "play[ed] down the significance of the law" (p. 701). But, as we have seen throughout, he did a good deal more than simply present it as relatively unattractive.

Seyoon Kim (*The Origin of Paul's Gospel* [Tübingen: J. C. B. Mohr (Paul Siebeck), 1981], esp. pp. 269–311) provides a sound discussion with a bibliography. As the alternative to the Damascus experience as the origin of Paul's thought about the law (the view Kim himself favors), he poses the debate with the Jewish Christians

CONCLUSION

in Galatia. It would seem that these are not truly alternative possibilities for the ultimate source of Paul's thought about the law. The day he took up his mission to the Gentiles, he must have made some decisions about the law, and his call to be apostle to the Gentiles he saw as having clear application to the law. The formulation "righteoused by faith and not by law," however, first meets us in Galatians, and that particular formula and the arguments which support it could well have originated in the Galatian conflict.

32. Peter Brown, writing of a slightly later period, says this: "To sin was no longer merely to err: it was to allow oneself to be overcome by unseen forces. To err was not to be mistaken: it was to be unconsciously manipulated by some invisible malign power." (*The World of Late Antiquity* [New York: Harcourt Brace Jovanovich, 1971], pp. 53f.)

33. Cf. Peter Stuhlmacher, "Das Gesetz als Thema biblischer Theologie," *ZTK* 75 (1978): 267.

34. Gal. 2:21 seems to indicate that Paul himself saw his negative conclusions about the law to be required by the death of Christ. Similarly he depicted Peter's willingness to preserve distinctions between Jews and Gentiles as hypocrisy (Gal. 2:11–14), which implies that he regarded his own position as the only possible one. The present point is that others did not see it this way. For the point that Paul saw his position as logically necessitated by faith in Christ, cf. Karl Hoheisel, *Das antike Judentum in christlicher Sicht* (Wiesbaden: O. Harrassowitz, 1978), p. 182: the recognition that "there is salvation only in faith in Jesus Christ — the pivot of his thought and the motivating power of his life — excludes purely logically every other way to salvation." See also Franz Mussner, "'Christus (ist) des Gesetzes Ende zur Gerechtigkeit für jeden, der glaubt' (Röm. 10, 4)," in *Paulus — Apostat oder Apostel* (Regensburg, 1977), pp. 35f.; Eckert, *Verkündigung*, p. 108.

35. This would also apply to other explanations of the source of Paul's thought, e.g. that he had an apocalyptic view of the law or that Jewish messianism led to the expectation that the law would be altered or abrogated (references in *PPJ*, p. 479 and notes). Other Jewish Christians viewed the events of their time through the lens of eschatology, and they all thought that Jesus was the messiah, without drawing Paul's conclusions about the law. Gager ("Some Notes on Paul's Conversion," p. 702) points to Paul's biography as explaining Paul's position on the law, and this is, as he observes, better than tracing "righteousness" from the Bible through Jewish apocalypticism. Even so, a puzzle remains. Was he the only devout follower of the law who came to have faith in Christ?

36. P. 47 above. Cf. Hoheisel, *Das antike Judentum*, pp. 184–87.

37. W. D. Davies, *Paul and Rabbinic Judaism*, 4th ed. (Philadelphia: Fortress Press, 1980), pp. xxxv–xxxvii.

38. E.g., G. B. Caird, review of *PPJ*, *JTS* 29 (1978): 542. See above, chapter 1, nn. 142 and 148.

Since several colleagues have taken the italicized sentence at the top of p. 552 of *PPJ* (what Paul finds wrong in Judaism is that it is not Christianity) in a way in which it was not intended, I should make two further clarifying remarks: (1) I meant that that is *all* that he found wrong, not that he saw Christianity as being entirely discontinuous with Judaism; (2) the sentence comes at the end of a summary which begins on p. 550, in which Paul's denial of the Jewish covenant (that is, of covenantal nomism) is highlighted, and the concluding sentence should be read in the light of the preceding pages.

39. Cf. Herman Ridderbos, *Paul: An Outline of His Theology* (Grand Rapids: Wm. B. Eerdmans, 1975), p. 139.

40. We should note that in Rom. 11:6 Paul actually does contrast grace with works, so that doing the law can be regarded as a rejection of grace on the assumption that election can be earned. The usual contrast is between faith (in Christ) and doing the law as the correct condition for receiving God's mercy. We should not, however, latch on to Rom. 11:6 as the verse on the basis of which everything else that Paul says about Jews and the law is to be evaluated. The thrust of Rom. 11:1–12 is the election. If the election depends on "works," it is not by the free choice of God, who elects some and hardens others. If works were the correct condition for receiving the election, Paul could not explain why law-abiding Jews who do not have faith in Christ are not in the elect. Even here, that is, the contrast between grace and works does not focus on individual self-righteousness. He is still explaining why Jews who obey the law are, at least temporarily, not in the people of God, as in Rom. 9:30 – 10:13. It is nevertheless striking that here the formulation is not christological, as it is in 9:30 – 10:13, but focuses on "grace" and "works" as if they were religious abstractions. In the light of all his other discussions, however, it is doubtful that we should read Rom. 11:6 in the individualized and generalized terms which are so common in discussions of the law and the fault of the Jews.

41. Cf., for example, Hans Hübner, "Identitätsverlust und paulinische Theologie," *KuD* 24 (1978): 181–93; "Das ganze und das eine Gesetz," *KuD* 21 (1975): 244f.; Heinrich Schlier, *Der Brief an der Galater*, 5th ed. (Göttingen: Vandenhoeck & Ruprecht, 1971), p. 132 ("die Menschen, die das Prinzip ihrer Existenz in den Gebotserfüllungen haben, sind dem Fluch unterworfen"); Franz Mussner, *Der Galaterbrief* (Freiburg: Herder, 1974), p. 223. Compare the criticism in Ulrich Wilckens, *Rechtfertigung als Freiheit: Paulusstudien* (Neukirchen-Vluyn, Neukirchener Verlag, 1974), p. 9.

42. Leander Keck, *Paul and his Letters* (Philadelphia: Fortress Press, 1979).

43. In favor of phenomenological thinking about "the lawness of law," at least in Galatians, see Hübner, "Das ganze und das eine Gesetz," p. 242.

44. For the natural Jewish assumption, see *PPJ*, p. 87. The rabbis wrestled with the problem of God's favoritism, but they did not deny it: ibid., pp. 87–101.

45. Nils A. Dahl, "The One God of Jews and Gentiles (Romans 3:29–30)," in *Studies in Paul* (Minneapolis: Augsburg Publishing House, 1977), p. 191.

46. Dahl (ibid.) correctly points out that in Judaism the idea of election – and, I would add, acceptance of election – mediates between universal monotheism and particularism.

47. I leave aside the question of how well Judaism's form of particularism serves humanity. See the discussion by E. E. Urbach, "Self-Isolation or Self-Affirmation in Judaism in the First Three Centuries: Theory and Practice," in *Jewish and Christian Self-Definition*, vol. 2, (Philadelphia: Fortress Press, 1981), pp. 269–98, esp. pp. 269–71 on Baeck and Guttmann.

48. Otto Michel, *Paulus und seine Bibel* (Darmstadt: Wissenschaftliche Buchgesellschaft, 1972), pp. 142, 145. This means, he points out, that the Bible testifies against the Old Testament religion and for the new Christian religion. Cf.

Peter Stuhlmacher, "Theologische Probleme des Römerbriefpräscripts," *EvTh* 27 (1967): 378: "The Old Testment is for Paul a book which in its deepest meaning contradicts the Mosaic law and bears witness to the Gospel." On Paul's continuing to use Scripture (as interpreted by him) as authoritative, see H.-J. van der Minde, *Schrift und Tradition bei Paulus* (Munich: F. Schöningh, 1976).

49. A. T. Hanson, *Studies in Paul's Technique and Theology* (London: SPCK, 1974), pp. 136–45.

50. Beker, *Paul the Apostle*, p. 252.

51. Cf. Räisänen, *Paul and the Law*.

52. Details and passages in *PPJ*, pp. 158–60.

53. George Foot Moore, *Judaism in the First Three Centuries of the Common Era*, vol. 3 (Cambridge, Mass.: Harvard University Press, 1930), p. 151.

54. *PPJ*, pp. 499–501.

PART TWO

PAUL AND THE JEWISH PEOPLE

6

Paul as Apostle of Christ and Member of Israel

Introduction

Now we take up the related questions of Paul's thought about and relationship with his own people. These two topics also involve us in discussing Paul's self-understanding, how he thought of himself, his life, and his work. These questions are as intricate and often as ambiguous as those which appeared in Part One. If the attempt to respond to them takes less space than was spent on the law, it is not because the problems are less momentous or less difficult, but because there are fewer passages and there is wider agreement about them. We shall begin with Paul's conception of the "body of Christ" and its relationship to Israel, then turn to Paul's manner of life and missionary practice, and finally consider the statement that all Israel will be saved (Rom. 11:26).

The Third Race[1]

There is wide agreement on how Paul viewed his work. The single clearest statement, which explains a lot not only about Paul but also about the early Christian movement, is Rom. 15:16: ". . . to be a minister of Christ Jesus unto the Gentiles, serving the Gospel of God as a priest, in order that the offering of the Gentiles might be acceptable, hallowed by the Holy Spirit." The solemn, sacerdotal language,[2] especially the phrase "offering of the Gentiles," points to the setting in which the apostles worked: The reign of God has come, Israel is being established, and the time has arrived for Gentiles to enter the people of God.[3] Most often Paul couches the reason for the financial offering which he is taking up in terms of need (Rom. 15:25–27; 2 Cor. 9:12 and elsewhere), but Rom. 15:16 shows how he, and doubtless the "pillars" in Jerusalem, saw the matter: it betokened the tribute of the Gentiles. This is the case even though "offering of the Gentiles" in Rom. 15:16 refers to the Gentiles themselves.[4] Paul's entire work, both evangelizing and collecting money, had its setting in the expected pilgrimage of the Gentiles to Mount Zion in the last days.[5]

We saw above that not only Peter and the other leading apostles in Jerusalem, but also those whom Paul calls "false brethren," agreed that Gentiles should be persuaded, or at least allowed, to enter the people of God. The issue at stake in Galatians was the condition of their entry: faith in Christ or also acceptance of the Mosaic law. Paul's insistence on "faith alone" for the Gentiles, however, is not what justifies the heading of this section. Peter and James apparently agreed that faith in Jesus Christ was adequate for the Gentiles ("they added nothing," Gal. 2:6). Paul, unlike Acts 15:29, does not say that minimal standards of behavior were also agreed to, but it may be that he and the Jerusalem apostles could have reached a consensus on that matter. A fair part of Part One was taken up with noting how Jewish Paul's views of correct behavior were. At any rate, it is not primarily the fact that Paul's Gentile converts partially, but only partially, observed the Jewish law that allows us to speak of a third race.

The crucial point is that Paul applied the entrance requirement "faith in Jesus Christ" to Jews as well as to Gentiles.[6] Even Peter and Paul, who had lived as righteous Jews, had to do *something else* in order to be members of the people of God; they had to have faith in Christ (Gal. 2:15f.). Paul did not count people who were as Jewish as they could be (such as himself, Phil. 3:4–6) among "the seed of Abraham."

In this, as in other respects, as we shall see, the messianic framework was substantially revised by Paul. Gentiles who enter the people of God do not, after all, in Paul's view, join Israel according to the flesh. It is not the case that Israel is established and that Gentiles are admitted to it on its own terms. The terms change. But moreover the new terms apply also to the chosen people: righteousness is by faith in Jesus Christ and not by works of law whether one is Jewish or Gentile; one is a true descendant of Abraham who belongs to Christ (Gal. 3:29), not otherwise. Paul's view that those who already belong to Israel must still join the new movement stands out in sharper relief when one considers the phrasing of a writer of the Pauline school. In Eph. 2:11 – 22 it sounds as if Gentiles were adopted into Israel according to the flesh: you Gentiles are no longer strangers, but *fellow* citizens (2:19). Paul's own view was that, with regard to access to membership in the people of God, Jew and Gentile were on equal ground and both had to join what was, in effect, a third entity.

We should immediately note a second way in which Paul modified the traditional view of the eschatological pilgrimage of the Gentiles. Gentiles are not subservient. Paul may pay token homage to the view that the Gentiles should come, bringing their wealth and making supplication to

Israel (Isa. 45:14), but his letters show a very energetic denial of Jewish superiority within the eschatological people of God: Rom. 3:9; 3:22, 29; 10:12; Gal. 3:28.

Only once in the extant correspondence does Paul explicitly use tripartite terminology. In 1 Cor. 10:32 he refers to Jews, Greeks, and the Church of God. Yet I do not doubt that he would have been horrified to read that, in claiming that both Jew and Greek had to have faith in Christ, he had made of the Christian movement a third race. In the first place, he viewed the movement of which he was a part as aiming toward a "new creation" which would not be merely one group among others, but which would transcend and replace the old humanity, which consisted of circumcised and uncircumcised, slave and free, and male and female.[7] Yet he knew that not everyone was in fact entering the new creation, and he frequently used bipolar distinctions — descendant of Abraham or not, my people or not my people (Rom. 9:25, quoting Hosea), those who are being changed and those who are perishing (2 Cor. 3:18 — 4:3; cf. Phil. 3:18–20), and the like. Often in the bipolar distinctions it is evident that his thought is informed by the conception of "true Israel," although that phrase does not appear. When he makes use of the conception of true Israel, it is equally clear that he would reject the view that his thought moves in the direction of a third race, since, as we shall see more fully below, he thought that all Israel would be included in true Israel.

That Paul considered the members of the church to be true Israel will not be universally conceded, and so some attention must be given to this point before we return to the question of the church as the third entity. The most debated passage is Gal. 6:16, where the phrase "Israel of God" appears. The RSV translates thus: "Peace and mercy be upon all who walk by this rule, upon the Israel of God." The Jerusalem Bible is even more explicit: "Peace and mercy to all who follow this rule, who form the Israel of God." These translations rely on two exegetical decisions: (1) that the phrase "and mercy," which follows "upon them" in Greek, is to be taken together with "peace," which precedes. (2) The *kai* (usually translated "and") before "Israel of God" is epexegetical, serving to describe "those who follow this rule," rather than to name a second group. The translators of the NEB came to a different conclusion with regard to the phrase "*kai* the Israel of God": "Whoever they are who take this principle for their guide, peace and mercy be upon them, and upon the whole Israel of God." Several scholars have understood "Israel of God" to be a second group. In Ernest de Witt Burton's view the expression applies "not to the Christian community, but to Jews; yet, in view of *tou theou*, not to the whole Jewish nation, but to the pious Israel, the remnant according to the election of grace (Rom. 11:5), including even those who had not seen the truth as Paul saw it. . . ."[8]

Most scholars, however, have viewed the *kai* before "the Israel of God" as epexegetical and thus have read the phrase as referring to "those who walk by this rule" earlier in 6:16 and "the new creation" in 6:15; that is, the phrase refers to Christians.[9] Two arguments seem to me to make this reading overwhelmingly probable. In the first place, as Gerd Lüdemann has pointed out, Gal. 6:16 is part of the postscript, which summarizes the main thrust of the letter.[10] Thus, for example, 6:12–13 recall 2:14, and 6:14 recalls 2:20. The "rule" (6:16) is that neither circumcision nor uncircumcision matters, which is a mild form of the earlier argument that circumcision is not required. Those who had pressed for the circumcision of the Gentiles Paul had earlier anathematized (1:8f.). We can hardly think that he now includes his opponents as receiving the same blessing as those who walk by the rule that circumcision does not matter. Secondly, a large part of the body of Galatians is devoted to the argument that those who have faith in Christ, and only they, are descendants of Abraham (3:6–29). It would not be much of a leap to call Christians the Israel of God.

The second point leads to the conclusion that, even without understanding the phrase "Israel of God" as referring to Christians as such, there is substantial evidence that Paul considered Christians to be "true Israel." The discussion of Abraham in both Galatians 3 and Romans 4 means that those who have faith in Christ, not Jews as such, can, in Paul's view, claim that inheritance. This view is reiterated in Romans 9. Paul first argues on the basis of precedent. It has always been the case, he states, that "not all who are descended from Israel belong to Israel, and not all are children of Abraham because they are his descendants" (9:6f.), and he refers to Isaac and Jacob, both of whom inherited to the *exclusion* of their brothers, to prove the point (9:7–13).[11]

Yet there is an ambiguity. Paul does not deny that non-Christian Jews should bear the title "Israel." In Rom. 9:24 he speaks of "us": "we," he writes, are composed of Jews as well as of Gentiles. "We," then, have not appropriated the title "Jews." But neither does this third group, composed of some of the other two, receive the title "Israel" (apart from Gal. 6:16). In the same chapter of Romans he speaks of the inherited privileges of the "Israelites" (9:4) and of the failure of "Israel" to attain righteousness (9:31). In 9:6 he seems to be headed toward a distinction of two "Israels": those who are descended from Israel and those who belong to Israel, but the terminology is not carried through.

174

It is well known that Paul did not have a title for "us." The term "Christian" had not been coined, and Paul might have rejected it if it had. Throughout Part One, I spoke of Paul's "Christian" convictions and of the "Christian" movement. Many will object to that word as applied to the church in Paul's conception, as to the phrase "a third race." Were Paul here he might be first among them. Yet one may press him. Who, then, are "we" in Rom. 9:24? As far as that goes, who are "we" in 2 Cor. 3:18? Certainly not Israel according to the flesh. They read Moses with the veil unlifted; "we," who have turned to the Lord, read Moses with the veil removed (2 Cor. 3:14–16). In 1 Cor. 12:13 Paul speaks of "us" as being baptized into one body, composed of both Jews and Greeks, but obviously neither Jews nor Greeks as such.[12] Further, in Gal. 1:13 Paul can speak of "his former life in Judaism." Does he not reveal here that there is a sense in which he is no longer fully described by the appellation "Jew" or "Israelite"?

The situation is quite clear, even if the terminology is confusing. Paul thought that those who "turned to the Lord" (2 Cor. 3:16) were the sole inheritors of the promises to Abraham. The way to be a descendant of Abraham is to be "in" the true descendant, Christ (Gal. 3:16, 29). Conceptually, then, those in Christ are "true Israel."[13] But that term is not used by Paul, for he knows that real Israelites, real Jews, are alive, well, and not in Christ. The church does not actually include them. He may propose that the inheritance has passed from those originally called "my people" to those formerly "not my people," but he at least stops short of transferring the actual designation. Thus he has no set collective name for those in Christ, although there are plenty of phrases: "new creation," "body of Christ," and "temple of God" being notable among them.[14] But often he simply uses the emphatic "we."

The Dead Sea Scrolls offer some help in understanding the substantial adoption by Paul of the concept of "true Israel" and the unwillingness to call the members of the new group simply "Israel."[15] The covenanters at Qumran thought that only they were truly obedient to the covenant with Moses, yet they knew that there were other Israelites. They called themselves not "Israel" or "true Israel," but "sons of light" and numerous other descriptive titles. Jews outside the community were "the wicked of Israel" or "the wicked of Ephraim and Manasseh."[16] According to 1QSa the time would come when the rest of the Jews would come over to the sect, and then the title "Israel" would be quite appropriate.[17] The War Scroll also calls the participants in the final war "Israel," but that designation comes after the predicted destruction of the wicked among Israel.[18] "Remnant" or "true Israel" theology originally depended on the physical destruction of those who did not constitute the remnant. In both Qumran and Paul we see that when destruction did not take place there was reluctance to deny to the unconverted the title "Israel" and to appropriate it for a new group or a sub-group.

Thus, although Paul thought of the members of the church as heirs of the promises to Israel, he did not (with one exception) give them the name. The title "Israel of God" would be truly appropriate only when all the physical descendants of Jacob had been accounted for, at the end, when the polar distinction "my people" and "not my people" would cover everyone. Meanwhile, however, we must recognize the extent to which the church constituted, in Paul's view, a third entity, which stood over against both the obdurate part of Israel and unconverted Gentiles.[19]

If conceptually Paul, despite himself, had to make the church a third entity, it is all the more the case that it was a third entity in concrete social reality. That Gentile converts could not fully participate as normal members of the Greco-Roman *oikoumenē* is evident. They could not treat Christianity as one among several religions in which they participated (1 Cor. 10:21), even though their nonparticipation, when it became publicly evident, might be construed as treason.[20] But it is equally clear that meetings of the church were not meetings of the synagogue. Church and synagogue meetings may have had the reading of Scripture in common (1 Cor. 14:26; cf. 2 Cor. 3:14), but the Corinthian correspondence shows that church and synagogue were socially distinct (1 Cor. 5:1–5; 11:17–22; 14:23–36). We see again that Gentiles who entered the people of God did not simply join Israel. There was a separate entrance requirement (faith), a separate entry rite (baptism),[21] and a separate social reality (the church).

We should also note the degree to which it is incorrect to speak of Christianity as a new *religion*.[22] I have thus far spoken of "conversion" as being required of both Jew and Gentile. W. D. Davies, however, has pointed out that if the term implies abandonment (as he takes it to do), it should not be applied to Jews.[23] He further argues that "Paul was not thinking in terms of what we normally call conversion from one religion to another but of the recognition by Jews of the final or true form of their own religion."[24] Paul Meyer has remarked that "Paul nowhere suggests that the way to obedience to God for the Israelite lies in abandoning the Torah."[25] As far as they go, these statements are entirely accurate. In Pauline theory, Jews who enter the Christian movement renounce nothing. They certainly do not, as the Gentiles must, turn to another God (1 Thess. 1:9; cf. 1 Cor. 6:9–11; 12:2). Nor does Paul call on them to cease obeying the law. The points of law which must not be accepted as essential to membership in the church may, if understood differently, be observed: circumcision, days, and food are optional (Gal. 6:15; 1 Cor. 7:19; Rom. 14:1-6). Paul even depicts himself as sometimes living Jewishly (1 Cor. 9:20). Jews are required to renounce neither God nor the law.

Yet in 2 Cor. 3:16, where Paul adapts Exod. 34:34, he alters "when Moses entered before the Lord" to "if someone turns to the Lord."[26] Those who "turn" (*epistrephō*) and have the veil which obscures the true meaning of the law removed must include Jewish Christians, and thus Paul can use the same verb for them as for Gentiles (1 Thess. 1:9).[27] It should also be noted that Paul uses "to win," *kerdainō*, for the mission to both Jews and Gentiles — whether or not 1 Cor. 9:19-23 refers to his own efforts to win Jews. Both Jew and Gentile need to be won in the sense of "converted."[28]

We should also in this connection recall the language of "dying," which appears especially in Rom. 6:1 — 7:6. One of the things to which Christians die is "the law." That is the language of conversion in the sense of abandonment. We know from other passages, especially Rom. 14:1-6, that what Meyer and Davies say is correct, that Paul did not insist that Jews who entered the church start disobeying the law. But in and of itself the language of dying to the old self, symbolized by law and epitomized as sin, in order to live "to God in Christ Jesus" (Rom. 6:11), is the language of conversion. One gives something up in order to accept something else.

I said earlier that in theory Jews who entered the Christian movement, in Paul's view, renounced nothing. His own description of himself as living according to the law around Jews and as "lawless" when around Gentiles (1 Cor. 9:20) would seem to confirm that. That, he says, was his stance as an apostle, "so that [he] could win the more" (9:19). We shall later inquire if that was in fact his behavior as an apostle. We should just now observe that there would be occasions when neither Paul nor any other Jewish Christian could do *both*. If Jewish and Gentile Christians were to eat together, one would have to decide whether to live as a Jew or as a Gentile. Paul might conceivably act one way in Jerusalem and another in Asia Minor and Greece, or one way in the Jewish section of a city and another way in the remainder of it, but even he, artful though he was, could not do both simultaneously. And neither could Peter. When the issue was pressed in Antioch, Peter decided that he had better live like a Jew "in order to win Jews" (I presume that such was his motive), and Paul accused him of not being true to the gospel (Gal. 2:11-14). It is seen in 1 Cor. 11:17-34 that Paul expected all Christians to share meals (presumably the Lord's supper). The Antioch incident would seem to show that, if Jews were present, Paul would expect them not to observe the Jewish dietary laws.

When it came to cases Paul's easy tolerance, which he effortlessly maintained in theory — it is a matter of individual conscience what one eats and whether one observes "days" — could not work. It was not only a matter of individual conscience, it turned out, but of Christian unity, and he judged one form of behavior to be wrong. The wrong form was living according to the law. We can hardly think, with Galatians before us, that in a mixed church Paul would have lived according to the law in order to please and win Jews. Given a direct conflict between living as a Gentile and as a Jew, with no possibility of changing one's practice to suit present company, Paul viewed it as the only behavior in accord with the truth of the gospel to live as a Gentile. Can we still say that Jews were never asked to give anything up? If Paul's view were to be accepted, Jewish Christians could live strictly as Jews only as long as they remained in an unmixed community. In the presence of Gentiles, they should drop those aspects of the law which stand as social barriers. Thus it seems that we must modify somewhat Davies's statement that "In Christ Jews remain Jews and Greeks remain Greeks. Ethnic peculiarities are honoured."[29] That is true as long as ethnic peculiarities did not come into conflict. When they did, the factors which separated Jews from Greeks must be given up by the Jews.[30]

Paul, then, we cannot doubt, thought of the church as the fulfillment of the promises to Abraham. In that sense it was not at all a new religion. Jews who entered the Christian movement did not have to convert in the way Gentiles did: they did not have to renounce their God, nor, at least in theory, observance of the law. Nevertheless in very important ways the church was, in Paul's view and even more in his practice, a third entity. It was not established by admitting Gentiles to Israel according to the flesh (as standard Jewish eschatological expectation would have it), but by admitting all, whether Jew or Greek, into the body of Christ by faith in him. Admission was sealed by baptism, most emphatically not by circumcision and acceptance of the law. The worship of the church was not worship in the synagogue (though quite conceivably some members could have done both). The rules governing behavior were partly Jewish, but not entirely, and thus in this way too Paul's Gentile churches were a third entity. Gentile converts definitely had to separate themselves from important aspects of Greco-Roman life, but they were not Jewish enough to make them socially acceptable to observant Jews, whether Christian or non-Christian. Christian Jews would have to give up aspects of the law if they were to associate with Gentile Christians. Paul's view of the church, supported by his practice, against his own conscious intention, was substantially that it was a third entity, not just because it was composed of both Jew and Greek, but also because it was in important ways neither Jewish nor Greek.

Paul's Missionary Practice

In Rom. 15:16, we have seen, Paul placed his own work within a well-known eschatological scheme in which, in the last days, Gentiles would make pilgrimage to Zion to worship the God of Israel. His own role as minister to the Gentiles was to see to it that the "offering of the Gentiles" was acceptable. Yet most scholars have seen Paul as missionary to both Jew and Gentile, partly on the basis of the depictions of his missionary activity in Acts and partly because of 1 Cor. 9:19–23, where he says of himself that at least some of the time he lived as a Jew "in order to win Jews." Johannes Munck, for example, wrote:

> It is probably true that in Peter's sphere of work this geographical division [Gal. 2:9] was also a religious one. He represented, in fact, the Jerusalem point of view that when Israel was won, the salvation of the Gentiles would be thereby guaranteed. . . . With Paul it was different. He certainly knew (Romans 11) that the salvation of the Gentiles would not be brought about by the conversion of the Jews, but that on the contrary the fullness of the Gentiles would lead to the saving of all Israel. But, as we know from Acts, Paul did not cease to preach in the Jews' synagogues.[31]

Munck cited as evidence, in addition to Acts, principally 1 Cor. 9:20. In Munck's view Paul's mission to the Jews was not very successful. He took with him from the synagogue, as a rule, "at most a few of the proselytes and God-fearing Gentiles," with the consequence that his churches were predominantly Gentile.[32] Munck wavered somewhat on this picture. On a later page in his book on Paul he wrote that the churches were "purely Gentile Christians," "even if a few Jewish Christians were to be found in them here and there."[33] In his companion volume on Romans 9 – 11 he said that

> Both Paul's letters and the picture given of the Pauline churches in Acts show that these churches consist of Gentile Christians. There is no reason to assume, as was formerly done, that the Pauline churches were mixed churches.[34]

Allowing for a few variations in formulation, Munck's view was that Paul attempted to win Jews by preaching in the synagogue, failed to do so, with only a few exceptions, and turned to Gentiles with success.

Davies, in criticizing Hans Dieter Betz's assumption that Galatians was addressed to Gentiles, argued that he should have recognized that the Galatian churches

> were largely made up of proselytes living on the fringe of the synagogue. . . .
> [Betz] has a tendency to ignore or at least to minimize a fundamental fact
> of early Christian, including Pauline, expansion. . . . We refer to the truism
> that it was the Hellenized Jewish communities of the Greco-Roman world
> and their *pro-Jewish* peripheries of God-fearing semiproselytes and proselytes
> who harbored the earliest Christian cells and served as bases of operation for
> Paul and other Christian missionaries. Paul was first an apostle to the Greek-
> *Jewish* communities.[35]

Günther Bornkamm saw 1 Cor. 9:19–23 as "Paul's classical formulation" which governed his missionary activity,[36] and Philipp Vielhauer, discussing the division of labor between Peter and Paul (Gal. 2:9), argued that it does not "contradict Paul's missionary practice of beginning at the synagogue," since it reflects a geographical division.[37]

Scholars have also pointed to the contents of the letters as helping to decide the nature of Paul's missionary activity. Thus H. J. Schoeps took it to be the case that Paul's use of the Bible in arguments points to the fact that the churches contained many native Jews.[38] Davies's view of the matter reveals some ambiguity:

> We have no letters of Paul to Jews or to Jewish Christians but only to largely
> Gentile churches. But these Christian communities were probably composed
> of Jews and Gentiles who had been attached to Judaism through the
> synagogues.[39]

In reviewing Betz, however, Davies puts his view more precisely. Betz's argument is that the form of Galatians is sophisticated by Hellenistic literary standards and points toward an audience of Gauls which was Hellenized and Romanized, and also fairly well educated.[40] Davies, making the same assumption as Betz that the audience can be inferred from the letter, but fixing on the contents rather than the form, argues that Paul's use of Scripture points "to readers not only highly sophisticated but familiar with the Greek translation of the Jewish scriptures and with the niceties, on a simple level at least, of synagogal biblical study."[41] Later he states that "the substance of Galatians in its form demands an audience of former proselytes, God-fearers and Jews."[42]

Almost all the essential points to be considered in determining Paul's missionary activity have now been touched on: (1) the descriptions of Paul's activities; (2) the contents of the letters; (3) the agreement between Peter, James, and Paul. To these we should add Paul's characterizations of his converts. We shall see that the predominant view of Paul's activity is at every point either uncertain or dubious.[43]

The evidence of Acts is itself neither dubious nor uncertain. Paul uniformly went first to the synagogue. That was, says Acts 17:2, "his custom." He would preach there for a while (e.g., for three Sabbaths, according to the same verse), persuading some Jews as well as "pious Greeks" who attended the synagogue (17:4), until he ran into some difficulty (17:5–10). Most scholarly reconstructions depict him as then turning to other Gentiles, although in this particular case Acts says that he had to leave the city. This procedure, we have seen, is generally regarded as historically Paul's own, even when it is acknowledged that the author of Acts presents it schematically.

Scholars who would not consider Acts as a source for Paul's thought or for his activity in other respects (five trips to Jerusalem rather than the three of Galatians) nevertheless regard Acts as reliable for helping to establish Paul's missionary practice. Yet it seems to me that we should apply to the question of Paul's missionary practice the principle established by John Knox for defining his chronology and travels:[44] the primary evidence is Paul's letters. Acts should be disregarded if it is in conflict. If we look simply at Paul's letters quite a different picture emerges.

Paul, in discussing his ministry, speaks exclusively of Gentiles (with the exception of 1 Cor. 9:20).[45] He is apostle to the Gentiles (Rom. 11:13), and he was called in order that he might preach Christ among the Gentiles (Gal. 1:16; cf. 2:2: "the gospel which I preach among the Gentiles"). The agreement between himself, Peter, and James was that he, Paul, would go to the "uncircumcised" or "Gentiles" (Gal. 2:7, 9), not simply to areas outside of Palestine. His task was to win obedience among all the Gentiles (Rom. 1:5), and he could report success: Christ had worked through him to win obedience from the Gentiles (Rom. 15:18). He wished to go to Rome in order that he might "reap some harvest among [the Romans] as well as among the rest of the Gentiles," since he was under obligation to all Gentiles, both Greeks and barbarians (Rom. 1:13f.). He does not say that Jews disrupted his preaching to Jews (as Acts has it), but rather that they hindered him in his efforts to preach to Gentiles (1 Thess. 2:16). Whatever Peter thought of the agreement with Paul, Paul himself appears to have taken it in the ethnic sense.[46] His mission was "to be a minister of Christ Jesus to the Gentiles . . . , so that the offering of the Gentiles would be acceptable" (Rom. 15:16).

The picture does not vary when we consider his characterizations of his converts. It is noteworthy that, of those definitely known to have been won by Paul, not a single one can be identified from his letters as being Jewish. Acts, for example, identifies Crispus as Jewish, but Paul does not (Acts 18:8; 1 Cor. 1:14).[47] Even if one agrees with Acts that Prisca and Aquila were Jewish one should also note that Acts does not explicitly say that they were Paul's converts (Acts 18:2; cf. Rom. 16:3; 1 Cor. 16:19).[48] The missionary couple explicitly said by Paul to be Jewish, Andronicus and Junia, are also said to have been "in Christ before [him]" (Rom. 16:7). That leaves only Herodian (Rom. 16:11); and he can be counted as having been won by Paul only if one assumes that Romans 16 was not sent to Rome, but to one of Paul's own churches, or that several of his converts had moved to Rome. It may be argued that some of the other names in Romans 16 are Jewish, but we must still note that tallying Jews in the Roman congregation results in only questionable evidence for Paul's own missionary activity.

Further, Paul's descriptions of the former lives of his converts do not lend support to the view that they were largely Jews or even proselytes and God-fearers.[49] The Galatians are said formerly to have worshiped "beings which are no gods"(Gal. 4:8). The Corinthians had been heathens who worshiped dumb idols (1 Cor. 12:2; cf. 6:9–11). The Thessalonians had turned to God from idols (1 Thess. 1:9), and it would appear that the Philippians were not circumcised (Phil. 3:2).

Johannes Munck, who recognized the conflicting character of the evidence, viewed the presentation in Acts as accurate with regard to Paul's procedure, but took the contents of the letters as showing that Paul failed in his attempt to win Jews.[50] Munck was, in my view, correct in thinking that the contents of the letters need not reflect the presence of Jews, whether natives or proselytes, in Paul's churches. Paul's quotation of Scripture does not require that his readers themselves be adept at arguing from Scripture. They had only to realize *that* he was quoting an authoritative text, not to be able to appreciate how cleverly he argued, much less to be able to formulate counter arguments. Galatians is the supreme example. Of the extant correspondence written to Paul's own churches (that is, leaving Romans out of account), Galatians depends most heavily on scriptural argumentation. Yet Paul characterizes the Galatian converts as former idolaters (Gal. 4:8). The level of the argument is required, as Munck saw, by the fact that he opposed Judaizers, who themselves doubtless quoted Scripture.[51] His argumentation reveals partly his own education — he argues the way he was taught — and partly the education of his third party opponents ("they," "some," Gal. 1:7; 5:12, etc.), not the education of his Galatian Gentile converts.[52]

What Paul's manner of argument and vocabulary reveal about him on the one hand and his audience on the other probably deserves more attention than it receives. I believe that J. A. T. Robinson speaks for the vast majority: Romans "presupposes a Jewish, Old Testament and rabbinic background and would be unintelligible to those who knew nothing of it."[53] Discussing vocabulary, Walter Bauer entertained the possibility of unintelligibility: When Paul writes of sacrifice, wrath, and righteousness, "it is quite correct to understand his words from the standpoint of Judaism. But what about his public, who have heard these words before, but with different connotations and associations?" He gives some examples and adds: "Sometimes one gets the distinct impression that the Greek must have failed to understand the basic meaning of a New Testament author."[54]

But would Paul really have been unintelligible to an audience largely or entirely composed of people without a Jewish education? It seems that Paul's "basic meaning" is usually clear enough. In Galatians, for example, which is perhaps the hardest letter for a Gentile audience, it is evident that Paul is against circumcision and the law as essential to righteousness and that he appeals to an authoritative text to prove his point. Even the proof-texting in 3:10–12 might have been sufficiently clear, since the necessary terms are on the page before us. It now requires a concordance to comprehend the niceties of Paul's technique, but the main points are stated in a straightforward fashion.

In any case, Paul wrote from the Jewish perspective. We saw in Part One (pp. 81–83) that he put Gentiles "under the law"; that is, he conformed their situation to the Jewish one, rather than vice versa. This might have puzzled them, just as might the Jewish mode of argument, but Paul still seems to have been able to get his main points across.

The attempt to draw inferences about the makeup of the Roman church from the contents of Romans helps us see how thoroughly Gentile Paul's own churches were. On the one hand, the Roman church as a whole is clearly placed within the bounds of the Gentile mission; and thus it is a suitable church for Paul's own ministry, whether performed in person or by letter (Rom. 1:13–15; 15:14–16). The clearest address to readers is 11:13, where Paul speaks to Gentiles. Throughout Romans Paul, as was his habit, wrote from his own Jewish perspective, and Rom. 4:1 (Abraham our forefather according to the flesh) says nothing about the presumed audience. Nevertheless, scholars universally and doubtless correctly conclude that Rome was a mixed church. Not only does Romans 16 (which may or may not have been originally sent to Rome) mention Jews, there are two addresses to Jews, one apparently largely rhetorical, but the other less so (Rom. 2:17; 7:1; in this context the law in 7:1 is to be interpreted as the Jewish law). Moreover, the general argument of the letter, which is so much concerned with the equality of Jew and Gentile, both before and after Christ, shows that Paul is here concerned to address the Jewish situation. This is in considerable measure to be explained by the fact that Paul is thinking about the coming confrontation in Jerusalem, but it may also point toward the fact that Paul envisages some of the Roman Christians as being Jewish. But what is noteworthy is that Romans is unique in the Pauline correspondence in containing so many clues to the presence of Jewish Christians among the readership. The other letters contain no such clues. Thus one should agree with Munck that the contents of the letters to Paul's own churches do not presuppose a Jewish Christian readership.

Munck, then, tried to harmonize Acts and the letters by accepting Acts for determining Paul's efforts and the letters for determining the results. Paul tried to win Jews but won only Gentiles. But this seems unlikely. Paul describes himself, we have seen, as apostle to the Gentiles. But there is a more telling argument. It is not until Romans, probably the last of Paul's surviving letters, that he reflects on the failure of the mission to Israel. It is striking that the charge against the Jews in 1 Thess. 2:14–16 has nothing to do with their rejecting Paul's gospel. Their fault, rather, was opposing Paul's mission to the Gentiles. It is only when the collection is in hand, when he has ready[55] the "offering of the Gentiles" (except for his planned last effort in Spain), and when he is about to travel to Jerusalem that he raises the question of the significance of Israel's refusal of the gospel. The traditional scheme has gone awry. The restoration of Israel has not taken place, and so he revises the scheme, as is well known: God will save the Jews after the Gentiles enter, not before (Rom. 11:13–16). Further, *it is only in this way that he assigns to himself any role in the redemption of Israel.* His successful mission to the Gentiles, which he is prepared to magnify, gives him a role *indirectly* in the salvation of Israel.[56] At least some Jews, seeing the Gentiles enter upon the inheritance promised to them, will be made jealous and thus accept the gospel.

The entirety of Romans is based on the assumption that Paul's mission, which has been a success, has been to the uncircumcised:

> In Christ Jesus, then, I have reason to be proud of my work for God. For I will not venture to speak of anything except what Christ has wrought through me to win obedience from the Gentiles. . . ." (Rom. 15:17f.)

Paul compares his own work favorably to that of the other apostles in 1 Cor. 15:10. Other apostles could pose a threat (2 Corinthians 11), and certainly not all who heard Paul believed (2 Cor. 2:14–16), but he seems to have regarded his own work among the uncircumcised as successful — he and the gospel proceed in triumph (2 Cor. 2:14). But it is in Romans — the very letter in which he reflects on Jewish rejection of the gospel — that he presents his own mission as successful, as being almost complete, and as relating only indirectly to the salvation of the Jews.

In contrast, the mission of Peter and others to the circumcised (Gal. 2:9) had largely failed, and Paul's reflection on and anguish over that failure is expressed precisely when he is about to travel to Jerusalem (Romans 9 — 11), which he considers to be the home of "unbelievers," apparently with relatively few "saints" (Rom. 15:31). Had he spent his own life in an unsuccessful effort to win Jews, one would have expected the Jewish "no" to the gospel to have been registered earlier than Romans and Paul's own feeling of failure to be reflected in Romans.

We see, thus far, a consistent picture: Paul was an apostle to the Gentiles, his mission was a success, the mission to the Jews was relatively unsuccessful, he addresses that failure as a fresh problem for the first time in Romans 9 — 11, he rearranges the eschatological sequence so that it accords with the facts, and only indirectly does he give himself a role in the salvation of Israel. What, then, shall we make of 1 Cor. 9:19–23, where Paul says that some of the time he lived according to the law in order to win Jews? We should first consider the difficulty of accepting those verses as a literal description of Paul's life and work. If taken as such they would mean that, in each city, Paul was Torah-observant for a short period of time, and then stopped observing at least aspects of the law when the first Gentile entered the church. The majority opinion regards Paul as having done just that, despite the intrinsic improbability — almost impossibility — of his having done so.[57] The problem is not the theological one of whether or not Paul was consistent in his stance toward the law.[58] We have seen that Pauline *theory* does not require Jews to abandon the law. Nor is the problem whether or not Paul, as a good missionary, would accommodate himself to different environments. Doubtless he could do so.[59] The problem is the practical one which we noted above: how could he have been a Jew to the Jews and Gentile to the Gentiles *in the same church?*

We may put the matter this way: Paul doubtless observed the laws of *kashrut* when he was in Jerusalem. But where else would he have been in a strictly Jewish environment? Obviously in the Diaspora synagogues. But Paul's purpose in the Diaspora was to win Gentiles, and, on the basis of Gal. 2:11–14, we can be sure that, when with Gentiles, he did not observe the dietary laws. In other words, to consider 1 Cor. 9:19–23 to be literal description of his behavior, we would have to suppose that he observed the law for a token period of time in each new city, intending to give it up as soon as a Gentile was attracted to the gospel, or that he established two different churches and commuted between them, observing the law in one and not in the other. To my knowledge, no one has ever proposed the second of these possibilities as the way in which Paul actually behaved. But is the first any more likely?

It will be helpful to consider another passage in which Paul describes his work in order to gain light on the present problem. In Rom. 15:19 he says that he "completed" (*peplērōkenai*) preaching the gospel from Jerusalem "in a circle" (or "in an arc") to Illyricum. Here he depicts himself as evangelist to a large part of the Mediterranean basin. It is generally acknowledged that the statement is meant representatively. He did not preach the gospel everywhere in that area. But it is also hyperbolic. By his own account in Galatians, he did not preach in Jerusalem, or even in Judea, at least up to the "apostolic conference" (Gal. 1:11–24). He emphasizes that he had a private meeting with Peter and James and was not known by sight to the churches in Judea (1:19, 22). But he also did not preach on his second trip to Jerusalem, where it was agreed that he would go to the uncircumcised (Gal. 2:7–9). That the division of labor was ethnographic rather than geographic is made probable by the terms used — the circumcised and the uncircumcised.[60] But whether it was geographic or ethnographic, it is highly unlikely that Paul preached in Jerusalem. It is also probable that he did not preach in Illyricum, although the phrase may mean only "as far as Illyricum," that is, Macedonia.[61] Rom. 15:19, then, is a hyperbolic account of Paul's missionary work.

I think that the best reading of 1 Cor. 9:19–23 is that it is also hyperbolic. In the two statements taken together, Paul depicts himself as apostle to everyone in the Mediterranean area. One can understand that he could sometimes think of himself in that way, and even sympathize with the breadth of his view, without thinking that the two statements are literally true. It is, of course, true that Paul sometimes "lived as a Jew" — when he went to Jerusalem, where he would have had to exert himself in order not to do so. If he were asked, he might justify the phrase "in order to win Jews" as meaning "so as not to give unnecessary offence" (see 1 Cor. 10:32). But I doubt that in each city where he worked he switched back and forth in the way that would have been required if 1 Cor. 9:19–23 were a literal description of his practice. In all probability, when he entered each city, he went to Gentiles, he preached to them with some success, and he lived like a Gentile. The evidence of all the other comments which Paul makes about his work and his churches seems to be too consistent for it to be completely reversed by 1 Cor. 9:20, which, especially in light of Rom. 15:19, is better read as hyperbole.

There is, however, a substantial remaining problem. Although some other scholars have seen the discrepancy between Paul's accounts of his work (expressed or implied) and those of Acts,[62] Walther Schmithals is to be credited with coming up with a comprehensive scheme.[63] It is as follows: Stephen preached a gospel which required Jews to abandon the law; it was this gospel to which Paul converted.[64] At the Jerusalem conference Paul agreed to stop preaching the Torah-free gospel to Jews and to confine his activities to Gentiles, since it was the conversion of Jews to such a gospel which led to persecution. The conversion of Gentiles to a Torah-less Christianity would not have been a matter of concern to Jews.[65] Following the Jerusalem agreement, Paul and Peter conducted separate missions, often, perhaps, in the same locations, to Gentiles and Jews respectively.[66]

I do not cite Schmithals's position in order to agree with it. On the contrary, I think that the evidence is entirely against attributing to Paul a gospel which required Jews not to obey the law.[67] Schmithals has, however, tried to take account of most of the problems involved in understanding early Christian missionary activity.[68] The point which requires attention here is the last: what about the Jews in Paul's cities? If he did not preach to them, who did? Bornkamm has noted the problem and used it to attempt to reestablish the traditional view of Paul's work:

> There is therefore not the slightest reason to contest in a wholesale manner the picture, drawn by Acts (admitting that it is heavily schematized), which shows Paul (a) as a rule using the synagogues as a base of operation for his mission and (b) seeking to remain within the realm of the synagogue, until a final conflict rendered that impossible. This view has recently been challenged by W. Schmithals. Calling attention to the agreement of the Apostolic Council, "that we should go to the Gentiles and they to the circumcised" (Gal. 2:9), he advanced the thesis that Paul consistently renounced any mission to the Jews. But it is historically unthinkable that Paul should have counted on a mission to the Jews to be carried out by others in the very places and towns where he was engaged in a mission to the Gentiles. As far as I can see, such an idea is not indicated in his letters. Indeed, there are some clear statements which refute it. . . ."[69]

He cites, as the clear statements, 2 Cor. 11:24 (the thirty-nine stripes) and 1 Cor. 9:20.

Despite Bornkamm's statement that there are no reasons for contesting the picture drawn by Acts, we have seen very good reasons to do so — everything that Paul says about his work except 1 Cor. 9:20 and also the inference about his mission which is to be drawn from Romans, particularly Romans 9 – 11, and still more particularly 11:13–16. But we must grant that Bornkamm's argument against the view that Peter sometimes worked to win Jews in the same city where Paul was winning Gentiles is forceful. It is not a matter of economy and practicality (though Bornkamm seems to think that such a policy would be "unthinkable" historically, which probably means as a practical matter). The early Christians lived in a world of eschatological dogma, not one in which the practical and convenient management of the missionary endeavor counted for much. The point to note, though Bornkamm does not actually note it, is that Paul himself would certainly have objected to the establishment of two churches, one Jewish and one Gentile, side by side. Jews and Gentiles in Christ should be members of one body (Gal. 3:28; 1 Cor. 12:13), and Paul meant that in more than just a mystical sense. The whole point of the controversy in Antioch is that Peter's action would lead to two separate Christian communities. Paul could never have agreed to a policy which would guarantee the result against which he fought in Antioch.

We appear to have confronted a problem with no clear solution. There seem to be five choices: (1) 1 Cor. 9:19–23 is a literal description of Paul's missionary activity. His self-description as apostle to the Gentiles, and his assigning to himself only an indirect role in the salvation of Israel, conceal a massive failure – actually he had sought for years to win Jews, had not done so, and in Romans portrays himself as a successful apostle to the Gentiles, while lamenting the nonconversion of the Jews and implicitly denying his own failure (the implication of Munck's position). (2) Acts is correct. Paul preached in synagogues, and his converts were almost entirely Jews, proselytes, and "God-fearers" (W. D. Davies, J. Christiaan Beker, and others). (3) We can accept his predominant self-description and read 1 Cor. 9:19–23 as hyperbole. This leaves the problem of the Jews in the Diaspora. (4) We can throw up our hands in dismay. (5) We can accept possibility no. 3 and speculate about the Diaspora Jews.

No. 5, of course, was Schmithals's course, and it is the unsuccessful character of his speculation which leaves us in a dilemma. I think that the reader will not be surprised to learn that I regard no. 1 as more than slightly unlikely. No. 2 is worse. It must deny the evidence of the letters themselves, not just Paul's self-descriptions, but his characterizations of his converts and the contents. We are left, then, with nos. 3–5. I shall attempt a combination of them.

No. 4 should be accepted to a substantial degree. We just do not know, and we probably never shall. We do not know precisely what Paul did in each city, what stance he took toward his fellow Jews of the Dispersion (except for one point, that derived from 2 Cor. 11:24, to be discussed below), nor what efforts others made to win them. Having confessed ignorance, I shall proceed to a speculation, one which will at first make Paul appear callous, almost impious. It is probable that all the apostles, not just Paul, thought in representative terms. Paul can ask how people can come to faith without having heard the gospel (Rom. 10:14), which sounds as if he were concerned with every individual. Doubtless in a sense he was. But in another sense he was not. He wanted to win "the full number" of the Gentiles (Rom. 11:25), and it is certain that neither Paul nor other missionaries succeeded in reaching every town and village — or rather that they would not have done so in the short period of time which they thought they had before the end. Paul was desperate to get on to Spain, but he surely knew that not every Gentile in Asia Minor and Greece had heard the gospel, and he was prepared to leave the area when many had had no opportunity to turn to the Lord. We should recall the wording of Rom. 15:19: Paul had "completed" (the perfect tense of *plēroō*) the gospel in the area from Jerusalem to Illyricum. That part of the task was over, no matter how many individuals had not been reached. The "complete number" (*plērōma*) of Gentiles was almost ready (Rom. 11:25).[70] The only task which he mentions as still to be done was the mission to Spain (Rom. 15:24–28).

It seems to me conceivable, in fact to be the best answer to a question which may have no certain answer, that Paul, Peter, and the others, in their urgent desire to carry out their respective representative missions, made no special provision for Diaspora Jews. We should note that those who formed what was perhaps the largest single group, the Jews of Alexandria, are not mentioned at all in the New Testament, and certainly not in the division of labor referred to in Gal. 2:9. How Christianity reached Egypt remains unknown. Paul, the apostle to the Gentiles, spoke of completing a circle (possibly "arc") (Rom. 15:19) which notably does not include Egypt and North Africa. It would seem that Peter thought of preaching to the circumcised without counting noses and realizing that there were more in Egypt than in Palestine. Paul and the Jerusalem pillars could do only so much. A majority of the people in the civilized world, not just the Jews in Asia Minor and Greece, seem to have had no apostle sent to them. Paul and the others could still think of "the full number" of the Gentiles and of "all Israel" being saved.

It may also be that, despite Rom. 10:14, the apostles were willing to leave the destiny of many to God's action at the end. The "mystery" which Paul reveals in Rom. 11:25f. offers a clue which should, at least on this point, be followed. At the end, when the Deliverer comes from Zion, "*he* will banish ungodliness from Jacob." Although we have learned not to rely on the precise wording of his proof-texts to establish Paul's own view, we perhaps should rely on this one to establish at least one point: God, not the apostles, would accomplish the salvation of Israel.

I do not wish to argue that Paul would have refused to admit Jews to his churches, only that there are virtually no signs of them. Occasional or opportunistic proclamation to Jews need not be outside the scope of the apostle to the Gentiles.[71] I am persuaded, however, that to make Paul first and foremost an apostle to the Jews in the Diaspora who failed and only then turned to the Gentiles is to distort our picture of him. We also need not restrict Peter to Palestine. C. K. Barrett has argued that Peter is the real opponent in the Corinthian correspondence,[72] and it would appear from 1 Cor. 9:5 that Peter, as well as the other apostles and the brothers of the Lord, traveled. He may even have meddled in Paul's churches. Exceptions to the rule and breaches of the agreement, however, should not be allowed to distort the main picture: Paul was apostle to the Gentiles. So he styled himself, and so he acted.

Conflicts with His Own People

Apart from the final conflict in Jerusalem, we have two other bits of information about Paul's relationship with his own people. Both show conflict, and one shows his own continuing commitment to Judaism. In 1 Thess. 2:16 Paul says that the Jews hinder "us" from "speaking to the Gentiles so that they would be saved."[73] In 2 Cor. 11:24, 26 Paul mentions being in danger from his own people, among others, and says that five times he had received the Jewish punishment of thirty-nine stripes. 2 Cor. 11:21–29 may be, to be sure, an example of Paul's rhetorical exaggeration: Paul depicts himself as in danger from all groups other than Pauline Christians and in every conceivable place. Perhaps it was not really so bad as that. The reference to the thirty-nine stripes, however, seems specific enough, and helps make sense of the numerous references to "persecution" in the Pauline letters. What Paul and others (see Matt. 10:23) called "persecution" was probably regarded by the administrators of it as "punishment."

There is rather a lot about persecution in the Pauline correspondence.[74] In some instances it is hard to know if actual persecution were taking place or if Paul simply had the habit of depicting himself and the Christian churches as subject to persecution by the outside world (thus, for example, 1 Cor. 4:12; 2 Cor. 4:9; 8:2). Some references, however, are more concrete. Paul himself persecuted the church, apparently in his role as zealous Pharisee (Gal. 1:13, 23; Phil. 3:6; 1 Cor. 15:9). Further, Paul wrote that if he still preached circumcision as a Christian apostle he would avoid persecution (Gal. 5:11). The evangelists who preached circumcision, Paul charged, did so to avoid persecution (Gal. 6:12). Finally, there is an allegorical or typological reference to persecution of Christians (or possibly only Pauline Christians) by others, designated those "born according to the flesh" (Gal. 4:29).

The point which emerges with most certainty from considering these passages is that at least some non-Christian Jews persecuted (that is, punished) at least some Christian Jews in at least some places. The best-attested fact is that Paul himself carried out such persecution. It is less certain that all the references to persecution refer to Jewish punishment of some in the Christian movement, although that is the most likely assumption. From Galatians (especially 5:11 and 6:12), and from 1 Thess. 2:16, it also appears likely that the issue was circumcision; that is, the admission of Gentiles to the people of God without requiring them to make full proselytization to Judaism.

Schmithals argued that Paul was punished for urging Jews to abandon the Torah,[75] and many scholars see the confession of a criminal (that is, one executed as a criminal) as messiah as the cause of persecution.[76] The only firsthand evidence, however, Paul's, points to the mission to the Gentiles and to "circumcision" as the issue which led to persecution.

It should be carefully noted that I am assuming that 1 Thess. 2:16; 2 Cor. 11:24; Gal. 5:11; and Gal. 6:12 all point to the same reality. That cannot be proved decisively to be the case. Perhaps Paul received the thirty-nine lashes for some offense other than that which he specifies in Gal. 5:11 and 6:12. Perhaps the Jews in Thessalonica "hindered" Paul from preaching to the Gentiles in some way other than punishing him. Perhaps they only yelled loudly at public meetings. The most likely path for the interpreter to follow, however, is to combine these bits of evidence: at least some other Jews, possibly including some Christian Jews (2 Cor. 11:26, "false brethren"), objected to Paul's preaching to Gentiles enough to administer to him the thirty-nine stripes. He was punished, that is to say, for doing what lay at the heart of his call and his life's work—bringing Gentiles into the people of God without requiring full obedience to the Torah. Thus he kept on getting punished, just as he kept on evangelizing the Gentiles. If Paul persecuted the church on the same issue as the one which subsequently brought down punishment on him, we would have to conclude that he did not initiate the Torah-free mission to the Gentiles.

Following these leads, we arrive at the following reconstruction: some Jewish Christian evangelists admitted Gentiles to the messianic movement without requiring proselytization; they were persecuted by some Jews. Other Jewish Christians escaped Jewish punishment either because they did not admit Gentiles (probably the situation of James and Peter) or because they did, but insisted on circumcision (the position of Paul's opponents in Galatia). Thus we can understand why Paul was persecuted, while the Jerusalem apostles lived for the most part in peace.[77] Paul accused those who admitted Gentiles, but required circumcision and acceptance of the rest of the law, of doing so in order to avoid persecution; but it is much more reasonable to think that they were, in their own view, following the will of God as revealed in Scripture.

We earlier noted that 2 Cor. 11:24 shows Paul's continuing commitment to Judaism. He kept attending the synagogue. Arland J. Hultgren has argued that Paul did not accept the punishment, but it is apparent that he did.[78] He kept showing up, and obviously he submitted to the thirty-nine stripes. He undoubtedly thought that those who judged him deserving of punishment were wrong, but had he wished he could have withdrawn from Jewish society altogether and thus not have been punished.

The most important point to be derived from 2 Cor. 11:24 is that both Paul and the Jews who punished him regarded the Christian movement as falling within Judaism.[79] Paul's converts were taken seriously enough by synagogue authorities to lead them to discipline the one who brought them into the people of God without requiring circumcision. Paul told them that they were heirs to the promises made to Abraham, and both he and non-Christian Jews regarded that as a serious issue. They punished Paul, and he submitted to the punishment, because they all agreed that the question of who constitutes Israel was a matter of crucial importance. Thus we see again that Paul was not consciously aiding in the foundation of a new religion. None of the parties who emerge in Paul's letters — Paul himself, his Gentile converts, the "false brethren," Peter and the other Jerusalem apostles, and the non-Christian Jews — looked on the Christian movement as outside the bounds of Judaism. *Punishment implies inclusion.* If Paul had considered that he had withdrawn from Judaism, he would not have attended synagogue. If the members of the synagogue had considered him an outsider, they would not have punished him.

The Salvation of Israel

We have earlier observed that when he is preparing to travel to Jerusalem, in fulfillment of his role as the priest who is to present "the offering of the Gentiles," Paul discusses, for the only time in his extant correspondence, the fate of his own people. The power and poignancy of Romans 9 — 11 are so great that one pauses before attempting an examination of them. Although it is certainly beyond the interpreter's poor power to add to them, it may not be beyond it to detract from them. More than any other part of the Pauline correspondence, their meaning depends on direct individual reading. That is the case because the feelings which they convey — concern, anguish, and triumphant expectation — are far more important than the ideas which they contain.[80]

In recent years the question of "two-covenant theology" has emerged in the Jewish-Christian dialogue. This has naturally led to the question of whether or not Paul can be read in such a way as to support the idea of two people of God. Franz Mussner, we have seen above, reads Rom. 10:4 to mean that Christ is the end of the law for the righteousness of those who have faith in Christ, but not for Jews, who can still come to righteousness through the law.[81] Krister Stendahl is the most forceful interpreter of Romans 11 along this line.[82] Out of pastoral concern, Paul relents from his exclusivism.[83] The meaning of Rom. 11:25f. is that Israel will be saved apart from faith in Christ.

I think that all interpreters of Paul are aware of the dangers of anachronism and of trying too hard to make an ancient author relevant for the modern world. Yet we also naturally address the text with our own questions in mind: that cannot be avoided. What I shall attempt is a brief account of the meaning of the closing section of Romans 11, with first-century concerns, and only first-century concerns, in mind, as far as I am able.

Understanding the setting of the section in Paul's career is crucial to understanding it, but we have said what that setting is often enough and need only recall it: it is the failure of the mission to the Jews in the light of Paul's relative success among the Gentiles and of his impending trip to Jerusalem.[84] As soon as Paul gets to Spain, it would appear, he can finish the Gentile mission. When the full number of the Gentiles is complete, it will be time for the Parousia. There is, however, a problem: Israel is not ready. But for the problem Paul has a solution: God has intentionally "hardened" part of Israel to allow the completion of the Gentile mission (Rom. 11:25). Further, he will use the Gentile mission itself to win Israel, through jealousy (11:13–16).

In Rom. 11:25–26a the salvation of the Gentiles is intimately connected with the salvation of Israel, and the connection is causative. Part of Israel is hardened until the full number of Gentiles comes in, and thus — in that manner[85] — all Israel will be saved: as a consequence of the Gentile mission, as Paul had already said (11:13–16). The same point is repeated in

11:31: *by means of* the mercy shown to you (the Gentiles), they, the Jews, will now receive mercy. The mystery which Paul reveals, then, at least in 11:25–26a, is that Israel will be saved in an unexpected manner, *after* the full number of the Gentiles has been won, and *through* the Gentile mission, not as a result of the mission of Peter and the others. The connection with the Gentile mission shows that the salvation of Israel does not take place apart from Christ.[86]

Despite the surprising character of the mystery, the explanation of the salvation of Israel in 11:26a is still "historical"; that is, it is connected with the missions of the apostles. But the proof-text which Paul quotes to establish the fact that all Israel will be saved has nothing to do with the Gentile mission. It speaks of the Parousia and depicts the redemption of Israel as being accomplished not within the historical period of the apostolic missions, but at the end, directly by the Deliverer himself. We return to an aspect of this point below, and here consider only the relevance of the quotation for the question of two paths to salvation.

"The Deliverer," as most scholars agree, is almost certainly Christ in Paul's understanding.[87] It is Christ who is God's end-time agent in 1 Cor. 15:20–28, and "the Lord" in 1 Thess. 4:13–18 is probably also "the Lord Jesus." Eschatological expectation need not be precisely uniform. In this case, however, since Paul thought that Jesus was the Jewish messiah and, more, Lord of the living and the dead (Rom. 14:9; cf. 1 Thess. 5:9f.), it is likely that he thought of Christ as coming at the end, before the kingdom was handed over to God (1 Cor. 15:24).

But for the present question, whether or not Paul thought of the salvation of Israel apart from Christ, it matters little whether he understands "the Deliverer" to be God or Christ; for it is incredible that he thought of "God apart from Christ," just as it is that he thought of "Christ apart from God." This is where the interpretation of Rom. 11:25f. as offering two ways to salvation seems to me to go astray. It requires Paul to have made just that distinction.[88] By the time we meet him in his letters, however, Paul knew only one God, the one who sent Christ and who "raised from the dead Jesus our Lord" (Rom. 4:24). To suppose that "the Deliverer" could be for Paul "God apart from Christ" seems to expect of him an unthinkable abstraction. He was not a *logos* theologian. We return here to a point made earlier. There should be no hard distinction between "theocentric" and "christocentric" strains in Paul's thought (above, pp. 41f.). It is God's will that all be saved through Christ. It is God who hardened part of Israel, it is God whose word will not fail (Rom. 9:6), and it is God who will see to it that all Israel is saved, though this does not happen apart from Christ.

That Rom. 11:25f. does not predict salvation for Israel apart from Christ is also seen when we note the verses which immediately precede and follow. The metaphor of the olive tree makes it clear that Paul is not thinking of a separate path to salvation. There is only one olive tree, and the condition of being a "branch" is "faith" (11:23). "Faith" may not come to Israel as a result of the mission of Peter, but it is a mistake to think that Paul is thinking of salvation, of regrafting, apart from faith.[89] In the section which immediately follows the quotation in 11:26f. Paul returns to one of his favorite themes: Jew and Gentile are equal and will be equally saved by God's mercy (11:32). But just as the salvation of Gentiles depends on faith (11:20), we should conclude that so does that of Israel.[90]

The main thrust of Paul's argument should now be summarized: the eschatological scheme has been reversed; Israel will be saved not first, but as a result of the Gentile mission, through faith in Christ. The figure of the olive tree says it very well. Some of Israel has been broken off, and this allows time for the completion of the Gentile mission; but if Gentiles are grafted into the olive tree, "all the more" will the natural branches be regrafted (11:24). In any case Jew and Gentile may be "in" the olive tree only on the condition of faith.

While this main thrust is entirely consonant with Paul's views elsewhere about what is required to be a descendant of Abraham, in two ways Rom. 11:25–27 raises questions. One we have already noted. Although Paul three times in Romans 11 connects the salvation of Israel with his own mission to the Gentiles, the quotation in 11:26b–27 assigns that salvation to the Redeemer; that is, it puts it outside the bounds of the apostolic missions altogether. Paul treats the quotation in 11:26b–27 as if it proves the point that the Jews will be saved as a result of the Gentile mission, but it does not do so. Should we read Paul as meaning that "some" of Israel would be saved as a result of jealousy (11:14), while the salvation of "all" would await the Parousia (11:26b–27)?

The second question is whether or not Paul consistently maintains the equality of Jew and Gentile. We have just seen that equality is part of the main thrust of the argument, figuring largely in the section about the olive tree and also at the conclusion of the chapter. Yet in 11:25f. there is a possible distinction between "the full number" of the Gentiles and "all Israel." These two points can be coalesced into one question: does Paul after all maintain the favored status of Israel, not by providing for their salvation apart from Christ, but by providing for their salvation apart from the apostolic missions, at the end, by Christ himself?

It would not surprise me a great deal to discover — although such a discovery will always lie beyond the powers of exegesis — that the quotation in Rom. 11:26b–27 represents Paul's "real" view. In this case we would come to this understanding of that view: The only way to become a member of the people of God, as long as ordinary history endures, is through faith. Even Peter and Paul, if they did not have faith, would not be righteoused. During the period of evangelization all are on equal footing and can be admitted on one ground alone. Jews have no more chance of finding righteousness by the law than Gentiles do of being saved by pagan deities. But when the term of Paul's mission to the Gentiles and of Peter's mission to the Jews is over, the Jews after all can count on the irrevocability of God's promises. They are provided for in a special way, being saved directly by Christ.

On this reading "all Israel" in 11:26 does not have to mean "the fullness of Israel" (cf. 11:12), but could mean "every Jew." By his own terms and definitions, Paul thought that within history only some Jews were truly descendants of Abraham. Some are in the olive tree and some are out. Most are out. The only way to be part of the olive tree is by faith. *Some* (11:14) will be regrafted because they come to faith as the result of jealousy, but at the end God will act through Christ, apart from even the Gentile mission, to save *all* Israel. Although it is God's intention to have mercy equally on all (11:32) there is no special eschatological salvation of all Gentiles.[91] At the end "the fullness" of the Gentiles and "all" Israel will be saved.

While it would not surprise me a great deal to discover that this is the correct interpretation of Paul's thought, I am not persuaded. It seems to rest too heavily on finding a second mystery in the quotation from Scripture,[92] while Paul's intention in using the proof-text may have been more limited. He seems to have quoted Scripture to prove what he had just said, that all Israel would be saved as a consequence of the Gentile mission. Even on this reading, however, there could be an intended contrast between the fullness of the Gentiles and all Israel, although it is perhaps preferable to understand "all Israel" as "the full number of Israel," as in 11:12.[93]

The simplest reading of 11:13–36 seems to be this: the only way to enter the body of those who will be saved is by faith in Christ; the mission to the Gentiles will indirectly lead to the salvation of "all Israel" (that is, "their fullness");[94] thus at the eschaton God's entire plan will be fulfilled and the full number of both Jews and Gentiles will be saved, and saved on the same basis; the Gentiles and the Jews are inextricably intertwined — Jewish disobedience leads to Gentile salvation, which in turn leads to Jewish salvation (11:30f.). It is God's intent to have mercy on all, but mercy has faith as its condition.

It perhaps should go without saying (though I shall nevertheless make the comment) that Paul's view does not provide an adequate basis for a Jewish-Christian dialogue. Generations have come and gone, and Paul's expectations have not been fulfilled. His references to the fullness of the Gentiles and to all Israel depend on his expectation that the Redeemer would come soon, and they have in view only the generation during which Paul worked. Thus they cannot be used in any simple way to determine what Paul would have thought of the fate of future generations of either Gentiles or Jews. We may put the matter this way: what Paul would have thought, had he foreseen that God would not do what he based his entire life on expecting him to do, is simply imponderable. That will not, however, keep us from pondering it. Some years ago, in discussing this issue, I wrote this:

> I do not know what Paul would have thought if he had lived for 2,000 years, or if he had foreseen the length of time between his own ministry and the eschaton. I think I know what he thought in the particular circumstances in which he wrote. He thought that the only way to be saved was through Christ Jesus. If it were to be proposed that Christians today should think the same thing, and accordingly that the Jews who have not converted should be considered cut off from God, and if such a proposal came before a body in which I had a vote, I would vote against it.[95]

I still would. I am now inclined to think that perhaps Paul would too. The reason is this: the anguish of Romans 9 – 11 is caused, as anguish often is, by a dilemma. The dilemma reminds us more than slightly of Romans 7, since it is really a dilemma about God and since it arises from Paul's twin sets of convictions, those native to him and those revealed. What God was up to had human consequences, and Paul worried about them, too. As in Romans 7 the theological problem about the purpose of the law and its connection with sin had led him to a vivid description of humanity under the requirement to fulfill the law without the indwelling Spirit, so also in Romans 9 – 11 a theological problem involves him in human anguish. Certainly he loved his own people profoundly. But that is not all that lies behind these chapters. He also worried about God, his will, and his constancy. How could God have willed the election and ultimately the redemption of Israel *and* have appointed Jesus Christ, whom most Jews were rejecting, for the salvation of all without distinction? The problem of how to hold these two convictions together runs throughout Romans 9 – 11. Paul keeps asking about God's constancy to his own word, to his expressed intent (9:6; 11:1). Finally, Paul put the two together with ingenuity. The Jews would come in as a result of the success of the Christian mission to the Gentiles.

197

The analogy with the problem about the law, sin, and God's will in Romans 7 continues. Paul's solution to the problem posed by Israel's unfaith is to be seen as a somewhat desperate expedient. Does he really think that jealousy will succeed where Peter failed? How can the promise be irrevocable if it is conditional on a requirement which most Jews reject? He has a problem, a problem of conflicting convictions which can be better asserted than explained: salvation is by faith; God's promise to Israel is irrevocable.[96] So what would he do if he had lived beyond the first generation? Hold his convictions, keep asserting them, and try ever new ways to combine them. At least that is what he did during the short period of which we have acquaintance.

Conclusion

Part Two has taken Rom. 15:16 as its leitmotif. Paul was engaged in a thoroughly Jewish task, bringing the Gentiles into the eschatological people of God. But we cannot look back on his efforts without the feeling of pathos. He intended to be helping complete the Israel of God. He was in fact engaged in a mission which helped lead to the separation of those in Christ from Israel according to the flesh. The problem was, first of all, the Gentiles. If it was thoroughly Jewish to win them during the messianic age, it was not evident to all that it was thoroughly Jewish to say that they should be admitted without accepting the law given by God to Moses. But Paul went further: Jews and Gentiles must be equal, both before and after admission. Therefore Jews themselves must be righteoused by faith in Christ; and they also must be prepared to give up aspects of the law if keeping it would sever the body of Christ.

Paul's stance on the Gentiles — and on the Jews — understandably led to conflict both with his "own people" and with "false brethren" (2 Cor. 11:24–26; Rom. 15:31; Gal. 2:4). He held his convictions with remarkable persistence. Almost everybody, or so he could portray the situation, opposed him. And perhaps he did not exaggerate very much. A Jew who, in fulfillment of a Jewish eschatological expectation, becomes in fact engaged in creating something other than Judaism will not have many supporters. But he had other, deeper problems, than "fighting without" (2 Cor. 7:5). He had "fear," and perhaps even doubt, within. Somehow everything was not quite right. He sounds confident enough in Galatians about God, sin, and the law. God gave the law to provoke sin so that he could subsequently save. But it was not that easy for Paul. Did God really give the law for such a reason?

A similar doubt may have lurked in his mind about his own people.

He sometimes sounds quite glib about transferring the promises made to Abraham to those in Christ, but it worried him. God made those promises, and he made them to a historical people. And Paul knew it. As he neared what by his own calculation must have been the last phase of his career, his doubts surfaced. And thus we have Romans; and thus New Testament professors have a continuing occupation. What is interesting is how far Paul was from denying anything that he held deeply, even when he could not maintain all his convictions at once without both anguish and finally a lack of logic. It is thus no accident that the most difficult chapters for interpreters are also the most anguished. It is in Romans 7 and 9 – 11 that his partially conflicting convictions come to full expression.

Paul becomes most human when he encounters difficulty, and the sections which show Paul at his most human are 2 Cor. 11:16–29, where the problems are external, and Romans 7 and 9 – 11, where his Jewish and his Christian convictions come into conflict in his own mind. Once we see past the exegetical difficulties to the troubles of the man who wrote them, a moving picture emerges, one that is partly poignant and partly stirring. We see Paul the Jew and Paul the apostle of Christ, convinced that God's will is that he be both at once, and therefore never questioning their compatibility, but sometimes having more than a little difficulty reconciling his native convictions with those which he had received by revelation. He was a loyal member of the synagogue, but was flogged by his own people. He saw himself as helping to fulfill God's eternal plan, already announced in Genesis, but he was thereby pushing the Christian movement toward becoming a third entity. He knew that righteousness is only by faith in Christ, but he still tried repeatedly to find a place for the law in God's plan. The most poignant point is the last one considered: he desperately sought a formula which would keep God's promises to Israel intact, while insisting on faith in Jesus Christ.

NOTES

1. On the third race, see Adolf von Harnack, *Die Mission und Ausbreitung des Christentums in den ersten drei Jahrhunderten*, 4th ed. (Leipzig: J. C. Hinrichs, 1924), pp. 259–81. (*The Expansion of Christianity in the First Three Centuries*, pp. 300–35).

2. Paul elsewhere depicts himself in priestly terms: Rom. 1:9; esp. Phil. 4:17f. He draws an analogy between priests and apostles in 1 Cor. 9:13f. There is an excellent discussion in Michael Newton, "The Concept of Purity at Qumran and in the Letters of Paul" (Ph.D. diss., McMaster University, 1980), pp. 139–53.

3. Dieter Zeller, *Juden und Heiden in der Mission des Paulus*, 2d. ed. (Stuttgart:

Verlag Katholisches Bibelwerk, 1976), pp. 255, 272–75, 284 argues, especially against Peter Stuhlmacher ("Interpretation von Römer 11:25–32," in *Probleme biblischer Theologie* [Munich: Chr. Kaiser, 1971], esp. pp. 560f., and "Erwägungen zum Problem von Gegenwart und Zukunft in der paulinischen Eschatologie," *ZTK* 64 [1967]: 430f.) that the setting of Paul's work is not the pilgrimage of Gentiles to Zion. He notes that the pagans are not streaming to Zion and that Israel, in Paul's view, is not exalted and victorious. Both points are correct, but Zeller is only pointing to some of the ways in which Paul altered the traditional picture, a picture presupposed by the alterations themselves.

While this eschatological view is crucial to Paul's view of his career, the inclusion of the Gentiles in the people of God does not exhaust his eschatological expectations. Especially to be remarked is the view that Christians are in the process of becoming "a new creation": 2 Cor. 3:18; 4:16; 5:17. The eschatological expectation includes the whole cosmos: Rom. 8:18–25.

4. See William Sanday and Arthur C. Headlam, *The Epistle to the Romans*, 5th ed. (Edinburgh: T. & T. Clark, 1902), p. 405; C. E. B. Cranfield, *The Epistle to the Romans*, vol. 2, (Edinburgh: T. & T. Clark, 1979), p. 756 ("the sacrifice consisting of the Gentiles"); Ernst Käsemann, *Commentary on Romans*, (Grand Rapids: Wm. B. Eerdmans, 1980), p. 393 ("the Gentile world itself is the offering").

5. On the pilgrimage, see n. 3 above and the discussion in W. D. Davies, *The Gospel and the Land*, (Berkeley and Los Angeles: University of California Press, 1974), esp. p. 217. Davies points out that "the centre of gravity of Paul's ministry has shifted away from geographic eschatology" to "the communities 'in Christ'."

6. Lloyd Gaston ("Paul and the Torah," in *Anti-Semitism and the Foundations of Christianity* [New York: Paulist Press, 1979], pp. 66), Franz Mussner ("'Christus [ist] des Gesetzes Ende zur Gerechtigkeit für jeden, der glaubt' [Röm. 10, 4]," in *Paulus — Apostat oder Apostel* [Regensburg, 1977], pp. 31–44), and others hold that faith in Christ was the entrance requirement only for Gentiles and provided a second means of access to membership in the people of God. We saw above, however, that Paul applied it also to Jews (above, pp. 29f., 34).

7. Gal. 3:28; 6:15; 1 Cor. 12:13; 2 Cor. 5:17. Cf. Harnack, *Mission*, pp. 304f.

8. See Ernest deWitt Burton, *The Epistle to the Galatians*, (Edinburgh: T. & T. Clark, 1921), pp. 357f. Cf. Peter Richardson, *Israel in the Apostolic Church* (New York: Cambridge University Press, 1969), pp. 74–84.

9. See J. B. Lightfoot, *Saint Paul's Epistle to the Galatians*, 10th ed. (London: Macmillan, 1892), pp. 224f. (the phrase "stands here not for the faithful converts from the circumcision alone, but for the spiritual Israel generally, the whole body of believers whether Jew or Gentile; and thus kai is *epexegetic*, i.e. it introduces the same thing under a new aspect"); Pierre Bonnard, *L' Epitre de Saint Paul aux Galâtes²*, 2d ed. (Neuchâtel and Paris: Delachaux & Niestlé, 1972), p. 131 ("those who follow that rule constitute now the elect people, the Israel of the new covenant"); Heinrich Schlier, *Der Brief an die Galater*, 5th ed. (Göttingen: Vandenhoeck & Ruprecht, 1971), p. 283 (who cites numerous names on both sides of the dispute); Gerd Lüdmann, 'Paulus und das Judentum' (forthcoming).

10. Gerd Lüdmann, "Paulus und das Judentum" (forthcoming).

11. Cf. Käsemann, *Romans*, p. 262: in Rom. 9:6ff. the conception is that of the true Israel, which is a variation of the motif of the seed of Abraham.

12. The emphatic "we" also refers to Christians in 2 Cor. 5:21; 6:16 (we are the temple of God); Gal. 4:28; 5:5. Most of the other uses of the emphatic *hēmeis* in the extant correspondence refer to Paul or Paul and his co-workers as distinct from other Christians. In any case it means "we as distinct from others"; when applied to the church it means "we as distinct from other Jews and Gentiles."

13. Cf. Davies (chapter 1, n. 20 above); Johannes Munck, *Paul and the Salvation of Mankind* (Atlanta: John Knox Press, 1977), p. 279; H. J. Schoeps, *Paul: The Theology of the Apostle in the Light of Jewish Religious History* (Philadelphia: Westminster Press, 1961), p. 237; Leonhard Goppelt, *Typos* (Gütersloh: Gerd Mohn, 1939), p. 169.

14. 2 Cor. 5:17; Gal. 6:15 (neither circumcision nor uncircumcision as such); 1 Cor. 12:27; 1 Cor. 3:16; 2 Cor. 6:16.

15. E. P. Sanders, *Paul and Palestinian Judaism* (Philadelphia: Fortress Press, 1977), pp. 244–55 (hereafter cited as *PPJ*).

16. 4QpPs37 3.12; 2.17; cf. 1 QM 1.2, "offenders against the covenant."

17. 1QSa 1.1–6, 20.

18. E.g., 1QM 15.1f.

19. Cf. Ulrich Wilckens, "Über Abfassungszweck und Aufau des Römerbriefs," in *Rechtfertigung als Freiheit: Paulusstudien* (Neukirchen-Vluyn: Neukirchener Verlag, 1974), p. 169: The church composed of Jews and Gentiles stands over against the obdurate part of Israel.

20. That Paul's Gentile converts, at least those who were Roman citizens, would have been considered as traitors to the empire is especially emphasized by Richard Freund, "Principia Politica: The Political Dimensions of Jewish and Christian Self-Definition in the Greco-Roman Period," (Ph.D. diss.; New York: Jewish Theological Seminary, 1982).

21. Even though Paul did not baptize all his converts himself (1 Cor. 1:14–17), he considered all members of the Christian movement to have been baptized (1 Cor. 12:13; Rom. 6:4).

22. Arland J. Hultgren ("Paul's Pre-Christian Persecutions of the Church: Their Purpose, Locale, and Nature," *JBL* 95 [1976]: 101f.) argued that Paul considered Christianity to be a rival religion to Judaism. I cannot agree *if* the subject is Paul's conscious intent.

23. W. D. Davies, "Paul and the People of Israel," *NTS* 24 (1977):24.

24. Ibid., p. 27.

25. Paul Meyer, "Romans 10:4 and the End of the Law," in *The Divine Helmsman* New York: KTAV, 1980). p. 66.

26. The LXX of Exod. 34:34 agrees with the Hebrew.

27. *Epistrephō* also means "convert" — more precisely, "reconvert" — in Gal. 4:9.

28. On *kerdainō* to mean "convert," see David Daube, *The New Testament and Rabbinic Judaism* (London: University of London, Athlone Press, 1973), pp. 348, 352–61. W. D. Davies (*Paul and Rabbinic Judaism*, 4th ed. [Philadelphia: Fortress Press, 1980], p. xxxvi), however, argues that "the vocabulary of conversion is absent from the epistles."

29. W. D. Davies, "Paul and the People of Israel," *NTS* 24 (1977): 23.

30. Except, of course, in the realm of ethical, especially sexual, practice, where Jewish mores should, as Paul saw it, be accepted by Gentiles. Michael Newton

("Purity," pp. 212–16) has recently discussed this in an illuminating way. He points out that Paul was concerned with the church's *unity* (and thus denied the parts of the law which separate Jew from Gentile), and also with its *purity* (and thus insisted on keeping aspects of the law which kept the church pure from the contagion brought by idolatry and sexual immorality).

31. Munck, *Paul*, pp. 119f.

32. Ibid., p. 120.

33. Ibid., p. 200. He continues, "The fact that the Jews were preached to does not mean that they believed" (ibid., p. 202).

34. Johannes Munck, *Christ and Israel* (Philadelphia: Fortress Press, 1967), p. 125.

35. W. D. Davies, review of *Galatians* by H. D. Betz, *RSR* 7 (1981): 311.

36. Günther Bornkamm, "The Missionary Stance of Paul in I Corinthians 9 and in Acts," in *Studies in Luke-Acts* (Philadelphia: Fortress Press, 1980), p. 194.

37. Phillip Vielhauer, "On the 'Paulinism' of Acts," in *Studies in Luke-Acts*, p. 38. He takes 1 Cor. 9:19–23 as literally describing Paul's missionary activity (p. 39). This view of Paul's missionary activity is very common. Thus, for example, Richardson (*Israel*, p. 136): it was Paul's practice to go "always to the Jewish synagogue in each city he visited before taking up his responsibility to the Gentiles"; F. F. Bruce, *Peter, Stephen, James, and John* (Grand Rapids: Wm. B. Eerdmans, 1980), p. 32; E. Haenchen, *The Acts of the Apostles* (Philadelphia: Westminster Press, 1971), p. 414; cf. H. Conzelmann, *1 Corinthians* (Philadelphia: Fortress Press, 1975), pp. 160f.

38. Schoeps, *Paul*, p. 40.

39. Davies, "Paul and the People of Israel," p. 19.

40. H. D. Betz, *Galatians* (Philadelphia: Fortress Press, 1979), p. 2. See above, chapter 1, n. 25.

41. Davies, review of Betz's *Galatians*, p. 312.

42. Ibid. Cf. also Robert Jewett, *A Chronology of Paul's Life* (Philadelphia: Fortress Press, 1979), p. 83 (he discusses "the evidence concerning the mixed composition of the Corinthian congregation," but it all comes from Acts, esp. 18:2–4; cf. also Jewett, pp. 36–38); J. Christiaan Beker, *Paul the Apostle* (Philadelphia: Fortress Press, 1980), p. 6: *the* apostle to the Gentiles was apostle to Jew and Gentile alike; p. 76: "The *ethnē* in the Pauline letters and Acts are on the whole not pure Gentiles but those 'God-fearers' among the Gentiles who had been attracted to the synagogue. . . ."; John H. Elliott, *A Home for the Homeless* (Philadelphia: Fortress Press, 1981), chap. 1 at n. 80: the rapid advance of Christianity in Asia Minor is "undoubtedly" to be attributed to the fact that it made gains "among Jewish converts and former Gentile proselytes to Judaism." "This is obvious from the Pauline letters and Acts"; Folker Siegert, "Gottesfürchtige und Sympathisanten," *JSJ* 4 (1973): 109–64, esp. 109. Siegert, as does Davies, points to the "astonishing familiarity with the Old Testament" which Paul appears to presuppose.

It is not necessary to discuss the adequacy of the term "God-fearers." See on this Siegert's article, just cited, and Neil J. McEleney, "Conversion, Circumcision and the Law," *NTS* 20 (1974): pp. 325–28.

43. Others have questioned the dominant view in favor of the one which emerges from Paul's own descriptions of himself and his mission. Thus Lüdemann, *Paulus der Heidenapostel*, vol. 1, p. 96 (with references to literature); Gaston, "Paul and

the Torah," p. 55; Peter Stuhlmacher, "Das Gesetz als Thema biblischer Theologie," *ZTK* 75 (1980): 270f.; *Das paulinische Evangelium*, vol. 1 (Göttingen: Vandenhoeck & Ruprecht, 1968), p. 99; and especially Schmithals, whose view will be discussed more fully below. Cf. also Claus Bussman *Themen der paulinischen Missionspredigt auf dem Hintergrund der spätjudisch-hellenistischen Missionsliteratur* (Frankfurt and Bern: H. Lang, 1971), p. 38, who contrasts Acts 17:1–4 with 1 Thess. 1:9; 2:14–16.

44. John Knox, *Chapters in a Life of Paul* (Nashville: Abingdon Press, 1950). It appears that Knox's view of how to assess the evidence of Acts and of Paul's letters for reconstructing Paul's life and work is now being taken up systematically, especially by Lüdemann (see the preceding note). Jewett's recent work on the chronology of Paul also shows that Knox's view is making headway.

45. Pp. 181f. are adapted from Sanders, "Philippians 3 and 2 Corinthians 11" (forthcoming publication).

46. See Lüdemann, *Paulus der Heidenapostel*, vol. 1, p. 96; Zeller, *Juden und Heiden*, pp. 270f.

47. It should be noted as a caveat to this argument from silence that Paul may have wanted not to distinguish his converts by race.

48. Paul's description of them as co-workers (Rom. 16:3) does not decide whether or not he won them, although the fact that a church met in their house (1 Cor. 16:19) may point in that direction.

49. Gaston ("Paul and the Torah," p. 55) cites the evidence which follows and curiously concludes that Paul's converts were former God-fearers.

50. Munck, *Paul*, pp. 204–6.

51. Ibid.

52. I think that the same consideration applies against Betz's view that they *must* have been well-educated in the Greco-Roman tradition. See Betz, *Galatians*, p. 2; n. 39 above.

53. J. A. T. Robinson, *Wrestling with Romans* (Philadelphia: Westminster Press, 1979), p. 7.

54. Walter Bauer, *A Greek-English Lexicon of the New Testament*, 2d ed. (Chicago: University of Chicago Press, 1979), p. xxiv.

55. "Has ready": note *peplērōkenai in* Rom. 15:19. The point is returned to below.

56. So also Käsemann, *Romans*, on Rom. 11:11–24.

57. W. L. Knox, whose view was accepted by Davies, also saw the improbability of Paul's having behaved in such a way, but he drew the opposite conclusion from ours. Paul, he said, "could not both behave as a Jew when dealing with Jews and as free from the Law when dealing with Gentiles. . . ." Knox, however, thought that Paul was always Torah-observant (despite Gal. 2:11–14). See W. L. Knox, *St. Paul and the Church of Jerusalem* (Cambridge: Cambridge University Press, 1925), p. 122; Davies, *Paul and Rabbinic Judaism*, p. 70 and n.3.

58. That is the problem which Conzelmann sees with 1 Cor. 9:20–22. He correctly observes that there is no problem. See *1 Corinthians*, pp. 160f.

59. The point is brilliantly made by Henry Chadwick, "All Things to All Men," *NTS* 1 (1954–55): 261–75. For accommodation in missionary practice generally, see Daube, *The New Testament and Rabbinic Judaism*, pp. 336–46. Paul's concern for making a favorable impression on outsiders is evident in 1 Cor. 14:16–25.

60. Above, at n. 45.

61. Cf. Käsemann, *Romans*, pp. 394f.; Sanday and Headlam, *Romans*, pp. 407f.; Cranfield, *Romans*, pp. 760–62.

62. N. 42 above.

63. W. Schmithals, *Paul and James* (London: SCM Press, 1965), pp. 16–62.

64. Ibid., p. 28.

65. Ibid., pp. 24, 25, 43f.

66. Ibid., pp. 50f.

67. In part 1 we noted several times that he regarded obedience to aspects of the law to be a matter of indifference *except* when they were considered to be necessary for membership. See Gal. 6:15, 1 Cor. 7:19; Rom. 14:1–6.

68. Schmithals continues to accept Acts for one point: Paul's converts were former "God-fearers" (*Paul and James*, pp. 60f.). Cf. the remark on Gaston, n. 49 above.

69. Bornkamm, "Missionary Stance," p. 200.

70. For the connection between *peplērōkenai* and *plēroma*, see Stuhlmacher, "Erwägungen zum Problem von Gegenwart und Zukunft," pp. 430f. For the point that Paul has "completed" his work in the area described in Rom. 15:19, see C. K. Barrett, *A Commentary on the Epistle to the Romans* (New York: Harper & Row, 1957), pp. 276f.

71. So Zeller, *Juden und Heiden*, pp. 270f.; cf. Munck, *Paul*, pp. 46f. In a much briefer treatment of this problem I wrote that "it would be silly to claim that Paul would decline to preach to a Jew or some Jews" ("Paul's Attitude toward the Jewish People," *USQR* 33 [1978]:177), a position which I still hold. In "A Response" (ibid, p. 190), Krister Stendahl replied that it would be unrealistic to "harden" the position that Paul was apostle to the Gentiles into the statement "he never witnessed to a Jew."

72. C. K. Barrett, "ΨΕΥΔΑΠΟΣΤΟΛΟΙ (2 Cor. 11:13)," in *Mélanges Bibliques en homage au R. P. Béda Rigaux* (Gembloux: Duculot, 1970), pp. 378–96.

73. I accept the authenticity of the passage. On how 1 Thess. 2:16b can be understood as pre-70, see Ernst Bammel, "Judenverfolgung und Naherwartung," *ZTK* 56 (1959):294–315. See also John Hurd, "Paul Ahead of His Time: I Thess. 2:13–16," forthcoming publication.

74. Pp. 190–92 are adapted from Sanders "Philippians 3 and 2 Corinthians 11."

75. Above, p. 187.

76. Hultgren, "Paul's Pre-Christian Persecutions," pp. 97–104; Beker, *Paul the Apostle*, pp. 143f., 182–84, 202. See the next note.

77. 1 Thess. 2:15 (still assuming its authenticity) raises the possibility of persecution of the Christian movement in Jerusalem. The wording is ambiguous. It is probable that the prophets who were killed were pre-Jesus prophets, not Christian prophets (cf. Matt. 23:37). "Drove us out" is especially problematic. Paul may here identify himself with others who favor a Torah-free mission (cf. Acts 8:1, "they were all scattered"). The main thrust of the criticism of the Jews, however, is that they hinder Paul and others from preaching to the Gentiles (2:16). In any case, Peter and the others were *not* driven out of Jerusalem — or if so, for an extremely short period — and on the whole lived there in peace. Cf. S. G. F. Brandon, *The Fall of Jerusalem and the Christian Church*, 2d ed. (London: SPCK, 1957), pp. 88–100. The general freedom of the Jerusalem apostles from punishment seems decisive

against the view of Beker, Hultgren, and others (see the preceding note) that the cause of persecution was the confession of a condemned man as messiah.

78. Hultgren, "Paul's Pre-Christian Persecutions," p. 101 n. 8 (where he disputes the view of Vielhauer).

79. Against Hultgren, ibid., p. 102.

80. I shall here not rehearse the history of criticism of Romans 9 – 11. For this see especially Zeller, *Juden und Heiden*, pp. 108ff. There are other summaries of views, coupled with exegetical treatments of the section, in Richardson, *Israel*, pp. 126–36; Ulrich Luz, *Das Geschichtsverständnis des Paulus* (Munich: Chr. Kaiser, 1968), pp. 19–37; Dahl, "The Future of Israel," in *Studies in Paul* (Minneapolis: Augsburg Publishing House, 1977), pp. 137–158; Peter Stuhlmacher, "Interpretation von Römer 11:25–32," in *Probleme biblischer Theologie* (Munich: Chr. Kaiser, 1971), pp. 555–70).

81. Above, chapter 1, nn. 111, 112.

82. Krister Stendahl, *Paul among Jews and Gentiles and Other Essays* (Philadelphia: Fortress Press, 1976); "A Response," *USQR* 33 (1978): 189–91.

83. See especially *Paul among Jews and Gentiles*, p. 40; "A Response," p. 190.

84. On Romans 9 – 11 as Paul's treatment of the failure of the mission to the Jews in the light of his trip to Jerusalem, the Gentiles, and the nearness of the Parousia, see Davies, "Paul and the People of Israel," p. 13, 28; Zeller, *Juden und Heiden*, pp. 77, 110. See above, on the setting of Romans, pp. 30–32.

85. Luz (*Geschichtsverständnis*, pp. 293f.) notes that 11:26 reads *kai outōs*, not *kai tote*. Paul does not lay emphasis on the temporal sequence, but on the manner of Israel's redemption. One may note that nevertheless a temporal sequence is implied. On "thus," see also Dahl, "The Future of Israel," pp. 152–54: "The mystery which Paul reveals is not Israel's ultimate salvation, but rather the way in which Israel will achieve that ultimate salvation." He continues, "Paul identifies the people's disobedience with their rejection of Christ and looks forward to the disappearance of this disbelief. . . ."

86. Cf. Zeller, *Juden und Heiden*, p. 257.

87. Luz, *Geschichtsverständnis*, pp. 294f.; Stuhlmacher, "Interpretation," pp. 562–64; Zeller, *Juden und Heiden*, pp. 259f.

88. This seems to be the implication of Stendahl's argument. Thus he observes that "Paul writes this whole section of Romans (10:17 – 11:36) without using the name of Jesus Christ" (*Paul among Jews and Gentiles*, p. 40).

89. On the importance of the figure of the olive tree for understanding 11:25f., see especially Richardson, *Israel*, p. 129. On the origin and also what may be called the socio-political significance of the figure, see W. D. Davies, "Romans 11:13–24: A Suggestion," in *Paganisme, Judaïsme, Christianisme* (Paris: Boccard, 1978), pp. 131–44.

90. V. 11:32 is the keystone to the entire mystery: see Richardson, *Israel*, p. 127; accepted by Stuhlmacher, "Interpretation," p. 567. Richardson parallels 11:28a, b with 11:30, 31 and 11:29 with 11:32. The result is an emphasis on the view that Jew and Gentile are saved on the same basis. As Munck puts it, "the Jews are now disobedient in order that they may in turn obtain mercy, the same mercy as shown to the Gentiles" (*Christ and Israel*, p. 139).

91. The dominant interpretation, which seems to me to be correct, is that "mercy

on all" in 11:32 does not mean "whether or not all have faith in Jesus Christ." Rom. 11:32 should be read in the light of the olive tree metaphor and of Paul's frequent statements that all stand on the same ground: Jew and Gentile alike are in sin and are righteoused only by faith (see the preceding note). It would take us too far afield to enter into a full discussion of the passages which indicate that all humanity, in fact the entire cosmos, will be redeemed. On the possibility of universal salvation in Paul's thought, cf. above, chapter 1, n. 64.

92. The first mystery is that Israel will be saved as a result of the Gentile mission. The second would be that at the end Israel will be saved apart from the work of the apostles.

93. So Beker, *Paul the Apostle*, p. 334.

94. This supposes that *plērōma* in 11:12, *tinas* in 11:14 and *pas* in 11:26 mutually interpret one another.

95. "Paul's Attitude toward the Jewish People," p. 185.

96. Several scholars have seen the principal problem of Romans 9 – 11, especially 11:25–32, to be Paul's desire to hold together faith in Christ with God's promises to Israel. See, for example, Richardson, *Israel*, pp. 132 and n. 4, 136, 147; Beker, *Paul the Apostle*, pp. 334f.

Conclusion: Paul and the Break with Judaism

It is beyond the scope of this monograph to attempt an assessment of the relative importance of Paul's role in the emergence of Christianity as a separate religion, with its own center and boundary markers. One may suspect that Paul's influence on the development of Christianity has been overemphasized. We may note, for example, that neither the church at Antioch nor the one at Rome was founded by him. Both were presumably mixed churches (Antioch certainly, Rome probably), and they show that other people were engaged in the mission to the Gentiles. At Antioch, further, we know that the law was not enforced, at least not until the arrival of emissaries from James. Thus Paul cannot be thought to have engineered single-handedly the departure from the law which, if nothing else did, clinched the separation of the Christian movement from Judaism. Nevertheless, it is appropriate here to summarize the nature of the break between the new movement and Judaism as it emerges in Paul's letters and, one presumes, in his churches.

Paul's thought was largely Jewish, and his work as apostle to the Gentiles is to be understood within the framework of Jewish eschatological speculation, as Rom. 15:16 makes clear. Paul interpreted his task of bringing the Gentiles into the people of God in such a way, however, that the church, in both his understanding and practice, became in effect a third entity — although he seems not to have perceived that his gospel and his missionary activity imply a break with Judaism. There are, nevertheless, two points at which the break is clearly perceptible. One is the traditional Jewish doctrine of election, which Paul denies. He appeals, to be sure, to God's covenant with Abraham, and thus his language is often appropriate to understanding the church as "true Israel." But his argument that the covenant "skips" from Abraham to Christ, and now includes those in Christ, but not Jews by descent, is in fact a flat denial of the election of Israel. The second point at which the break is especially clear is his insistence that it is through faith in Christ, not by accepting the law, that one enters the people of God. Thus he denies two pillars common to all forms of Judaism: the election of Israel and faithfulness to the Mosaic law.

While we can see that Paul, in discussing membership in the people of God, always insists on the equality of Jew and Gentile and faith in Christ alone, and thus conclude that these are the two interrelated convictions which lie immediately behind his denial of righteousness by law, there is a real sense in which we cannot explain in detail why Paul came to that position. He appeals to revelation. God revealed his son to (or in) him, and as a result he knew that it was through faith in Christ that God intended to save the world. That, he was convinced, had always been God's intention, and he had stated it clearly in advance (e.g. Gal. 3:8). God had never intended to make the law the condition of life (Gal. 3:21). If acceptance of the law were the condition of salvation, Christ would have died in vain (Gal. 2:21). It was the experience of the resurrection which convinced Paul that Christ had not died in vain, and thus it is that experience which is the source of Paul's denial of righteousness by the law, to the degree that we can know it.

In denying Jewish privilege as the elect of God, Paul makes the church in theory universal; it is God's intention to have mercy on all. But faith in Christ is necessary for membership in the people of God. Further, members of the body of Christ should behave accordingly. Heinous sin, unrepented of, may lead to expulsion (though not to damnation), and behavior which denies Christ, such as worshiping idols as if they were real gods or accepting some requirement other than faith as essential for membership, results in being cut off. Thus Christ is both the center of the "new creation" and also defines its parameters.

In Paul's discussion of behavior in the Corinthian correspondence we see aspects of a new "covenantal nomism," according to which membership entails correct behavior, incorrect behavior is punished, punishment leads to restoration (even if only at the judgment), and the like. There are, however, limits to this analogy. There is an important respect in which behavior is not conceived in the manner common in Judaism. Paul understands it to be the "fruit of the Spirit." Despite his well-known lists of vices and virtues, his general tendency was not to give concrete rules for living; and we discover most clearly that he had some when someone strays too far from the sort of behavior which should flow from the indwelling Spirit. But the principal point is that, in Pauline theory, deeds do flow from the Spirit, not from commandments.[1]

There are two more important, and also more elusive ways in which an analogy with convenantal nomism does not hold: the entrance rite and the new entity are different in kind — at least on a conceptual level. Baptism, in Paul's interpretation of it, does not represent "true, inner circumcision." It represents dying with Christ, sharing his sufferings so as to share his life (Rom. 6:5–11; cf. 8:17; Phil. 3:10f. [where, however, the sharing is presented as partly in the future]). Certainly Paul believed that Christians should turn and submit to God with commitment, love, and devotion (cf. Rom. 6:15–19). If that were all he thought, his conception of the Christian life would have stayed within the bounds of covenantal thought. But he also thought that, in dying with Christ, the Christian became one with him, so that his death and resurrection not only count for the believer's debts, but provide the means of the believer's own death to the power of sin and new life to God.

Similarly the church: there are some minimal procedures and a few rules (cf. 1 Cor. 11:17–34). The Scripture is read, as it is in the synagogue (1 Cor. 14:26; cf. 2 Cor. 3:16). The church, again like the Jewish community, should avoid recourse to outsiders to settle disputes (1 Cor. 6:1–8). If the church lacks Israel's history and its sense of solidarity of experience and ancestry, Paul is prepared, at least in part, to borrow them (1 Cor. 10:1; Rom. 4:1). But the church — again in Paul's conception of it — is more than a community bound together with common ties of history, commitment, devotion, prayer, Scripture, and descent. It is the body of Christ, in which all — Jew and Greek, male and female, slave and free — become one person.

There is no claim here that in Paul's churches his view was realized. The Corinthians had "the Spirit," but not necessarily with the desired result. Paul — and early Christianity — may well have succeeded better than could have been anticipated in abolishing distinctions even on a practical level (see Rom. 16:3, 7 [in 16:7 "Junia" should be read]); but some distinctions, such as the one with which we began our study (1 Cor. 11:5–16), still crop up. In any case, what I intend to point to is the fact that Paul's mind did not run entirely in ways familiar from the Bible or from most forms of Jewish thought known to us. Not all his mental furniture is from the same workshop. There are important ways in which his thought about Christian life and experience does not stay within the categories which are familiar in Jewish covenantal thought. Many things essential there are absent, and some of Paul's key concepts move into a different realm of thinking and discourse.

Knowing the outcome, we can see in the Pauline letters the nucleus of much of Christianity's understanding of itself. It would appropriate Israelite history and also claim to transcend it. It would rely on Jewish Scripture and find its truth therein, but it would not hesitate to dismiss unwanted parts and to supplement it with new words, some "from the Lord" and some on human authority. Many aspects of Jewish thought and tradition would be retained, but new patterns of thinking would emerge. The development of a new covenantal nomism would proceed. It would be too much to say that in these and other matters Christianity was conscious of following Paul. Nevertheless in many ways it achieved its own identity by pursuing the course which we have seen in this study, a course which involved the simultaneous appropriation and rejection of Judaism.

NOTES

1. Morna D. Hooker, commenting on my description of the "pattern" of Paul's thought, has urged that it is closer to Jewish "covenantal nomism" than I allowed. One of her principal points is this: " . . . just as Palestinian Judaism understood obedience to the Law to be the proper response of Israel to the covenant on Sinai, so Paul assumes that there is an appropriate response for Christians who have experienced God's saving activity in Christ" (Morna D. Hooker, "Paul and 'Covenantal Nomism,'" in *Paul and Paulinism: Essays in honour of C. K. Barrett* [London: SPCK, 1982], pp. 47–56, quotation from p. 48). I appreciate her emphasis on this point, which in fact I asserted: " . . . on the point at which many have found the decisive contrast between Paul and Judaism — grace and works — Paul is in agreement with Palestinian Judaism. . . ." (E. P. Sanders, *Paul and Palestinian Judaism* (Philadelphia: Fortress Press, 1977), p. 543; cf. p. 513.) Hooker's principal point, however, is that the correspondence between grace and requirement should have been made central to Paul's pattern of religion. In *PPJ* (pp. 513f.) I attempted to explain why I did not make the covenantal scheme central to Paul's thought, while arguing that this aspect of it is there.

Bibliography

Bammel, Ernst. "Judenverfolgung und Naherwartung." *ZTK* 56 (1959): 294–315.

Barrett, C. K. "ΨΕΥΔΑΠΟΣΤΟΛΟΙ (2 Cor. 11:13)." In *Mélanges Bibliques en homage au R. P. Beda Rigaux*, edited by A. Deschamps and A. de Halleaux, pp. 378–96. Gembloux: Duculot, 1970.

———. *A Commentary on the Epistle to the Romans*. HNTC [= BNTC]. New York: Harper & Row; London: A. & C. Black, 1957.

———. *Essays on Paul*. Philadelphia: Westminster Press; London: SPCK, 1982.

Barth, Markus. "Die Stellung des Paulus zu Gesetz und Ordnung." *EvTh* 33 (1976): 466–526.

Bauer, Walter. *A Greek-English Lexicon of the New Testament and Other Early Christian Literature*. ET, W. F. Arndt and F. W. Gingrich, 2d ed. Rev. Gingrich and F. W. Danker. Chicago and London: University of Chicago Press, 1979.

Beker, J. Christiaan. *Paul the Apostle: The Triumph of God in Life and Thought*. Philadelphia: Fortress Press, 1980.

Betz, Hans Dieter. *Galatians: A Commentary on Paul's Letter to the Churches in Galatia*. Hermeneia. Philadelphia: Fortress Press, 1979.

Bonnard, Pierre. *L' Épitre de Saint Paul aux Galâtes*. CNT 9. 2d ed. Neuchâtel and Paris: Delachaux & Niestlé, 1972.

Borgen, Peder. "Observations on the Theme 'Paul and Philo': Paul's preaching of circumcision in Galatia (Gal. 5:11) and debates on circumcision in Philo." In *Die Paulinische Literatur und Theologie*, edited by S. Pederson, pp. 85–102. Skandinavische Beiträge. Aarhus: Forlaget Aros, 1980.

Bornkamm, Günther. "Gesetz und Natur (Röm. 2, 14–16)." In *Studien zu Antike und Urchristentum. Gesammelte Aufsätze II*, pp. 93–118. BEvTh 28. Munich: Chr. Kaiser, 1963.

———. "The Missionary Stance of Paul in I Corinthians 9 and in Acts." In *Studies in Luke–Acts*, edited by L. E. Keck and J. L. Martyn, pp. 194–207. Reprint. Philadelphia: Fortress Press, 1980.

———. "The Revelation of God's Wrath." In *Early Christian Experience*, ET P. L. Hammer, pp. 47–70. New York and London: Harper & Row, 1969.

———. "Der Römerbrief als Testament des Paulus." In *Geschichte und Glaube*, vol. 2, *Gesammelte Aufsätze IV*, pp. 120–39. BEvTh 53. Munich: Chr. Kaiser, 1971.

Borse, Udo. "Die geschichtliche und theologische Einordnung des Römerbriefes." *BZ* 16 (1972): 70–83.

———. *Der Standort des Galaterbriefes*. BBB 41. Bonn: Hanstein, 1972.

BIBLIOGRAPHY

Brandon, S. G. F. *The Fall of Jerusalem and the Christian Church.* 2d ed. London: SPCK, 1957.

Brown, Peter. *The World of Late Antiquity: From Marcus Aurelius to Muhammad.* New York: Harcourt Brace Jovanovich; London: Thames & Hudson, 1971.

Bruce, F. F. "The Curse of the Law." In *Paul and Paulinism: Essays in honour of C. K. Barrett,* edited by Morna D. Hooker and S. G. Wilson, pp. 27–36. London: SPCK, 1982.

——. *Paul: Apostle of the Heart Set Free.* Grand Rapids: Wm. B. Eerdmans; Exeter, Eng.: Paternoster Press, 1977.

——. *Peter, Stephen, James, and John.* Grand Rapids: Wm. B. Eerdmans, 1980.

Bultmann, Rudolf. "Pisteuō." In *TDNT* 6: 197–228. Grand Rapids: Wm. B. Eerdmans, 1968.

——. "Romans 7 and the Anthropology of Paul." In *Existence and Faith: Shorter Writings of Rudolf Bultmann,* ET, S. M. Ogden, pp. 147–57. Cleveland and New York: World Publishing Co., Meridian Books, 1960.

——. *Der Stil der paulinischen Predigt und die kynisch-stoische Diatribe.* FRLANT 13. Göttingen: Vandenhoeck & Ruprecht, 1910.

——. Theology of the New Testament. 2 vols. ET, Kendrik Grobel. New York: Charles Scribner's Sons, 1951–1955.

Burton, Ernest deWitt. *The Epistle to the Galatians.* ICC. Edinburgh: T. & T. Clark, 1921.

Bussmann, Claus. *Themen der paulinischen Missionspredigt auf dem Hintergrund der spätjudisch-hellenistischen Missionsliteratur.* Frankfurt and Bern: H. Lang, 1971.

Byrne, Brendan. *"Sons of God — Seed of Abraham": A Study of the Idea of the Sonship of God of All Christians in Paul against the Jewish Background.* Analecta Biblica 83. Rome: Biblical Institute Press, 1979.

Caird, G. B. Review of *Paul and Palestinian Judaism* by E. P. Sanders. *JTS* 29 (1978): 538–43.

Callan, Terrance. "Pauline Midrash: The Exegetical Background of Gal. 3.19b." *JBL* 99 (1980): 549–67.

Cambier, J. "Le jugement de tous les hommes." *ZNW* 67 (1976–77): 187–213.

Cavallin, H. C. C. "'The Righteous Shall Live by Faith.' A Decisive Argument for the Traditional Interpretation." *ST* 32 (1978): 33–43.

Chadwick, Henry. "All Things to All Men." *NTS* 1 (1954–55): 261–75.

Conzelmann, H. *1 Corinthians: A Commentary on the First Epistle to the Corinthians.* ET, J. W. Leitch. Hermeneia. Philadelphia: Fortress Press, 1975.

Cranfield, C. E. B. *The Epistle to the Romans.* 2 vols. ICC. Edinburgh: T. & T. Clark, 1979.

Dahl, Nils A. "The Future of Israel." In *Studies in Paul: Theology for the Early Christian Mission,* pp. 137–158. Minneapolis: Augsburg Publishing House, 1977.

——. "The One God of Jews and Gentiles (Romans 3:29–30)." In *Studies in Paul,* pp. 178–91.

Daniel, Jerry L. "Anti-Semitism in the Hellenistic-Roman Period." *JBL* 98 (1979): 45–65.

Daube, David. *The New Testament and Rabbinic Judaism.* 1956. Reprint. London: University of London, Athlone Press, 1973.

BIBLIOGRAPHY

Davies, W. D. *The Gospel and the Land: Early Christianity and Jewish Territorial Doctrine.* Berkeley and Los Angeles: University of California Press, 1974.
————. "Paul and the People of Israel." *NTS* 24 (1977): 4–39. Reprinted in *Jewish and Pauline Studies.* Philadelphia: Fortress Press, 1983.
————. *Paul and Rabbinic Judaism.* 4th ed. with new Preface. Philadelphia: Fortress Press, 1980.
————. "Paul: From the Semitic Point of View." In *Cambridge History of Judaism II.* (Forthcoming publication from Cambridge University Press.)
————. Review of Galatians by H. D. Betz. *RSR* 7 (1981): 310–18.
————. "Romans 11:13–24: A Suggestion." In *Paganisme, Judaïsme, Christianisme: Influences et affrontements dans le monde antique. Mélanges offerts à Marcel Simon,* edited by A. Benoit, M. Philonenko, C. Vogel, pp. 131–44. Paris: Boccard, 1978.
Didier, Georges. *Désintéressement du Chrétien: La rétribution dans la morale de saint Paul.* Éditions Montaigne, 1955.
Dodd, C. H. *The Parables of the Kingdom.* Rev. ed. London: William Collins Sons, Fontana Books, 1961.
Donfried, Karl P. "Justification and Last Judgment in Paul." *ZNW* 67 (1976): 90–110.
————, ed. *The Romans Debate.* Minneapolis: Augsburg Publishing House, 1977.
Drane, John W. *Paul: Libertine or Legalist? A Study in the Theology of the Major Pauline Epistles.* London: SPCK, 1975.
Dülmen, Andrea van. *Die Theologie des Gesetzes bei Paulus.* Stuttgarter biblische Monographien 5. Stuttgart: Verlag Katholisches Bibelwerk, 1968.
Dunn, James D. G. "Rom. 7, 14–25 in the Theology of Paul." *TZ* 31 (1975): 257–73.
————. *Unity and Diversity in the New Testament: An Inquiry Into the Character of Earliest Christianity.* Philadelphia: Westminster Press; London: SCM Press, 1977.
Eckert, Jost. *Die urchristliche Verkündigung im Streit zwischen Paulus und seinen Gegnern nach dem Galaterbrief.* Biblische Untersuchungen 6. Regensburg: F. Pustet, 1971.
Eichholz, Georg. *Die Theologie des Paulus im Umriss.* Neukirchen-Vluyn: Neukirchener Verlag, 1972.
Elliott, John H. *A Home for the Homeless: A Sociological Exegesis of I Peter — Its Situation and Strategy.* Philadelphia: Fortress Press; London: SCM Press, 1981.
Filson, Floyd V. *St. Paul's Conception of Recompense.* UNT 21. Leipzig: J. C. Hinrichs, 1931.
Fitzmyer, J. A. "Saint Paul and the Law." *The Jurist* 27 (1967): 18–36.
Flückiger, F. "Zur Unterscheidung von Heiden und Jüden in Röm. 1, 18 – 2,3." *TZ* 10 (1954): 154–58.
————. "Die Werke des Gesetzes bei den Heiden." *TZ* 8 (1952): 17–42.
Forkman, Göran. *The Limits of the Religious Community.* ConBNT 5. Lund: CWK Gleerup, 1972.
Freund, Richard. "Principia Politica: The Political Dimensions of Jewish and Christian Self-Definition in the Greco-Roman Period." Ph.D. Dis. New York: Jewish Theological Seminary, 1982.
Fuller, D. P. "Paul and 'the Works of the Law'," *Westminster Theological Journal* 38 (1975): 28–42.
Gager, J. G. "Some Notes on Paul's Conversion." *NTS* 27 (1981): 697–704.

BIBLIOGRAPHY

Gaston, Lloyd. "Paul and the Torah." In *Anti-Semitism and the Foundations of Christianity*, edited by A. T. Davies, pp. 48–71. New York: Paulist Press, 1979.

Goppelt, Leonhard. *Typos: Die typologische Deutung des Alten Testaments im Neuen*. Gütersloh: Gerd Mohn, 1939. (ET: *Typos: The Typological Interpretation of the Old Testament in the New*. ET, D. H. Madvig. Grand Rapids: Wm. B. Eerdmans, 1982.)

Gundry, Robert H. "The Moral Frustration of Paul before His Conversion: Sexual Lust in Romans 7:7–25." In *Pauline Studies: Essays Presented to F. F. Bruce*, edited by D. A. Hagner and J. Murray, pp. 228–45. Grand Rapids: Wm. B. Eerdmans, 1980.

Haenchen, E. *The Acts of the Apostles*. ET R. McL. Wilson. Philadelphia: Westminster Press; Oxford: Basil Blackwell, 1971.

Hahn, Ferdinand. "Das Gesetzesverständnis im Römer und Galaterbrief." *ZNW* 67 (1976–77): 29–63.

Hanson, A. T. *Studies in Paul's Technique and Theology*. London: SPCK, 1974.

Harnack, Adolf von. *Die Mission und Ausbreitung des Christentums in den ersten drei Jahrhunderten*. 4th ed. Leipzig: J. C. Hinrichs, 1924. (ET: *The Mission and Expansion of Christianity in the First Three Centuries*. ET and edited by J. Mofatt. 2 vols. New York: Harper & Row, Torchbooks, 1962.)

Harvey, A. E. *Jesus and the Constraints of History*. Philadelphia: Westminster Press; London: Duckworth, 1982.

Hickling, C. J. A. "Centre and Periphery in the Thought of Paul." In *Studia Biblica 1978*, vol. 3, *Papers on Paul and Other New Testament Authors*, edited by E. A. Livingstone, pp. 199–214. *JSNT* Supplement Series 3. Sheffield: JSOT Press, 1980.

Hoheisel, Karl. *Das antike Judentum in christlicher Sicht: Ein Beitrag zur neueren Forschungsgeschichte*. Studies in Oriental Religions 2. Wiesbaden: O. Harrassowitz, 1978.

Hooker, Morna D. "Beyond the Things that are Written? St. Paul's use of Scripture." *NTS* 27 (1981): 295–309.

———. "Paul and 'Covenantal Nomism.'" In *Paul and Paulinism: Essays in honour of C. K. Barrett*, edited by Morna D. Hooker and S. G. Wilson, pp. 57–66. London: SPCK, 1982.

Horbury, W. Review of *Paul and Palestinian Judaism* by E. P. Sanders. *Expository Times* 96 (1979): 116–18.

Howard, George. "Christ the End of the Law: The Meaning of Romans 10:4ff." *JBL* 88 (1969): 331–37.

———. *Crisis in Galatia: A Study in Early Christian Theology*. SNTSMS 35. New York and Cambridge: Cambridge University Press, 1979.

———. "Romans 3:21–31 and the Inclusion of the Gentiles." *HTR* 63 (1970): 223–33.

Hübner, Hans. "Gal 3,10 und die Herkunft des Paulus." *KuD* 19 (1973): 215–31.

———. "Das ganze und das eine Gesetz." *KuD* 21 (1975): 248–56.

———. *Das Gesetz bei Paulus: Ein Beitrag zum Werden der paulinischen Theologie*. 2d ed. FRLANT 119. Göttingen: Vandenhoeck & Ruprecht, 1980. (ET: *Law in Paul's Thought: Studies in The New Testament and Its World*. Edinburgh: T. & T. Clark, 1983.)

———. "Identitätsverlust und paulinische Theologie." *KuD* 24 (1978): 181–93.

BIBLIOGRAPHY

————. "Pauli Theologiae Proprium." *NTS* 26 (1980): 445–73.

————. "Der theologische Umgang des Paulus mit dem Alten Testament im Römerbrief." A paper presented to the seminar on "The Use of the Old Testament in the New." SNTS annual meeting, Toronto, 1980.

Hultgren, Arland J. "Paul's Pre-Christian Persecutions of the Church: Their Purpose, Locale, and Nature." *JBL* 95 (1976): 97–111.

Hurd, John C., Jr. "Paul Ahead of His Time: I Thess. 2:13–16." (Forthcoming publication.)

Jeremias, J. *Jesus' Promise to the Nations*. ET, S. H. Hooke. Reprint. Philadelphia: Fortress Press, 1982; London: SCM Press, 1958.

Jervell, Jacob. "The Letter to Jerusalem." In *The Romans Debate*, edited by K. P. Donfried, pp. 61–74. Minneapolis: Augsburg Publishing House, 1977.

Jewett, Robert. "The Agitators and the Galatian Congregation." *NTS* 17 (1970–71): 198–212.

————. *A Chronology of Paul's Life*. Philadelphia: Fortress Press, 1979.

Käsemann, Ernst. *An die Römer*. HNT8a. Tübingen: J. C. B. Mohr (Paul Siebeck), 1974. (ET: *Commentary on Romans*. ET and edited by G. W. Bromiley. Grand Rapids: Wm. B. Eerdmans; London: SCM Press, 1980.)

Keck, Leander. "The Law and 'The Law of Sin and Death' (Rom. 8:1–4): Reflections on the Spirit and Ethics in Paul." In *The Divine Helmsman: Studies on God's Control of Human Events. Presented to Lou H. Silberman*, edited by J. L. Crenshaw and S. Sandmel, pp. 41–57. New York: KTAV, 1980.

————. *Paul and His Letters*. Fortress Press: Philadelphia, 1979.

Kim, Seyoon. *The Origin of Paul's Gospel*. WUNT Reihe 2,4. Tübingen: J. C. B. Mohr (Paul Siebeck), 1981; Grand Rapids: Wm. B. Eerdmans, 1982.

Knox, John. *Chapters in a Life of Paul*. Nashville: Abingdon Press, 1950.

Knox, W. L. *St. Paul and the Church of Jerusalem*. Cambridge: Cambridge University Press, 1925.

König, A. "Gentiles or Gentile Christians? On the Meaning of Rom. 2:12–16." *Journal of Theology for South Africa* 15 (1976): 53–60.

Léon-Dufour, Xavier. "Jugement de l'homme et jugement de Dieu. 1 Co 4, 1–5 dans le cadre de 3, 18 – 4, 5." In *Paola a una chiesa divisa (1 Co 1 – 4)*, edited by L. De Lorenzi, pp. 137–75. Rome: Abbazia di S. Paola, 1980.

Lightfoot, J. B. *Saint Paul's Epistle to the Galatians*. 10th ed. London: Macmillan, 1892.

Lindars, Barnabas. *New Testament Apologetic: the Doctrinal Significance of the Old Testament Quotations*. London: SCM Press, 1961.

Lohse, Eduard. "ὁ νόμος τοῦ πνεύματος τῆς ζωῆς, Exegetische Anmerkungen zu Röm 8,2." In *Neues Testament und Christliche Existenz: Festschrift für Herbert Braun zum 70. Geburtstag*, edited by H. D. Betz and L. Schottroff, pp. 279–87. Tübingen: J. C. B. Mohr (Paul Siebeck), 1973.

Longenecker, Richard. *Paul: Apostle of Liberty*. New York and London: Harper & Row, 1964.

Lüdemann, Gerd. *Paulus, der Heidenapostel*. Vol. 1: *Studien zur Chronologie*. FRLANT 123. Göttingen: Vandenhoeck & Ruprecht, 1980. (ET forthcoming from Fortress Press.)

————. "Paulus und das Judentum." (Forthcoming publication.)

215

Lull, David. Review of *Galatians* by H. D. Betz. *Perkins Journal* 34 (1981): 44–6.

Luz, Ulrich. *Das Geschichtsverständnis des Paulus.* BEvTh 49. Munich: Chr. Kaiser, 1968.

Lyonnet, S. "St. Paul: Liberty and Law." In *The Bridge: A Yearbook of Judaeo-Christian Studies* 4, edited by J. M. Oesterreicher, pp. 229–51. Newark, N. J.: The Institute of Judaeo-Christian Studies, Seton Hall University, 1962.

Malherbe, Abraham J. "ΜΗ ΓΕΝΟΙΤΟ in the Diatribe and Paul." *HTR* 73 (1980): 231–40.

Manson, T. W. "St. Paul's Letter to the Romans – and Others." *BJRL* 21 (1948): 224–40.

Marquardt, Friedrich-Wilhelm. *Die Juden im Römerbrief.* Theologische Studien 107. Zürich: Theologischer Verlag, 1971.

Mattern, L. *Das Verständnis des Gerichts bei Paulus.* ATANT 47. Zurich and Stuttgart: Zwingli Verlag, 1966.

Mattill, A. J., Jr. "Translation of Words with the Stem *Dik-* in Romans." *Andrews University Seminary Studies* 9 (1971): 89–98.

McEleney, Neil J. "Conversion, Circumcision and the Law." *NTS* 20 (1974): 319–41.

Meyer, Paul. "Romans 10:4 and the End of the Law." In *The Divine Helmsman: Studies on God's Control of Human Events*, edited by J. L. Crenshaw and S. Sandmel, pp. 59–78. New York: KTAV, 1980.

Michel, Otto. *Der Brief an die Römer.* 12th ed. KEK. Göttingen: Vandenhoeck & Ruprecht, 1963.

———. *Paulus und seine Bibel.* 1929. Reprint. Darmstadt: Wissenschaftliche Buchgesellschaft, 1972.

Minde, H. -J. van der. *Schrift und Tradition bei Paulus: Ihre Bedeutung und Funktion im Römerbrief.* Paderborner theologische Studien 3. Munich: F. Schöningh, 1976.

Moore, George Foot. *Judaism in the First Three Centuries of the Common Era: The Age of the Tannaim.* 3 vols. Cambridge, Mass.: Harvard University Press, 1927–1930.

Moule, C. F. D. *An Idiom Book of New Testament Greek.* 2d ed. New York and Cambridge: Cambridge University Press, 1959.

———. "The Judgment Theme in the Sacraments." In *The Background of the New Testament and its Eschatology; Studies in Honour of C. H. Dodd*, edited by D. Daube and W. D. Davies, pp. 464–81. New York and Cambridge: Cambridge University Press, 1956.

Munck, Johannes. *Christ and Israel: An Interpretation of Romans 9–11.* ET, I. Nixon. Philadelphia: Fortress Press, 1967.

———. *Paul and the Salvation of Mankind.* ET, F. Clarke. Atlanta: John Knox Press, 1977; London: SCM Press, 1959.

Murphy-O'Connor, J. "Corpus paulinien." *RB* 82 (1975): 130–58.

Mussner, Franz. "'Christus (ist) des Gesetzes Ende zur Gerechtigkeit für jeden, der glaubt' (Röm. 10,4)." In *Paulus – Apostat oder Apostel*, edited by M. Barth, J. Blank, J. Bloch, F. Mussner, and R. J. Zwi Werblowsky, pp. 31–44. Regensburg, 1977.

———. *Der Galaterbrief.* HTKNT. Freiburg: Herder, 1974.

BIBLIOGRAPHY

———. "Theologische 'Wiedergutmachung.' Am Beispiel der Auslegung des Galater-briefes." *Freiburger Rundbrief* 26 (1974): 7–11.

Newton, Michael. "The Concept of Purity at Qumran and in the Letters of Paul." Ph.D. Diss. Hamilton, Ontario; McMaster University, 1980.

O'Neill, J. C. *Paul's Letter to the Romans.* Baltimore and Harmondsworth, Eng.: Penguin, Pelican Books, 1975.

Osten-Sacken, Peter von der. "Das paulinische Verständnis des Gesetzes im Span-nungsfeld von Eschatologie und Geschichte." *EvTh* 37 (1977): 549–87.

Pfleiderer, Otto. *Paulinism: A Contribution to the History of Primitive Christian Theology.* Vol. 1. ET, E. Peters. London: Williams & Norgate, 1877.

Przybylski, Benno. *Righteousness in Matthew and His World of Thought.* SNTSMS 41. New York and Cambridge: Cambridge University Press, 1980.

Räisänen, Heikki. "Das 'Gesetz des Glaubens' (Röm. 3.27) und das 'Gesetz des Geistes' (Röm. 8.2)." *NTS* 26 (1979): 101–17.

———. "Legalism and Salvation by the Law." In *Die paulinische Literatur und Theologie,* edited by S. Pedersen, pp. 63–83. Scandinavische Beiträge. Aarhus: Forlaget Aros, 1980.

———. *Paul and the Law.* (Forthcoming publication.)

———. "Paul's Theological Difficulties with the Law." In *Studia Biblica 1978,* vol. 3, *Papers on Paul and Other New Testament Authors,* edited by E. A. Livingstone, pp. 301–20. JSNT Supplement Series 3. Sheffield: JSOT Press, 1980.

Ramarosan, L. "Un 'nouveau plan' de Rm 1, 16 – 11,36." *Nouvelle Revue Théolo-gique* 94 (1972): 943–58.

Reicke, Bo. "The Law and This World according to Paul." *JBL* 70 (1951): 259–76.

Richardson, Peter. *Israel in the Apostolic Church.* SNTSMS 10. New York and Cam-bridge: Cambridge University Press, 1969.

———. "Pauline Inconsistency: I Corinthians 9:19–23 and Galatians 2:11–14." *NTS* 26 (1980): 347–62.

Ridderbos, Herman. *Paul: An Outline of His Theology.* ET, J. R. De Witt. Grand Rapids: Wm. B. Eerdmans, 1975.

Rivkin, Ellis. *A Hidden Revolution: The Pharisees' Search for the Kingdom Within.* Nashville: Abingdon Press, 1978.

Robinson, J. A. T. *Wrestling with Romans.* Philadelphia: Westminster Press; Lon-don: SCM Press, 1979.

Roetzel, Calvin J. *Judgment in the Community: Eschatology and Ecclesiology in Paul.* Leiden: E. J. Brill, 1972.

Sanday, William and Arthur C. Headlam. *The Epistle to the Romans.* 5th ed. ICC. Edinburgh: T. & T. Clark, 1902.

Sanders, E. P. "On the Question of Fulfilling the Law in Paul and Rabbinic Judaism." In *Donum Gentilicium: New Testament Studies in Honour of David Daube,* edited by E. Bammel, C. K. Barrett, and W. D. Davies, pp. 103–26. Oxford: At the Clarendon Press, 1978.

———. *Paul and Palestinian Judaism: A Comparison of Patterns of Religion.* Philadelphia: Fortress Press; London: SCM Press, 1977.

———. "Paul's Attitude toward the Jewish People." *USQR* 33 (1978): 175–87.

———. "Philippians 3 and 2 Corinthians 11." (Forthcoming publication.)

Sanders, J. A. "Torah and Christ." *Interpretation* 29 (1975): 372–90.

Schiffman, Larry. "At the Crossroads: Tannaitic Perspectives on the Jewish-Christian Schism." In *Jewish and Christian Self-Definition*, Vol. 2, *Aspects of Judaism in the Graeco-Roman Period*, edited by E. P. Sanders, with A. I. Baumgarten and A. Mendelson, pp. 115–56, 338–52. Philadelphia: Fortress Press; London: SCM Press, 1981.

Schlier, Heinrich. *Der Brief an die Galater*. 5th ed. KEK. Göttingen: Vandenhoeck & Ruprecht, 1971.

Schmithals, Walther. *Paul and James*. SBT 46. ET D. M. Barton. London: SCM Press, 1965.

———. *Die theologische Anthropologie des Paulus: Auslegung von Röm. 7, 17 – 8, 39*. Taschenbücher 1021. Stuttgart: Kohlhamer Verlag, 1980.

Schoeps, H. J. *Paul: The Theology of the Apostle in the Light of Jewish Religious History*. ET H. Knight. Philadelphia: Westminster Press; London: Lutterworth, 1961.

Schrage, Wolfgang. *Die konkreten Einzelgebote in der paulinischen Paränese: Ein Beitrag zur neutestamentlichen Ethik*. Gütersloh: Gerd Mohn, 1961.

Schweitzer, Albert. *The Mysticism of Paul the Apostle*. ET, W. Montgomery. New York: Henry Holt; London: A. & C. Black, 1931.

Scroggs, Robin. "Paul as Rhetorician: Two Homilies in Romans 1 – 11." In *Jews, Greeks and Christians: Essays in Honor of W. D. Davies*, edited by R. Hamerton-Kelly and R. Scroggs, pp. 271–98. Studies in Judaism in Late Antiquity 21. Leiden: E. J. Brill, 1976.

Siegert, Folker. "Gottesfürchtige und Sympathisanten." *JSJ* 4 (1973): 109–64.

Stendahl, Krister. *Paul among Jews and Gentiles and Other Essays*. Philadelphia: Fortress Press, 1976.

———. "A Response [to E. P. Sanders]." *USQR* 33 (1978): 189–91.

Stern, M. "The Jews in Greek and Latin Literature." In *The Jewish People in the First Century*, I, 2, edited by S. Safrai and M. Stern, pp. 1101–59. Compendia Rerum Iudaicarum ad Novum Testamentum. Philadelphia: Fortress Press; Assen, Neth.: Van Gorcum, 1976.

Stowers, Stanley K. *A Critical Reassessment of Paul and the Diatribe: The Dialogical Element in Paul's Letter to the Romans*. SBLDS 57. Chico, Calif.: Scholars Press, 1982.

Stuhlmacher, Peter. "'Das Ende des Gesetzes' Über Ursprung und Ansatz der paulinische Theologie." *ZTK* 67 (1970): 14–39.

———. "Erwägungen zum Problem von Gegenwart und Zukunft in der paulinischen Eschatologie." *ZTK* 64 (1967): 423–50.

———. "Das Gesetz als Thema biblischer Theologie." *ZTK* 75 (1978): 251–80.

———. "Interpretation von Römer 11.25–32." In *Probleme biblischer Theologie: Festschrift für Gerhard von Rad zum 70. Geburtstag*, edited by H. W. Wolff, pp. 555–70. Munich: Chr. Kaiser, 1971.

———. *Das paulinische Evangelium*, Vol. 1, *Vorgeschichte*. FRLANT 95. Göttingen: Vandenhoeck & Ruprecht, 1968.

———. "Theologische Probleme des Römerbriefpräscripts." *EvTh* 27 (1967): 374–89.

———. *Versöhnung, Gesetz und Gerechtigkeit: Aufsätze zur biblischen Theologie*. Göttingen: Vandenhoeck & Ruprecht, 1981.

BIBLIOGRAPHY

Suggs, Jack. "' The Word is Near You': Romans 10.6–10 within the Purpose of the Letter." In *Christian History and Interpretation: Studies Presented to John Knox*, edited by W. R. Farmer, C. F. D. Moule, and R. R. Niebuhr, pp. 289–312. New York and Cambridge: Cambridge University Press, 1967.

Synofzik, Ernst. *Die Gerichts- und Vergeltungsaussagen bei Paulus: Eine traditionsgeschichtliche Untersuchung.* Göttinger theologische Arbeiten 8. Göttingen: Vandenhoeck & Ruprecht, 1977.

Theissen, Gerd. "Soteriologische Symbolik in den paulinischen Schriften." *KuD* 20 (1974): 282–304.

Townsend, John. "The Gospel of John and the Jews." In *Anti-Semitism and the Foundations of Christianity*, edited by A. T. Davies, pp. 72–97. New York: Paulist Press, 1979.

Tyson, Joseph B. "'Works of Law' in Galatians." *JBL* 92 (1973): 423–31.

Urbach, E. E. "Self-Isolation or Self-Affirmation in Judaism in the First Three Centuries: Theory and Practice." In *Jewish and Christian Self-Definition*, Vol. 2, *Aspects of Judaism in the Graeco-Roman Period*, edited by E. P. Sanders, with A. I. Baumgarten and A. Mendelson, pp. 269–98. Philadelphia: Fortress Press; London: SCM Press, 1981.

Vielhauer, Philipp. "On the 'Paulinism' of Acts." In *Studies in Luke-Acts*, edited by L. E. Keck and J. L. Martyn, pp. 33–50. Reprint. Philadelphia: Fortress Press, 1980.

Wagner, G. "Pour comprendre l'apôtre Paul." *Lumière et Vie* 27 (1978): 5–20.

Wernle, Paul. *Der Christ und die Sünde bei Paulus.* Freiburg: J. C. B. Mohr (Paul Siebeck), 1897.

Wetter, G. P. *Der Vergeltungsgedanke bei Paulus: Eine Studie zur Religion des Apostels.* Göttingen: Vandenhoeck & Ruprecht, 1912.

Wilckens, Ulrich. "Über Abfassungszweck und Aufbau des Römerbriefs." In *Rechtfertigung als Freiheit: Paulusstudien*, pp. 110–70. Neukirchen-Vluyn: Neukirchener Verlag, 1974.

———. "Was heisst bei Paulus: 'Aus Werken des Gesetzes wird kein Mensch gerecht?'" In *Rechtfertigung als Freiheit: Paulusstudien*, pp. 77–109.

Wuellner, Wilhelm. "Toposforschung und Torahinterpretation bei Paulus und Jesus." *NTS* 24 (1978): 463–83.

Zeller, Dieter. *Juden und Heiden in der Mission des Paulus: Studien zur Römerbrief.* 2d ed. Stuttgart: Verlag Katholisches Bibelwerk, 1976.

Indexes

INDEX OF PASSAGES

Bible

Apocrypha and Pseudepigrapha

Dead Sea Scrolls

Philo

Rabbinic Literature

INDEX OF NAMES

INDEX OF SUBJECTS

DATE DUE

JAN 0 8 1999			
FEB 1 3 1999			
MAR 2 5 1999			
JAN 3 1 2000			
7/14/00			
FEB 1 4 2001			
MAR 1 4 2001			
APR 1 6 2001			
GAYLORD			PRINTED IN U.S.A.